a brit's guide
to
DISNEYLAND®
Resort Paris

2004-2005

GW00597416

simon veness

foulsham
LONDON • NEW YORK • TORONTO • SYDNEY

foulsham

The Publishing House, Bennetts Close, Cippenham, Berkshire, SL1 5AP, England

ISBN 0-572-02949-7

Dedication
To Anthony and Mark – the best little research team a father could wish for.

Other books in this series:
A Brit's Guide to Orlando and Walt Disney World 2004, Simon Veness, 0-572-02925-X
Choosing A Cruise 6th edition, Simon Veness, 0-572-02946-2
A Brit's Guide to New York 2004, Karen Marchbank, 0-572-02917-9
A Brit's Guide to Las Vegas and the West 2004–5, Karen Marchbank, 0-572-02926-8

Printed in Great Britain by Creative Print & Design (Wales), Ebbw Vale.

Contents

8. Beyond the Theme Parks

(or, Let's Shop 'Til We Drop and Other Fun Pursuits). Exploring the restaurants and bars, entertainment and shopping opportunities in *Disney Village;* what's in store at Val d'Europe and La Vallée; Sea Life Centre, Manchester United Soccer School, and having a swing at *Golf Disneyland*.

9. The Attractions of Paris

(or, Getting an Eiffel of the City). The highlights of the real must-see and must-do opportunities of Paris, public transport in the city, trips on the Seine and sights further afield including Versailles and Provins.

10. Your Holiday Planner

Examples to help you plan a 3-day or 5-day stay in *Disneyland Resort Paris,* with blank forms for your holiday.

Foreword

Welcome to the second edition of the newest and brightest guidebook on Europe's No. 1 tourist attraction. This is something of a departure for me as I have tended to concentrate on Disney's American theme parks in general and Florida in particular. But I paid my first visit to Disneyland Resort Paris *in October 2001 and was instantly hooked on the contrasting style from the US version and the complementary, almost artistic, experience it offers. Yes, it is still a Disney experience, but it has been uniquely 'Europeanised' and given a different flavour as a result.*

The opening of the Walt Disney Studios Park *in March 2002 added a dramatic new depth and breadth to the offering, fully justifying the change of name to* Disneyland Resort Paris *and ensuring it is now a much more rounded – and time-consuming! – place to visit. Other developments have been springing up in parallel to Disney's, hence your choice for things to do in this corner of the world is now hugely varied and great fun.*

That means you need a good guidebook to steer you through this theme park wonderland – and beyond. You need practical, impartial advice and a real user-friendly companion, as opposed to all the meaningless words and hype of the glossy brochures. It is a world of fun and adventure, but it is also complicated, detailed and demanding – especially in the summer – so it is important you are armed with all the necessary insider information to tackle it.

To that end, the Brit's Guide *series is dedicated completely to you, the holidaymaker; to ensuring you get the most out of your trip, at the best price and with the least amount of hassle. This book aims to be your Good Companion throughout the Disney experience – from the moment you start planning, to your journey there, how to enjoy it all while you're on site, and on to all the extra things to appreciate in the vicinity, notably in the city of Paris itself.*

Therefore, turn the pages and let me be your guide to this magical place called Disneyland Resort Paris. *The prospect alone fills me with great anticipation, so let's not wait another moment – on to Neverland…!*

Simon Veness

---

1 Introduction
(or, An Open Invitation to the Mouse House)

There is a very simple reason why Disney's theme parks are the world's most-visited attractions, be they in America, Japan or, in this case, France. They are simply the best family entertainment you will find anywhere, bar none, guaranteed.

And the guaranteed fun is not restricted just to families either. For, while children find the allure of Mickey and Co almost irresistible, there is something for everyone in a Disney park, be they young or old, single, a couple or with the whole family in tow. In fact, I would go so far as to say there is more all-round entertainment value here than anywhere else I've seen.

It is a great short-break destination, a perfect location for a week (or even longer, given the additional attractions of the Paris region itself) and it is easy to reach; it is beautifully geared up for families (especially those with young children), yet it also attracts its fair share of honeymooners and other couples; and its appeal is totally timeless, harking back to a nostalgic yesteryear but also remaining contemporary in so many areas.

Pixie dust

It is a beguiling prospect, and it is also one that is sure to bring out the child in (nearly) everyone. If you can envisage grown-ups rushing to hug Mickey or Minnie, then you can imagine the effect the Disney 'Pixie dust' has on just about every person who walks through the gates.

Indeed, Roy Disney, nephew of the great Walt himself, opened the Paris park with a phrase that his uncle first used for the debut of *Disneyland California* way back in 1955. He said: 'To all who come to this happy place, welcome! This is your land. Here age relives fond memories of the past and here youth may savour the challenge and the promise of the future. We hope it will be a source of joy and inspiration to the world.' And it certainly shapes up that way.

But enough of this tantalising glimpse of make-believe. Let me paint a picture of the reality and try to provide a basic understanding of how it all works. Believe me, this can be a complicated business and you need to keep your wits about you at all times. When the crowds start to flock into those parks, it is quite a challenge to keep up with the ebb and flow of it all. When the queue for a ride tops an hour, you need strategy on your side and the essential tool of all Disney-goers – a plan!

In fact, *planning* is an essential component of your holiday. At quieter times of the year, you might just get away with a free-wheeling, make-it-up-as-you-go-along kind of approach if you are on your own or just a couple. But, at even moderately busy periods or with youngsters in tow, there are plenty of pitfalls that await the unwary or the unprepared. This is most definitely not like a day out to Alton Towers or Thorpe Park, where a day is usually enough to see everything on offer.

Now there are two fully fledged parks to the Disney experience, it means there is a significant element of choice. Behind that lies a matter of scale that is hard to convey fully in advance and which includes an attention to detail both breathtaking and a little bewildering. It is easy to get side-tracked by some of the clever scenery, shops and other frippery, so that's why planning is important.

Not for nothing did they change the name to *Disneyland Resort Paris* in 2002, for truly this is a resort experience *par excellence*, and that means a multi-dimensional approach in all things, from the attractions to the hotels, the restaurants and even the shops. There is some kind of fun almost every which way you turn and a host of competing attractions at any one time. Therefore, you need to do your homework carefully in advance, to be aware of all that lies in store.

Chequered history

The *Disneyland Resort Paris* story began in the mid-1980s when Michael Eisner, the new Chief Executive Officer of the Walt Disney Company, came to Europe in search of a new outlet for their theme park creativity. Both France and Spain were firmly in the frame, and the verdict came down heavily in favour of the former for a variety of reasons, not least the strong French connection in many Disney films (*Cinderella, Sleeping Beauty, Hunchback of Notre Dame*) and the wonderfully central location offered by the Paris region.

As far back as December 1985, Mr Eisner signed a letter of intent with the then Prime Minister of France, Laurent Fabius, to build a Disney park in Marne-la-Vallée, some 32km (20 miles) due east of Paris itself. That agreement was formalised with Jacques Chirac in March 1987 and what was then about 1,900 hectares (4,700 acres) of beet fields became the planning ground for a great adventure in architecture and engineering, or Imagineering, as the Walt Disney Company likes to call it.

The first earth-moving equipment moved in on 2 August 1988 and a 4-year construction period of no little toil and tribulation began. Despite all the challenges of mother nature (and some considerable hindrance from the weather), the Euro Disney park (as it was then known, it quickly changed to Euro Disneyland) opened on time – in a massive blaze of film and TV star publicity – on 12 April 1992.

Now, I would like to be able to report that the opening was greeted with universal acclaim and support, but that wasn't quite what happened. Despite the glittering launch, the combination of a sceptical British press, a certain amount of French hostility (going back to the project's announcement) aimed at the supposed 'Americanisation' of their culture and some over-optimistic attendance forecasts all meant that Euro Disneyland had a painful initiation.

The media focused on anything negative – long lines for meals and longer queues for some rides, high prices, rumours of empty hotels and staff unhappiness – and the combination of problems both real and perceived almost brought the whole place to its knees. The park and all its associated development – various hotels, shops and restaurants, all grouped around a 'village' core called Festival Disney – had actually soared heavily over budget, and the lack of the immediate huge profits forecast to pay off the short-term debt, coupled with a Europe-wide recession, meant there was a very real threat the whole place might close after little more than a year of operation – despite a first annual attendance of 10.8 million.

A major financial restructuring was necessary in 1994, at which time it was also decided to rebrand as Disneyland Paris and, from there, the story has been one of strong and steady growth. Attendances steadily built up through the late 1990s and, as the future of the resort looked assured, more development began to spring up all around Marne-la-Vallée, both commercial and residential.

The success of Disney's on-site hotels (six of them, plus the camping ground of *Disney's Davy Crockett Ranch®* a short drive away) encouraged a mini proliferation of hotels in the vicinity, while the development extended to a new town centre at neighbouring **Val d'Europe,** a combination business/shopping/housing expansion which promises to add even more to the picture locally. Here, the immaculate shopping mall jostles for attention with the excellent outlet shopping of **La Vallée,** the **Sea Life Centre** and some enticing restaurants.

At the same time, a Disney-run **golf complex**, with three nine-hole courses, was developed just 10 minutes' drive from the resort itself, offering yet another diversion for people wanting to combine their theme park experience with something more down to earth (but equally vital).

A new park

The original plans also called for a sister park, along the lines of Disney-MGM Studios in *Walt Disney World Resort in Florida*. This was scheduled to open just three years after the first park, but the financial and other headaches of 1994 meant the concept went into storage for a while. However, with things looking up a few years later, those plans were revived in 1998 and construction began in earnest shortly afterwards. The eagerly awaited *Walt Disney Studios Park* then opened on 16 March 2002, with another explosion of publicity – and a second rebranding to *Disneyland Resort Paris*.

Here, finally, was the true resort expansion as originally envisaged by Eisner and his team of Imagineers, completing a well-rounded picture of accommodation, shopping, restaurants and theme parks, and providing a multi-day experience, even out of busy periods. The Festival Disney, now known more appropriately as *Disney Village*, has grown to encompass seven restaurants, three bars, a multi-screen cinema complex, an adjoining dinner show (the exceptionally family-friendly Buffalo Bill's Wild West Show), a big nightclub and a choice of seven shops.

With the Marne-la-Vallée railway station at the heart of the whole development, linking the resort with central Paris, Charles de Gaulle airport and, ultimately, London via Eurostar, it is also a wonderfully convenient location, easy for arrival and well organised to allow for easy movement either straight to the

BRIT TIP: *Disneyland Resort Paris* is just under 2 hours from Ashford in Kent on the direct Eurostar service and only 2 hours 50 minutes from London Waterloo. For the great convenience the train provides, it's definitely worth considering.

1

Facts and figures

- The whole site of *Disneyland Resort Paris* covers 1,943 hectares (4,800 acres), or one-fifth the area of Paris
- Groundbreaking took place in August 1988
- 51km (32 miles) of roads were built and 120 million cubic metres (157 million cubic yards) of earth moved
- Around 450,000 trees and shrubs were planted
- It employs 12,500 people every year (on average)
- The *Disneyland Park* covers 57 hectares (140 acres)
- The *Walt Disney Studios Park* stands on 25 hectares (62 acres)
- The seven themed hotels have a total of 5,800 rooms
- There are 68 counter and full-service restaurants throughout the resort
- In all, there are 47 different shops and boutiques
- Some 120 million people have visited since it opened
- Around 40% of visitors are French, 23% British, 8% German, 8% Belgian, 8% Dutch, 8% Spanish and Italian, and 5% from other nations

Theme Parks, to the hotels (using an efficient bus service) or directly into *Disney Village*.

Anyone familiar with the Orlando resort set up – 12,173 hectares (30,080 acres) of four parks, two water parks, 22 hotels and a mini-town area called *Downtown Disney* – will almost certainly be impressed by the ease with which you can move around this resort by comparison. All of it is within reach by a 20-minute walk at most and the scale is big enough to be constantly exciting yet manageable enough not to be daunting. Indeed, it is a triumph of the designers' art in making this hugely complex development one of very human dimensions, a riot of visual stimulation and yet easy to negotiate and effortless in its convenience. Yes, there is a lot going on here, but it is not difficult to get around and enjoy.

Disney Village

Offering a positive riot of sights and sounds, both by day and night (when the contrast is quite startling, from the peaceful Lake Disney in early morning to the near-disco

proportions of the late-evening hubbub), *Disney Village* acts as a conduit between the Theme Parks and hotels. It is an exit for the weary park-goers (and you can be pretty weary by park closing, believe me!) and offers a new source of fun and frolics for all those who enjoy their nightlife.

It is a heady cocktail but it also requires a certain amount of forethought, especially if you have the family in tow, to ensure you get the most out of *Disney Village*, whether it be for a meal, some more shopping or the amusement of some of the fairground-type games before you head back to the hotel.

Of course, the *Disney Village* is not reserved purely for Disney's on-site hotel guests. It does attract a good number of locals of an evening (especially on Fridays and Saturdays) and its large car park makes it easily accessible for anyone staying at one of the nearby hotels, while the RER service (the main local train line, a combination of underground and commuter rail) runs until after midnight for those who prefer to avoid driving.

The European touch

Truly, *Disneyland Resort Paris* is a wonderfully impressive set-up and is easily the equal of any of Disney's other parks and resorts around the world. In fact, I think it is the clever 'Europeanisation' of the traditional Disney style that makes this most appealing. There is more than a hint of French flair, Italian chic, Spanish partying, German organisation and Dutch friendliness about the whole resort, but it comes together best in the Village.

Yes, there are some drawbacks – especially for non-smokers, as avoiding cigarette smoke can be difficult at times – and the mixture of cultures occasionally causes some awkwardness as well as empathy; and the toilets could certainly be kept cleaner in many instances (for some reason, this seems to be a bit of a blind spot in the *Disneyland Park* and *Disney Village*).

It is not a particularly restful holiday, unless you go out of season in winter and are blessed by mild, dry weather and it can make a serious dent in your bank balance. But, all in all, it offers superb value for money and richly rewards those who go with an open mind and the willingness to try those few words of school French you can dredge up from memory.

More importantly, it is guaranteed to put a smile on the faces of young and old alike and hopefully reaffirm simple family and friendly values. When Walt built Disneyland in California back in 1955, his most famous statement (now etched on the bronze Walt 'n Mickey statue in front of the Sleeping Beauty Castle) was: 'I think most of all what I want Disneyland to be is a happy place… where parents and children can have fun together.'

So, don't forget to take time out to reaffirm those values during your visit; watch your children's faces during one of the parades or on the Dumbo ride or in the queue to meet Mickey (or just look at the reaction of other children); and ensure you do things together, however silly they may be! There is artistry all around you, in the rides, the architecture and the Cast Members, but the most meaningful feeling you can invoke is the bond with your loved ones – and nowhere brings that to the fore quite like a Disney park, whether it be for kids of six or 60.

However, perhaps the question most seasoned Disney-goers will want to ask is: if I have already been to *Walt Disney World Resort in Florida*, do I need to go to *Disneyland Resort Paris*? I would say unequivocally yes. Apart from the obvious advantage of this being a much closer and more convenient short-visit destination (no 9-hour flights and long queues at Immigration to deal with), I believe the more luxurious theming of the *Disneyland Park*, the updated versions of classic rides like Space Mountain, Haunted Mansion and Big Thunder Mountain, and the all-new thrills of most of the *Walt Disney Studios Park* make it an absolute must to visit here as well as Florida at some stage in your holiday travels. For some, it is also a handy 'refresher' of Disney magic in between visits to Orlando (and it probably goes without saying it is cheaper to spend a few days visiting Paris than a week or more's long haul to America). Anyone familiar with the vast extent of the Florida wonderworld will also appreciate the simple convenience of being able to walk everywhere!

See the city

Another big bonus of the location is the nearby lure of Paris itself and you certainly do not need to have a car here to benefit (in fact, trying to drive into the city is not advisable at all). The reliability of the RER service and the local buses mean you can easily enjoy an evening along the Champs Elysées or the Bastille district and still get the train back to Disneyland. A highly recommended night out for couples is the **Lido de Paris** show in the Champs Elysées, while another recent development is the **Cityrama** bus tours of the city, picking up at *Disney's Hotel New York* every day. The latter provides an excellent whistle-stop visit of all the main features of this fabulous city, still with the great convenience of staying outside it. It is also only about 40 minutes on the RER train into central Paris, which is then easy to negotiate either on foot or by the Métro or bus. It is a truly fabulous city with a wealth of history, architecture, art and amazing monuments, plus a dazzling array of fine restaurants and shops. If you are planning a 4-day Disney visit, I would definitely think about having at least half a day and an evening in Paris itself, especially as there are a host of attractions geared to the family audience (see Chapter 9).

BRIT TIP: Need to find your way around Paris public transport? Well, you have the Métro (the underground), RER train service (regional rail, part underground), Transilien SNCF (suburban rail – not strictly relevant to *Disneyland Resort Paris*), bus and tram. Visit www.ratp.fr for more info in French and English.

Those who bring the car can benefit from exploring slightly further afield – and there are some wonderful towns and villages to visit in this region of France, notably the medieval walled town of **Provins** just to the southeast. The road links are good (France also has a system of toll roads which are quite superb) and rarely subject to the kind of congestion we experience in much of the UK – apart from in the centre of Paris itself.

You can also stock up with some wonderful food and wine along the way, as well as in Val d'Europe, where the **Auchan hypermarket** is a highly civilised alternative to the bunfights that often ensue around the rather tired supermarkets of Calais.

The main focus, however, should be the Theme Parks themselves. The original *Disneyland Park* remains the heart and soul of the Magic, especially for families with children under 10, while the new *Walt Disney Studios Park* has added an element of excitement and thrills for the older age group. The two parks provide a complementary experience, but the time requirements of each are quite different. Don't be fooled into thinking you can spend 2 days here and feel you have done it all, even during an off-peak time of the year. The older park will require at least 2 days to ensure you have seen and done most of what is on offer, while the Studios version usually needs a full day to absorb fully its variety of entertainments.

Seasonal fun

The *Disneyland Resort Paris* is unique in the Disney empire of theme parks in providing a huge range of seasonal celebrations. While all their other resorts can lay on a brilliantly themed backdrop for Christmas and Halloween, only here will you find a real in-depth and broadly arranged series of attractions throughout the year, with special winter festivities, the spring Lion King Carnival, a Latin Festival in June, the amazing and quite superb transformation of

Speaking French

The resort has been a multi-lingual operation since Day One and all Disney employees (or Cast Members, as they are known) should be able to speak at least two languages (many speak four or five). This means you shouldn't have any trouble being understood wherever you are from. However, it is still good practice (and simple good manners) to try to remember a few words of French to get by from time to time. All cast members wear a badge with their name and home country, so you can easily spot the occasional Brit working here but, for those who can't remember their basic school French, here is a quick guide to those handy vital words:

ENGLISH	FRENCH
Do you speak English?	Parlez-vous Anglais?
Good morning/Hello	Bonjour
Good evening	Bonsoir
Please	S'il vous plaît
Thank you	Merci
I would like…	Je voudrais…
Do you have…	Avez-vous…
How much is…	Quel est le prix de…
How much?	C'est combien?
A receipt	Un reçu
The bill, please	L'addition, s'il vous plaît
Coffee	Café
White coffee	Café au lait
Where are the toilets?	Ou sont les toilettes?
Toll booths	Les péages
Motorway service areas	Aires
Autoroutes (toll roads)	Autoroutes des péages
Hypermarket	Hypermarché

Frontierland to Halloweenland in October, a series of Bonfire Night specials and the magic of Christmas in full *Disneyland Resort Paris* style.

BRIT TIP: In keeping with their seasonal approach, the New Year period from January to Easter has become the great Family Value time to visit, with plenty of Kids Go Free (with each adult) deals.

There is even a special celebration now to mark Chinese New Year.

Rain and shine

This is still Western Europe and the climate can be depressingly like our own at times – wet, grey and cold. However, much of both parks have been built with rain and wind in mind, which means there is nearly always somewhere you can escape the elements when they turn nasty. Indeed, almost 80% of the new *Walt Disney Studios Park* is under cover, which means you don't have to worry overmuch about the vagaries of mother nature ruining your

Top 10 campaign tips

1   Decide what you want to do and try to plan a rough daily schedule (especially in summer).

2   Work out if you want to Do It All (remember in summer, when opening hours are longest, everything is available but queues are at their longest, too) or have a quieter time in spring or autumn (with shorter hours and more unpredictable weather).

3   Stay in the resort or outside? The former offers unequalled convenience and essential 'Magic', but the latter is cheaper.

4   Choose your mode of transport. Eurostar, car, coach or air – where you live will determine which one is the most convenient (see Chapter 3).

5   Long weekend or holiday. The temptation is to pack it all into a weekend, and the ease of the Eurostar makes this appealing. But the weekends are busier and going for 4 to 5 days instead allows you more variety (see page 16).

6   Whether you have a day in Paris, an outing to Provins or Versailles, or just a shopping expedition to Val d'Europe, you'll benefit from a Disney break at some stage.

7   Stop and admire the scenery. Often.

8   Enjoy the fact you can have a (good) glass of wine or a beer in the *Disneyland Park*. Alcohol is not served in Walt Disney World's *Magic Kingdom Park* in Florida.

9   Try a little French. The locals are usually more hospitable and forthcoming if you make even a token effort to speak their language.

10 Get everyone in your party to read this book!

holiday. Providing you pack a light raincoat (advisable for all but summer months – and even then it is not a bad idea!), you are well prepared to carry on enjoying all that the Theme Parks can provide.

In fact, spring and autumn can offer some of the best times for visiting *Disneyland Resort Paris* as they rarely come up with any seriously anti-social weather, while the crowds are far more manageable. And, while the delights of Paris in the springtime is a wonderful cliché, that doesn't mean it also isn't true –

hence the months of April (after Easter) and May are just about the best time to visit, with a heavenly combination of pleasant weather, convivial atmosphere and lower-than-average attendances.

Yes, this is the biggest tourist attraction in Europe – with 13.1 million visitors in 2002, some 2.75 million from the UK alone – but it can easily be a breeze of a place to visit if you get your tactics right.

And so, with that firmly in mind, let us move on to the vital area of planning…

2 Planning

(or, How to Do Disney and Stay Sane!)

It used to be the case just a few years ago that you could pop across the Channel to Marne-la-Vallée, have a fun day out and be back home again for tea the next day, safe in the knowledge you had 'done' Disney. Not any more.

The addition of the new *Walt Disney Studios Park* in March 2002, the expansion of the surrounding area and continuing influx of visitors mean this is now somewhere you need to consider carefully before you set out for that 'perfect' holiday. It is not quite the same as *Walt Disney World Resort in Florida*, where any visit has to be planned with the precision and accuracy of a military campaign (well, not far short, anyway!), but you do need to have a good idea of what you are letting yourself in for and it is still highly advisable to try to plan around some of the pitfalls that await the unwary.

First of all, the two parks are a complete contrast from each other, and therefore have different time requirements and appeal to different people. They provide a complementary experience for all but the youngest children (the new park has fewer attractions for under 5s), but you will probably need the best part of 2 full days to explore all of the *Disneyland Park*, while a day is usually sufficient at the *Walt Disney Studios Park*.

The Disneyland Park

The *Disneyland Park* follows the rough formula of the *Magic Kingdom* in Orlando, *Disneyland California*, near Los Angeles, and *Disneyland Tokyo*. It is subdivided into five 'lands' around a central hub and features a range of almost 50 attractions in the form of rides, shows, parades and other live entertainment. There is also an impressive cast of accompanying shops and restaurants, all themed to the various lands and offering some useful browsing opportunities. At 57 hectares (140 acres), it requires some serious shoe leather to see it all, and you will be amazed at how time-consuming it can be to get from land to land with the number of diversions you can encounter.

BRIT TIP: Can't find the characters? Check out Main Street USA in the *Disneyland Park* in the morning and the Animation Courtyard area of the *Walt Disney Studios Park* throughout the day. Better still, book one of the character meals at a restaurant like Café Mickey or the Lucky Nugget Saloon.

This is also the Theme Park where families tend to concentrate (although there are also several terrific thrill rides, most notably Space Mountain and Indiana Jones™ and The Temple of Peril: Backwards!). There is a huge choice for dining and some wonderful character meal opportunities (which kids adore), but you need to pace yourself more here as it's easy to get worn to a frazzle – and end up with fractious children – by too much unnecessary to-ing and fro-ing.

Walt Disney Studios Park

This park is subdivided into four areas and is slightly less than half the size of its sister park. It is therefore easier to negotiate. As the name suggests, *Walt Disney Studios Park* is geared around the magic of the film world, but it is a very different proposition to the *Disney-MGM Studios* in Orlando (although two of the rides are similar and another is a transplant from Orlando's *Magic Kingdom*). It is much more show-based, hence its attractions are geared around specific times of the day (like the amazing Stunt Show), and more of it is indoors, which is handy when the weather is too cold, too hot or too wet! There are fewer things to appeal to younger children here and the dining opportunities are distinctly ordinary compared to the *Disneyland Park*, but you will still encounter the all-important Disney characters and some wonderful street entertainment as well.

Beyond the Theme Parks

Once you have visited the Theme Parks, the delights of the *Disney Village* await you. Here you can dine, dance, shop, go to the cinema or catch a show in this lively, bustling hub which is a pure delight at night with the clever lighting effects. The choice of dining is terrific – the elaborate international theming of Planet Hollywood (one of my real favourites here), Rainforest Café, the 1950s' Americana of Annette's Diner, (a superb Steakhouse), the country and western style of Billy Bob's Saloon, an all-day character-fest at Café Mickey (with excellent food, too), a Sports Bar and a New York Sandwiches deli, plus a large McDonalds. A new Bavarian-style restaurant – King Ludwig's Castle – opened in May 2003, replacing the old Rock 'n' Roll America bar/diner and adding still further to the great variety on offer.

Live bands are an outstanding feature of Billy Bob's, while Hurricanes disco (free to Disney resort guests) starts bopping around midnight (although it can be quiet Sunday to Thursday out of season).

BRIT TIP: Too crowded for lunch in the Theme Parks? Step outside and enjoy a meal in *Disney Village*, with none of the long queues, at restaurants like Planet Hollywood, Café Mickey and Annette's Diner.

Nine fully-fledged boutique stores stay open usually until midnight, and the Central Stage is the venue for more live entertainment from time to time. The Gaumont Cinema is a 12-screen complex showing the latest movies but, unless you speak good French, there is only one English-language presentation – every Monday night. The new IMAX Cinema (due in summer 2004) should add an extra dimension here. There is also the inevitable video games arcade.

Finally, **Buffalo Bill's Wild West Show** is a real *Disney Village*

Four nights – barely enough

To get an idea of the full new resort set-up in summer 2002, I took my boys (then aged 4 and 6) on a standard 4-night/5-day package with Leger Holidays, the big coach tour operator. Staying at *Disney's Hotel Santa Fe*, I had semi-planned an itinerary for each day and found this was a valuable strategy (especially where meals were concerned), although I also had to keep our plans fairly fluid at times to allow for tired boys! This is how the trip worked out:

DAY ONE: Arrive at *Disney's Hotel Santa Fe* at 9.30pm after 8½-hour journey, including P&O Ferry crossing. Everyone straight to bed!

DAY TWO: Up at 8am for hotel breakfast and off to the *Disneyland Park* soon after. Full day in the Theme Park, with lunch (pre-booked) at The Lucky Nugget Saloon. Younger son in need of a break after 3pm parade, so back to the hotel for a rest. Dinner at Planet Hollywood at 6.30pm, followed by a slow wander back to the hotel through the *Disney Village* (with much to sidetrack both boys!).

DAY THREE: A late start – not up until 9.30am; hotel breakfast at 10, then off to the *Walt Disney Studios Park*, just in time to catch the 11am Stunt Show. Take in two more shows before lunch at Backlot Express (self service), then complete the full range of attractions by 5.30pm. Switch to *Disneyland Park* for dinner at Silver Spur Steakhouse at 6.30pm (pre-booked), then one last ride before catching bus back to hotel.

DAY FOUR: An 8am breakfast (pre-booked) in the *Disneyland Park* at Walt's – An American Restaurant (with various characters). Then spend 2 hours doing many of the rides in Fantasyland. Leave park to take RER one stop to Val d'Europe and visit the Sea Life Centre*. Have lunch and shop, and give the boys a chance to play in La Vallée play area, before catching the train back. Revisit the *Walt Disney Studios Park* for another chance to see the Stunt Show and Animagique before heading back to the other park for our planned late night. Dinner at 8pm watching a show at Videopolis, and both boys happily keep going on various rides until the 10.30 evening parade and fireworks.

DAY FIVE: Quite surprisingly, we make an 8am breakfast and pack our luggage back on to the coach. Visit the Esso petrol station next to the hotel to grab a few snacks for the long journey back to Calais. Coach departs at 10am, non-stop to Calais hypermarket. Home again – very tired but with very happy boys! – by 4.30pm UK time.

* If the boys had been a bit older, I would have considered the full-day Paris sight-seeing tour with Cityrama (see Chapter 9) for our break from the Theme Parks.

institution, a corny-but-fun dinner show which is usually a huge hit with kids (even grown-up ones!) and offers the chance to shout, cheer and wave your (free) cowboy hat in support of the various acts, who entertain you in the huge indoor auditorium during a typical cowboy dinner. In peak summer season there is also a daily Wild West parade outside before the first of the two shows of the day (around 6pm). For the full details on *Disney Village*, see Chapter 8.

On a different note, the opening of the new **Manchester United Soccer School** next to *Disney's Sequoia Lodge* hotel (in spring 2004) provides still more variety.

As if all that were not enough, you will also find the additional lure of **Val d'Europe** quite strong (it is developing all the time as a major business centre), and there is some excellent shopping in store here (most notably at the adjoining **La Vallée** outlet village). This is just 5 minutes away on the RER train (and free buses also run between the Disney resorts and Val d'Europe at various times) and can provide a refreshing break from the world of the Mouse after a few days.

Here you will find a huge indoor shopping mall, some excellent restaurants in an upmarket food court and the exceedingly child-friendly **Sea Life Centre**, a major aquarium run by the attraction chain that owns six similar attractions in the UK and another seven throughout Europe. It is a great diversion for kids from 2 to 12 especially and provides a good 2-hour break if Mum or Dad want to go shopping!

When to go

Unfortunately, the majority of people who visit do so in full family mode, hence they are usually there in the school holidays. Unfortunate because both the cost and the crowds increase during those times, while the summer can also be uncomfortably hot – in excess of 30°C (and two of the resort hotels, *Disney's Hotel Cheyenne* and *Disney's Hotel Santa Fe*, plus MyTravel's Explorers Hotel, do not have air-conditioning). That means you will need to consider all your options very carefully.

If you are still set on the main school holiday periods, try to opt for late Easter or late summer if you can. The spring and autumn half-term holidays are also prime opportunities, although, once again, the cost does increase at those times.

The one big pay-off with a summer visit, of course, is the bonus of extended opening hours (to 11pm) and a full show and parade

---

France on holiday

There are 11 public holidays in France. They are: 1 January, 1 May, 8 May, Easter Monday, Ascension day, Whit Monday, 14 July, 15 August, 1 November, 11 November and 25 December. All government departments, banks and shops are usually closed on these days.

French children – and their teachers – have FIVE holidays a year! They get 1 week at the end of October, 2 weeks at Christmas, 2 more in February, 2 in spring, and the whole of the summer in July and August. Consequently, *Disneyland Resort Paris* and the roads are noticeably busier during these periods.

For more details on French school holidays, look up: www.education.gouv.fr/prat/cal.htm

schedule. If you can avoid Le Weekend crowds, you still benefit from the pure magic of long nights in the *Disneyland Park* followed by the evening finale fireworks. As ever, it is a case of swings and roundabouts, and you really need to consider what might work best for you, or what appeals most.

Busy times

If you are able to visit in the non-peak times, you will really feel the benefit. And, by non-peak periods, I also mean weekdays rather than weekends. For, while the local populace didn't exactly embrace Disney with great eagerness at the beginning, the Theme Parks (and *Disney Village*) have developed into a major source of local recreation. So much so that the French attendance on a Saturday and Sunday can be 50% or more quite easily. Put simply, this is where much of suburban Paris comes to play at the weekend, and it can be very hectic, especially on Saturdays.

Both parks cope pretty well with the thousands who pour in during the first few hours of the day, but the queues do build up quickly at most of the main rides (and just about everywhere in Fantasyland in the *Disneyland Park*). The standard wait

BRIT TIP: Disney's FastPass system is an invaluable aid to your park visit, but many people neglect to use it because they don't understand it. It is FREE to use and simply gives you a time to return to the ride and bypass the main queue with only a short wait. It is fully explained in Chapter 5.

time for rides like Peter Pan's Flight and Dumbo can easily top an hour, and this can make for an uncomfortable period of standing in line, especially when it's hot and even more so if you have young children in tow. However, Disney has developed a wonderful virtual queuing system called **FastPass**, which takes a lot of sting out of the waits for many attractions, but even that has its limitations, which means, during Easter, summer and Christmas (and any weekend when the weather is fair), you will spend a lot of time on your feet.

So, if you need to avoid school holidays, most of the summer and the weekends, when *should* you go? Well, as I've already mentioned, the spring usually sees Paris at its best, and this tends to rub off on Disneyland, too. Of all Disney's parks all over the world, this one is designed and landscaped with distinctly European tastes in mind. Somehow, the architecture is a touch more elegant and lavish; there is less overt Americana and more emphasis on European art and history (especially cinematic history), the scale is more human and meandering; and there is a much greater emphasis on plants and greenery, providing a naturalistic element to the *Disneyland Park* in particular which is a joy to behold in the spring and early summer.

That is not to say both parks don't have a good deal of charm all year round (especially at Christmas and New Year, when Disney really lays on the charisma), or that you can't have as much fun on the rides in November as you can in April, but there is something genuinely special about a bright spring day that perfectly sets off the magic provided by the Imagineers. The Adventureland section of the *Disneyland Park* is particularly noticeable in this way, as it is an area which completely envelops you with

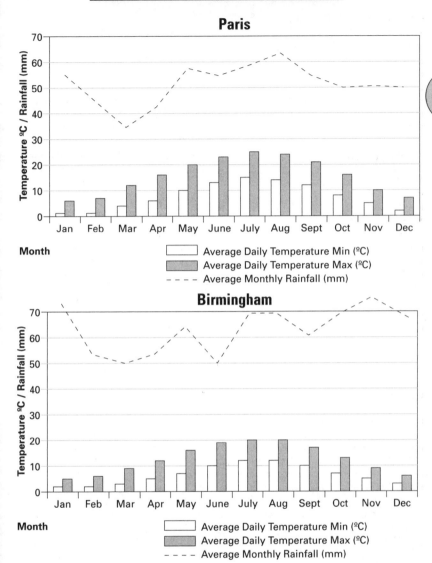

Paris

Month

☐ Average Daily Temperature Min (ºC)
▨ Average Daily Temperature Max (ºC)
- - - Average Monthly Rainfall (mm)

Birmingham

Month

☐ Average Daily Temperature Min (ºC)
▨ Average Daily Temperature Max (ºC)
- - - Average Monthly Rainfall (mm)

its sense of grand design and creativity.

Visiting off peak

The weather also tends to be more consistent in a Paris springtime than just across the Channel, too. Here you can compare the two typical temperature and rainfall charts for Paris and Birmingham. However,

the winters can be equally unpleasant as our own in terms of wet and cold, hence there are several factors you need to bear in mind if you opt to visit from November to February. The most obvious is the downturn in business in the winter, with not only the crowds dropping off appreciably, but some of the restaurants and attractions closing too. All Disney's rides, shows and attractions go through a regular process of refurbishment and much of this is carried out in the winter months, so you may well find one or two things shut down at this time. For example, if you enjoyed the Lion King-style dining at Hakuna Matata (in the *Disneyland Park*) during a summer visit, be aware it is frequently one of the counter-service outlets that close at off-peak times.

BRIT TIP: The excellent German/English website www.dlp-guidebook.de includes a section on Closed Attractions, which lists rides due for a revamp more than six months in advance.

Some entertainment is geared only to peak periods, when the Theme Parks are open longer. A nightly fireworks show and a special evening parade extravaganza in the *Disneyland Park* are real highlights in summer and at Christmas, while the Winnie The Pooh & Friends show is also high season only. Bad weather (notably heavy rain) can scupper some of the outdoor entertainment at any time of the year, but this is obviously going to be more likely to happen in the winter months.

However, a notable plus point for those wishing to visit out of season is the lack of any serious queues in many instances. I have been in the Theme Parks at a whole variety of different times and nothing beats being able to wander around places like Fantasyland and Discoveryland with the choice of any ride without queuing (and without tripping over toddlers or being run over by pushchairs!). The staff have more time for you, too, and the whole atmosphere is less frenetic, which definitely adds to the enjoyment.

The other big bonus is that it is *cheaper* at off-peak times as this is the only Disney operation which works seasonally. The Low Season is officially from early January (after the New Year festivities) to the end of March or early April (just prior to Easter) and entry ticket prices drop by around 20% for adults and 15% for children (3–11; under 3s are always free). The regular **'Kids Go Free'** season (another unique Disney feature here) also coincides with Low Season, whereby, with any Disney hotel package, every child stays and plays free with a full fare-paying adult, including free continental breakfast and park entry.

Of course, the Theme Park hours are shorter at this time of year (usually 10am–8pm at the *Disneyland Park* and 10am–6pm at the *Walt Disney Studios*), but it is that much easier to get around so you shouldn't feel short-changed at all (while 8pm is often late enough for many children anyway).

A weather eye

Ah, but what about the weather, you will be asking (well, someone might!). As I have already pointed out, *Disneyland Resort Paris* can organise many things, but they have yet to discover how to keep the rain at bay or order the right amount of sunshine for their guests' requirements. That means your day in the Theme Parks might fall foul of unwelcome precipitation that could literally rain on your parade. But don't fret! The park designers took the weather firmly into all their calculations when they were busy Imagineering and you will find more attractions protected from the elements than at any other theme park in the world. It is even possible to walk deep into the *Disneyland Park* mainly under cover (follow the special route in Chapter 6).

The provision of arcades down

both sides of Main Street USA (the entrance to the main park), some capacious indoor restaurants and very few real 'outdoor' rides (not to mention all the shops, which can provide welcome shelter from any wind and rain) mean much of your enjoyment should be unspoilt by the vagaries of the weather. Additionally, if you bring a waterproof (or buy one of the cheap plastic ponchos on sale throughout the resort) you will be able to continue enjoying the rides with fewer people.

Christmas events

You may want to take the resort's seasonal events into consideration when planning your visit. First and foremost is the **Christmas** programme, which features special shows, parades, fireworks, decorations and other events in the Theme Parks, hotels and *Disney Village* from around 9 November to the first week of January, plus the Enchanted Ball on the Sunday before Christmas Day.

Main Street USA in the *Disneyland Park* becomes the focus of all this festive fun as it is transformed into a genuine winter wonderland. There is an evening **Christmas Tree Lighting ceremony** in Town Square, which is led by Santa's reindeer-drawn sleigh and accompanied by a cast of toy soldiers and dancing dolls. Each evening, a child is chosen from the crowd to sprinkle a handful of 'pixie dust' to illuminate the tree and set off a breathtaking procession of lights all the way up Main Street USA to the castle. The **Lights of Winter** are strung all the way above Main Street USA, while the festive atmosphere is enhanced by elaborately decorated and themed window displays and Christmas carollers (not to mention a guaranteed snowfall five times a day,

BRIT TIP: Some of the Disney characters have different names in France, and will occasionally give their autograph in French fashion. Chip 'n' Dale are translated into Tic and Tac, Goofy can become Dingo and Winnie The Pooh is Winnie l'Ourson.

whether it's cold enough or not!). The Central Plaza area is decorated in individual style with the **Magical Christmas Tree Forest**, a series of fir trees that bear the hallmarks of characters like Pluto and Goofy.

Other highlights are the magnificent decorations throughout Fantasyland, topped off by the nightly **Sparkling Christmas Fireworks** spectacular over the castle, which is preceded by a special outing of the scintillating **Fantillusion** parade. In **Santa's Grotto**, children can meet Father Christmas and have a photo with him and his elves, while new in 2002 was **Belle's Christmas Village**, a medieval village themed after Beauty and the Beast, opened every day with a show led by Belle and friends, and a chance to meet the characters afterwards. On the Castle Stage at the top of Main Street USA, **'Santa' Goofy** leads another character meet 'n' greet, which always goes down well with children (11am–2.30pm and 4.30–6pm).

The daily Christmas Parade **Mickey's Nutcracker,** is a superb cavalcade of traditional Disney favourites themed around Tchaikovsky's seasonal masterpiece, and two additional shows – the 25-minute **Le Noel De Mickey** (or *'Twas The Night Before Christmas*) at the Fantasy Festival Stage. **Mickey's Winter Wonderland** provides 20 minutes of ice-skating fun and frolics with Mickey and the gang at the Chaparral Theatre in Frontierland (which is the one Christmas element that usually continues right through to the beginning of March).

At the *Walt Disney Studios Park*, the seasonal celebration is centred on the Front Lot, with another huge tree and some over-the-top decorations. Inside Disney Studio 1, the soundstage is set up for a festive production, with more Christmas carols and a snow-covered 'landscape'.

The highly decorated theme is recurrent through all areas of the resort, with a special Christmas market and a Santa show in *Disney Village*. Having seen how brilliantly Disney's Imagineers prepare the Theme Parks in Orlando, I can assure you that they take it to new heights in *Disneyland Resort Paris* and it is definitely worth braving the wintry elements for the experience.

You can enjoy another great winter touch at *Disney's Hotel New York*, with a clever **ice-skating rink** outside. Both *Disney's Hotel New York* and *Disney's Newport Bay Club* hotels also feature special **Christmas musical dinner shows** that are well worth booking in advance, *A Musical Evening with Mickey* at the former and *The Magical World of Tinker Bell* at *Disney's Newport Bay Club*. The final, one-off element is the new **Enchanted Christmas Ball**, a separate evening's fun and entertainment at the *Disneyland Park* at around £16 per person (under 3s free). Running from 9pm–2am, it features a Disney choir and ballroom dancers set in a Dickens' Victorian-style Christmas on Main Street USA, with three of the lands and all their rides open throughout the night. NB: the *Disneyland Park* closes at 8pm on Christmas Eve, but is open until 1am on **New Year's Eve**, when there are party festivities throughout the Theme Park and *Disney Village*.

> **BRIT TIP:** If you can visit in late November or the first 2 weeks of December, you will benefit from the full Christmas festivities but without the heavy crowds which they attract later in the month.

A new parade

February 2004 sees the arrival of a new celebration in the *Disneyland Park*, the **Lion King Carnival**, with the lovable Timon leading a daily parade along the main procession route, plus other musical fun and games. Dance with Pumba and enjoy the beat of the jungle tam-tams as all the Lion King characters join in the fun. The whole of Main Street is transformed into a party venue, with Mr Calypso leading a Samba-style mini-parade up to six times a day. You can see the Dixie Musicians in Town Square, and join Baloo and his friends in the **Jungle Boogie Party** twice daily in the Central Plaza.

Other events include a new January season marking **Disney's Chinese New Year,** the annual **St Patrick's Day** celebration (17 March) and the **Festival Latina** (salsa, samba, beautiful girls and Latin rhythms) every June, all centred on *Disney Village* and the Central Stage (and the bars, in the case of St Patrick's Day – and, yes, they do serve Guinness!).

Summer season

From early July until the end of August, the full range of park entertainment is up and running, the *Disneyland Park* is open until 11pm – and crowds are at their highest. At this time of year, the new **Fantillusion** parade is one of the main highlights, closely followed by the **Tinker Bell Fantasy in the Sky fireworks**, which bring down the curtain each evening.

Halloween

The next big landmark period is **Halloween** – and Disney makes a big feature of this. While the idea is certainly more American than European, the style with which *Disneyland Resort Paris* has adopted this tradition is quite breathtaking. Not only is there a daily **Halloween Happening** parade but the whole of Frontierland becomes Halloweenland for all of October, with a wonderfully imaginative series of tableaux (and it is amusing rather than scary for little children). The parade follows the same route as the usual daily Princess Parade, but it is a showcase for the Disney Villains (and is actually more fun!). Kids will also automatically gravitate towards the Halloween **face-painting** stalls, which are another notable feature here. Additionally, there are two late evening **Halloween Parties** where, for an extra fee, the Theme Park is open from 9pm–2am for more ghostly goings-on (see page 100), plus a late-night party in *Disney Village*.

Finally, the **Bonfire Night** specials run for 3–4 nights each year around 5 November in best Guy Fawkes tradition. This firework spectacular takes place above Lake Disney, adjacent to *Disney Village*.

How long do you need?

So, once you have worked out WHEN is the right time for you to visit, you need to work out HOW LONG you need to go for.

First time visitors will probably want to opt for the maximum time they can afford, especially at busy periods. The standard packages now offer 2, 3 and 4-night stays and, as indicated on page 16, the 4-night duration is only barely enough these days, especially if you have young children to consider. To my mind, if you can afford a week in summer, you will have the ideal amount of time to explore fully and see some of the surrounding area and Paris as well (and not return home frazzled!). However, because the majority book one of the standard packages, I have drawn up an example of how to plan for each in **Your Holiday Planner** in Chapter 10.

If you're already familiar with the *Disneyland Park* and have yet to see the *Walt Disney Studios Park*, you will probably be comfortable with a 2-night stay, concentrating on the new park during your full day on site. Couples without children or with older kids who can safely survive the demands of a bit of hectic park-hopping can probably negotiate both parks and, perhaps, Val d'Europe on a 3-night package. But let me stress – you simply will not be able to 'do it all' in one of the peak periods!

Ideally, you should gear your trip towards avoiding the weekends if at all possible. The perfect 4-night visit would run from Monday to Thursday, returning on the Friday before the place starts to get *seriously* busy.

However, if you can't go for long enough, or if you have to include a weekend, let me reassure you that you *can* still have a great time, and there are a number of dodges, tips and short cuts which *will* give you a head start over the rest of the crowds. These will all become obvious in the three chapters on the Theme Parks themselves.

Clothing and comfort

The most important part of your holiday wardrobe is your footwear – you will spend a lot of time on your feet, even during the off-peak periods. The two parks may not be gigantic but that is irrelevant to the amount of time you will spend going to and fro and queuing. This is not the time to break in those new sandals or trainers. Comfortable, well-worn shoes or trainers are essential. Otherwise, you need dress only as the climate dictates. T-shirts and shorts are quite acceptable in both parks when it's warm enough, and most restaurants and other eating establishments will happily accept informal dress. Shoes and shirts must be worn at all times in the Theme Parks, though. Warm, waterproof footwear is also advisable in winter, along with extra-thick (or thermal) socks.

If, after a long day, you feel the need to bring a change of clothes or some extra layers for the evening, you can leave them in a bag at the Luggage Check next to Guest Relations in both parks (€2 per bag). Both parks are also well equipped with pushchairs (or strollers, if you happen to get an American Cast Member) for a small charge and baby-changing areas are found in most toilets.

Disney with children

I am often asked what I think is the right age to take children to Disney for the first time, and there is no set answer, I'm afraid. Some toddlers take to it instantly, while some 6- or even 7-year-olds are left rather bemused. Quite often, the best attractions for young children are the hotel swimming pool or the long moving walkways from the car park! Some love the Disney characters at first sight, while others find their size quite frightening. There is simply no predicting how they will react, but I do know my eldest boy (then 4½) loved just about every second of his first experience (apart from the fireworks) and still talks about much of it. Yes, a 3-year-old may not remember much, but they

WILL have fun and provide YOU with some great memories, photos or video.

Here are a few tips, put together from personal experience and with advice from other parents:

The journey: try to look calm (even if you don't feel it) and relaxed. Small children soon pick up on any anxieties and make them worse! Pack a bag with plenty of little bits for them (comics, sweets, colouring books, small surprise toys, etc) and keep vital 'extras' like Calpol (in sachets, if possible), change of clothes, small first-aid kit (plasters, antiseptic cream, baby wipes), sunglasses, hat and sunscreen in your hand luggage. If they are fussy with their food, you may want to take a bottle of their favourite squash, etc. Ribena is unheard of in Europe, for example.

> BRIT TIP: Pushchairs are essential, even if your children are a year or two out of them. The distances involved around the Theme Parks wear kids out quickly, and a pushchair can save a lot of discomfort (for dads especially!). You can take your own, hire them at the Theme Parks or even buy one relatively cheaply at the Auchan supermarket in Val d'Europe.

Once there: take things slowly and let your children dictate the pace, to a large extent. **The summer heat can make children irritable in no time at all, so take breaks for drinks or go to attractions with air-conditioning.** Remember to carry your small first-aid kit with you. Things like baby wipes always come in handy and it is a good idea to take spare clothes, which you can leave at the Luggage Check at both parks. Going back to the hotel for an afternoon snooze is also well worthwhile – the late afternoon/early evening is usually the best time to be at the Theme Parks in terms of cooler temperatures (in summer), lower crowds and pure enjoyment. Both parks have a Lost Children meeting place (see page 88).

In the summer: carry suncream and sunblock at all times and use it frequently, in queues, on buses, etc. A children's after-sun cream is also a good idea and don't forget to drink a lot of water or non-fizzy drinks. Tiredness and irritability are often caused by mild dehydration.

Eating out: look for the all-you-can-eat buffets as these are a great way to fill the family up (you may get away with two meals a day) and cater for picky eaters. The Lucky Nugget Saloon, Plaza Gardens Restaurant and Billy Bob's (the latter in *Disney Village*) all offer some serious buffets. Also, try to let your children get used to the (size of the) characters before you go to one of the character meal opportunities.

BRIT TIP: Full Baby Care Centres (for changing, preparing food and feeding, with nappies and baby food for sale) can be found behind the Studio Services, just inside the entrance to the *Walt Disney Studios Park*, and next door to the Plaza Gardens Restaurant in the *Disneyland Park*.

Having fun: try to involve your children in some of the decision-making and be prepared to go with the flow if they find something unexpected they like (the vintage vehicles up and down Main Street

USA in the *Disneyland Park* are a good example).

With young children, the chances are you won't get to see and do everything, so just take your time and make the most of what you can all enjoy together.

Travellers with disabilities

Disney pays close attention to the needs of holiday-makers with disabilities, and even has a discounted entry price at the Theme Parks. There are few rides and attractions that cannot cater for them, while wheelchair availability and access is almost always good.

As the *Walt Disney Studios* is so new, much thought and care has gone into the arrangements for people with various kinds of disabilities (from the wheelchair-bound to those with autism and epileptic concerns), and it is worth taking a little time to familiarise yourself with all the ways in which you can take advantage of the facilities. The Cast Members should be fully prepared to help and assist, ensuring you get the full value from all the thoughtful extra touches.

All Disney hotels (except *Disney's Davy Crockett Ranch®*) have rooms accessible for guests with disabilities, while they also publish a free *Guide for Guests with Special Needs* (outlining all the necessary information for an enjoyable visit), which is available at hotel receptions and Guest Services offices at both Theme Parks. The guide can be sent to you in advance from: Disneyland Resort Paris, Guest Communication, PO Box 100, 77777 Marne-la-Vallée, Cedex, France.

Guidebooks in Braille are also provided and guide dogs are allowed in (although they are not permitted on certain attractions). Start by going to Guest Services at either park and asking for a copy of the *Guide for Guests with Special Needs*. You will also be given a Blue Card that allows you to access the special entrances for guests with disabilities (usually through the ride's exit – the main queue lines are not designed for wheelchair access), plus special seating for the shows and parades. However, you must be able to show a doctor's note or disabled pass to qualify for one.

Guests with hearing disabilities are not terribly well catered for, apart from a handful of attractions that have sub-titles on video screens rather than bi-lingual commentaries or headphone translators. The multi-lingual nature of the resort makes it difficult to use a close-captioning system effectively as they do so well in Disney's American parks and they seem to be still some way off from cracking this particular problem.

Disney for grown-ups

It may sound daft to include something specifically for adults but it is an often overlooked aspect that you don't need to have kids in tow to enjoy *Disneyland Resort Paris*. In fact, I've often felt the place is actually *too good* for kids! There is so much clever detail

and imagination which most youngsters miss in their eagerness for the next ride, it is usually the grown-ups who get the most out of the experience. In fact, there are just as many couples without children and young adults on their own visiting the Theme Parks (especially from countries like Holland and Germany), making it a legitimate holiday for *all* ages. Certainly, when you look at some of the sophisticated dining on offer and the evening entertainment at places like Billy Bob's and Hurricanes in *Disney Village* (although Billy Bob's often has an early evening session into which kids are allowed, and enjoy bopping along to), it is easy to see the attraction for those aged 21 and over.

Paris obviously makes a wonderful honeymoon destination and newly-weds are just as likely to visit one of Disney's parks as the Eiffel Tower. Restaurants like the Blue Lagoon and Auberge de Cendrillon in the *Disneyland Park*, The Steakhouse in *Disney Village*, the Hunter's Grill Restaurant at *Disney's Sequoia Lodge* and the superb California Grill at the *Disneyland Hotel* also offer a genuine romantic touch to dining à la Disney.

Top 10 things to do in Disneyland Resort Paris

Here is my guide to the 10 things you MUST do on any visit to this wonderful resort:

1 Have a character meal
2 Dine at the Blue Lagoon restaurant
3 See the daily parades (especially the Fantillusion parade)
4 Take a stroll around Lake Disney
5 Have dinner at Planet Hollywood and then check out the live music at Billy Bob's Saloon in *Disney Village*
6 See Buffalo Bill's Wild West Show
7 Have a drink in the Redwood Bar and Lounge at *Disney's Sequoia Lodge*
8 Go shopping at La Vallée
9 Watch the Rythmo Technico street percussion group in *Walt Disney Studios Park*
10 Moteurs... Action! Stunt Show Spectacular in *Walt Disney Studios Park*

Disney for seniors

If my parents are anything to go by, the over-60 age group can get a huge amount of enjoyment from *Disneyland Resort Paris*.

The greater ease of getting here (as opposed to the American parks) is high on their list of plus factors, while the convenience of just about everything being within walking distance or a short bus or train ride scores highly too. They preferred the *Disney Village* and hotel areas during the day when crowds were rare. Within 2 days they were fully *au fait* with the whole resort and extremely comfortable with the set-up. Here is their own Top 10 of attractions suitable for the over 60s:

1 Cinémagique (Walt Disney Studios)
2 Star Tours (Disneyland Park)
3 Pirates of the Caribbean (Disneyland Park)
4 Moteurs ... Action! Stunt Show (Walt Disney Studios)
5 Studio Tram Tour (Walt Disney Studios)
6 Haunted Mansion (Disneyland Park)
7 Animagique (Walt Disney Studios)
8 Tarzan Encounter (Disneyland Park)
9 'it's a small world' (Disneyland Park)
10 Flying Carpets Over Agrabah (Walt Disney Studios)

They would even go as far as listing the walk around Lake Disney as an attraction in its own right, while they also felt the more show-based style of the *Walt Disney Studios* suited them better than the rather more hectic ride-orientated nature of the original park. However, they still acknowledge the essential magic of the latter as totally unmissable.

Being practical

When it comes to the practicalities of your holiday, your obvious needs include **passports** for all the family (double-checking the name on your passport matches with that on your travel tickets) and remember that all children must have their OWN passport these days. Passports must also remain valid for 3 months after entering France, but no visas are required. For UK passport enquiries, call 08705 210410.

Travel insurance

You can get free or reduced cost treatment in all European Union countries. However, you must obtain an E111 form in advance from your Post Office and make sure it is stamped by a counter clerk to validate it. The E111 does not cover all medical expenses however, or the cost of bringing a person back to the UK in the event of illness or death, so it is essential to have adequate insurance cover as well.

Having said you should not travel without good insurance, you should also not pay over the odds for it. Tour operators can be expensive or may imply you need to buy their insurance policy when you don't. In all cases make sure your policy covers you for: **medical cover** up to £1million; **personal liability** up to £1million; **cancellation** or **curtailment** cover up to £3,000; **personal property** cover up to £1,500 (but check on expensive items, as most policies limit single articles to £250); **cash and document** cover, including your passport and tickets; and finally that the policy gives you a 24-hour **emergency helpline**.

A question of characters – where are they?

The biggest question on most visitors' lips (especially those with children!) is usually 'Where can we find the characters?' There are invariably some who leave frustrated because they simply miss out on this essential photo and autograph opportunity. Therefore, to give you a head start on your character hunting, here is a quick rundown of where you can usually meet Mickey and Co:

Disneyland Park: at the top of Main Street USA for the Main Street Park Opening at 9–9.30am every day; Meet Mickey just in front of the upper exit of the Liberty Arcade; at regular intervals in the Central Plaza area in front of the castle; in the morning on the stage of Le Théâtre du Château; periodically outside Colonel Hathi's Pizza Outpost in Adventureland; from time to time outside 'it's a small world' in Fantasyland; at breakfast at Walt's – An American Restaurant; at lunch in the Lucky Nugget Saloon and tea at the Plaza Gardens Restaurant.

Walt Disney Studios Park: in the entrance courtyard in front of Studio 1 for the first hour of the day, and periodically thereafter; at Meet Mickey in Animation Courtyard; every now and then throughout Animation Courtyard itself; during the daily Disney Cinema Parade.

Disney Village: at one of the character meals which are served throughout the day at Café Mickey (7.30 and 9.30am for breakfast, noon–2.30pm for lunch and 3–11pm for dinner).

Disneyland Hotel: at breakfast and dinner at the Inventions Restaurant.

All Disney Hotels (including *Disney's Davy Crockett Ranch®*): in the lobby area at regular intervals throughout the morning.

For all character meals, you need to make a reservation either when you book your Disney package, through reception at your Disney hotel or in advance by phoning (from the UK) 00 33 1 60 45 60 45 (just 01 60 45 60 45 in France). To check on when and where to meet the characters in the Theme Parks, always call in at **City Hall** at the *Disneyland Park* or **Guest Relations** at the *Walt Disney Studios Park*.

Shop around at reputable dealers like **American Express** (0800 700 737), **AA** (0191 235 6513), **Bradford & Bingley** (0800 435642), **Club Direct** (0800 0744 558), **Columbus** (0207 375 0011), **Direct Travel** (01903 812345), **GA Direct** (0800 121007), **Options** (0870 848 0870), **Premier Direct** (0990 133218), **Primary Direct** (0870 444 3434), **Thomas Cook** (0845 600 5454), **Travel Insurance Direct** (0990 168113), **Worldcover Direct** (0800 365121) and **Worldwide Travel Insurance** (01892 833338).

Medical matters

When it comes to anything of a medical nature, it is worth knowing that there are two fully English-speaking hospitals in Paris. **The American Hospital in Neuilly** is located at 63 Boulevard Victor Hugo, 92200 Neuilly sur Seine (Métro Porte Maillot); tel (in Paris) 46 41 25 25 or 47 47 70 15. And the **Hertford British Hospital** can be found at 3 Rue Barbès, 92300 Levallois-Perret (Métro Anatole France); tel 46 39 22 22.

For an after-hours chemist, the

Drugstore Champs-Elysées at 133 Avenue des Champs-Elysées (Métro Charles de Gaulle–Etoile), tel 47 20 39 25, is open until 2am daily, while the **Pharmacie Dhery** at 84 Avenue des Champs-Elysées (by Métro George V), tel 45 62 02 41, is open around the clock.

Emergencies

In the event of an emergency dial 17 for the police, 18 for the fire brigade or 15 for 24-hour medical emergencies. The public ambulance service can be called on 45 13 67 89. For a 24-hour doctor's service, call 47 07 77 77.

Safety first

Crime has never been a major issue at *Disneyland Resort Paris*, but it still pays to keep your common sense with you all the time, as you would in any city. Keep your hotel door locked at all times (even if you are just popping down the corridor) and don't leave things like cameras or camcorders on view in the car when you leave it parked.

Both parks have a Lost and Found office and Guest Services can advise you of any additional security requirements you may need (only the *Disneyland Hotel, Disney's Hotel New York* and *Disney's Newport Bay Club* have rooms equipped with safety deposit boxes).

The Paris **lost property office** is located at the Préfecture de Police, 36 Rue des Morillons, 75015 Paris (Métro Convention); tel 55 76 20 00. It is open Mondays and Wednesdays 8.30am–5pm, Tuesdays and Thursdays 8.30am–8pm and Fridays 8.30am–5.30pm.

If for any reason you need to contact the British Embassy in Paris, it can be found at 35 Rue du Faubourg Saint-Honoré, 75383 Paris; tel 44 51 31 00.

Money

As ever on a foreign holiday, it is advisable not to carry too much **cash** with you. Travellers cheques are better as they are easier to replace if lost or stolen (provided you have a note of the serial numbers), but generally speaking you can make do for a few days in *Disneyland Resort Paris* with cash and credit cards, which are almost universally accepted (although not by many small hotels and cafes in some areas of France). You can also use Switch, Visa and Mastercard at the several cash dispensers around the resort.

The **currency**, of course, is now the euro, which actually makes travelling through Western Europe so much easier. At the time of writing, £1 = €1.43, or €1 = 70 pence, so roughly speaking £5 would be €7. For those who have yet to encounter the euro, there are eight coins – 1 and 2 euros, and 1, 2, 5, 10, 20 and 50 cents – and seven notes in 5, 10, 20, 50, 100 and 200 denominations (the 100 and 200 are not practical in most places).

In France, a 15% service charge is sometimes added to restaurant and hotel bills but the usual practice of **tipping** is simply to leave a few euros at the end of a meal (it is not such an important practice as in the United States, for example). A taxi driver would expect a 10–15% tip, while a porter would expect to be given €1 a bag.

Phone calls

If you need to **phone home**, avoid using the hotel phones as they are fiendishly expensive (and Disney hotels are no exception). It is better to use a public payphone and pay via your BT Chargecard or another kind of phone card. To call the UK from France, dial 00 44 and then the UK number (omitting the first 0 from the area code).

Tourist info

And, if you are out and about in France, look for the local **Offices du Tourism** and **Syndicats d'Initiative** for maps, advice and info on the local sights and attractions. Most tourist attractions are open 10am–5pm, with one late opening day per week, but many close on public holidays (although not in *Disneyland Resort Paris*).

Know before you go

Before we go any further, I have compiled a list of useful websites to help in your planning and preparation at this stage. As hard as we work to keep this guide as up to date and accurate as possible, there are always going to be things that change after our deadlines, or areas we can't cover fully in such a relatively small volume. But you can stay on the ball by using the internet as much as possible and there are a good number of websites that can help you.

First and foremost is the official *Disneyland Paris Resort* website, www.disneylandparis.com, with the opportunity to book online and save money, while by far the most comprehensive and useful of the 'unofficial' sites is www.dlp-guidebook.de/index_e.htm, which is the English translation of a superb German fan site. This includes excellent sections on the resort's history, the current shows and parades, hours of operation, rumours, downloads and newsletters, plus the latest practical advice, and a chat and discussion forum.

Also just launched on the *Walt Disney World* website to which I contribute – look up www.disboards.com, then go to Disneyland Forums – is a special section on *Disneyland Resort Paris*, with more busy discussion boards and a chat forum. Who knows, I might 'see' you there! Other more general websites are: www.franceguide.com, www.paris-ile-de-france.com, www.parisbienvenue.com, www.paris-tourist-information.com or www.paris.org.

Well, I think that gives you enough food for thought in the planning stage for now. Let's move on to another vital subject in your preparations, that of actually getting there…

Getting There
(or, Trains, Planes and Automobiles; and Coaches and Ferries, and….!)

In many ways, your choice of when to go to *Disneyland Resort Paris* pales into insignificance compared to the issue of how you get there at all. The options for travel on what is, after all, just a 295km (183-mile) journey once you reach Calais on the other side of the Channel are almost as wide-ranging as the resort itself.

Obviously, your geographical location in the UK plays a large part in deciding what is best for you. The Eurostar service may be a wonderful method of transport but it is not necessarily your ideal means of getting there if you live in Newcastle or Bangor. Equally, going by coach and letting someone else do all the driving has a lot of appeal but it can seem a long-winded way of doing

things if you live in the South East (where Eurostar and Eurotunnel are quicker options). Flying is increasingly popular and affordable with the range of low-fare airlines now available and the advantages are especially noticeable from regional airports like Newcastle, Aberdeen, Bristol and even Southampton.

So here is an outline of each of the main possibilities along with their pros and cons. I should declare at this point that, living in the South East, the Eurostar from Ashford is my preferred means of transport. It most suits my requirements for getting there easily and efficiently, but it is probably not everyone's cup of tea and there are several viable alternatives, some of which happen to be cheaper.

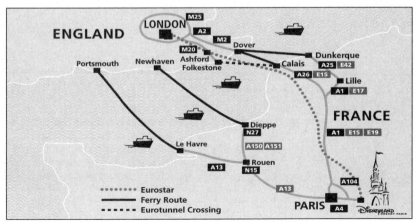

By car

With the opening of the Channel Tunnel in 1994, the dream of quick, reliable transport to the Continent became a reality. A permanent link was established and the companies which operate via the tunnel immediately created a whole new realm of Channel-hopping possibilities. Some 57 million people used the longest undersea tunnel in the world – 50km (31 miles) in length, 39km (24 miles) of them under the sea itself – in the first 6 years of its existence, and the yearly average is some 2.9 million cars, 83,000 coaches and 6.7 million Eurostar passengers.

And, while it obviously opened in direct competition with cross-Channel ferry businesses, it actually served to increase quite significantly the total traffic between the UK and Europe. Not only did the day-tripping habit pick up (and the number of British-orientated supermarkets in the Calais vicinity), but driving holidays to France, Belgium, Holland, Spain, Germany and even Italy also received a major boost. So, just 2 years after the opening of the *Disneyland Resort Paris*, it stands to reason the tunnel would swiftly become a prime route in getting people there (in fact, one of the many reasons why Disney eventually settled on the Paris site was because of the forthcoming tunnel link).

The combination of the tunnel and the well-established ferry links from Dover, Newhaven and Portsmouth now provides a wealth of opportunity for routes into France by both car and coach, and more people travel by car than any other mode of transport. France is also blessed with a series of well-organised and relatively smooth-flowing motorways (certainly compared to our M25), most of which are toll-road autoroutes, or *autoroutes des péages*. In 2003, it cost

Autoroutes des Péages

Tickets are issued at the beginning of each of the paid motorway networks. Payments are then calculated on the distance you travel and must be paid on leaving the motorway. You pay at the *péages* (or toll gates) with either cash or credit card. For short journeys locally it is a good idea to keep some small change handy to avoid the hassle of using your credit card. Payments also vary according to your vehicle, with different price bands for cars, vans, cars with trailers, lorries and motorbikes.

€17.20 one way to use this quickest and most convenient of routes (A26 from Calais, then A1, A104 and A4 – see maps on pages 31 and 33). Basically, it is 105km (65 miles) on the A26, 153km (95 miles) on the A1, 25.6km (16 miles) on the A104 and then another 11.5km (7 miles) on the A4 before the turn off (Exit 14) for 'Les Parcs Disneyland'.

From Calais ferry port, you are directed straight on to the A26 (via the E15 – follow the clear signs for Paris, Reims), while from the Channel Tunnel, you have a short 6km (3½ mile) stretch on the A16 (follow the signs for Calais) before picking up the A26.

BRIT TIP: Watch out for the A26 junction with the A1, as the signposting is not terribly clear here and it is easy to miss. The motorway turn-off signs are all in white (and set off to the right-hand side) and you need to follow the big blue overhead destination signs for Paris.

DISNEYLAND RESORT PARIS

DISNEYLAND PARK

DISNEY HOTELS

1 Disneyland Hotel
2 Disney's Hotel New York
3 Disney's Newport Bay Club
4 Disney's Sequoia Lodge
5 Disney's Hotel Cheyenne
6 Disney's Hotel Santa Fe
7 Disney's Davy Crockett Ranch
8 Val-de-France hotels
9 Pierre & Vacances

WALT DISNEY STUDIOS PARK

DISNEY VILLAGE

VAL D'EUROPE

SEA LIFE

LA VALLÉE

GOLF DISNEYLAND

©DISNEY

DISNEY HOTELS

Above: Disney's Hotel Cheyenne
Top left: Disney's Newport Bay Club
Top right: Disney's Sequoia Lodge
Above right: Disney's Hotel New York
Right: Disneyland Hotel
Below right: Disney's Davy Crockett Ranch
Below: Disney's Hotel Santa Fe

Around Disneyland Resort

Above: Explorers Hotel
Right and below: Novotel Collegien
Below right: Chanteloup Hotel
Bottom: Eurostar

Main Street & Parades

Above: Princess Parade
Top right: Fantillusion
Above right: Main Street
        vehicles
Below right: Liberty Arcade
Bottom right: Main Street
        Electrical Parade
Below: Cinema Parade

It is advisable to navigate by the directional signs rather than the route numbers, hence from Calais on the A26, initially follow the signs for Saint-Omer, Arras, Reims, Paris; at the junctions with the A1, follow signs for Paris, Arras Est; immediately after Charles de Gaulle Airport, follow signs for Bordeaux, Nantes, Lyon, Marne-la-Vallée, Paris Est, Bobigny; once on the A104, look for Lyon, Meaux, Marne-la-Vallée and 'Les Parcs Disneyland'; at the junction with the A4, follow signs for Meaux, Reims.

BRIT TIP: Although *Disneyland Resort Paris* is officially located in Marne-la-Vallée, the whole area along the A4 here is also designated Marne-la-Vallée, hence it is easy to get sidetracked. Once on the A104, you should follow the signs for 'Les Parcs Disneyland'.

The only other area to watch out for is switching from the A1 to the A104 at Charles de Gaulle Airport (the A1 actually becomes the A3 for 2km/1½ miles), although there is a sign for 'Les Parcs Disneyland' just before and after the airport, directing you on to the A104. Immediately after the airport, the autoroute splits, and you need to be in the right-hand lanes for Marne-la-Vallée; it then splits again, and the right two lanes bring you on to the A104 south (see map below).

It should take you a shade under 3 hours to drive from Calais, with the speed limit up to 130kph (80mph) on the autoroutes. You *can* save the toll money by taking the Routes Nationales (or N-roads), but for the amount you avoid in tolls, you would need to add the best part of another hour to your journey. The toll road system in France is split up into eight privately owned networks, but the one from Calais to Marne-la-Vallée is all under the control of SANEF (www.sanef.com), so it does make for an exceedingly simple journey. Check out

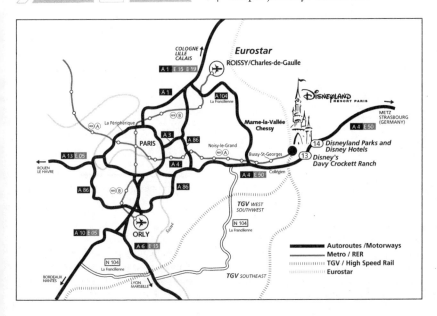

www.autoroutes.fr for more detail on your journey and a handy route planner, while the Eurotunnel website www.eurotunnel.com has some helpful route advice as well (see page 42). The www.multimap.co.uk site is also useful.

The first toll booths you come to on the A26 are after about 61km (38 miles) between Exits 4 and 5, and here you simply collect a ticket from the machine, which records the point at which you join the A-route system, and then you pay at the toll booths just north of Charles de Gaulle Airport (just after Exit 7). These are the only tolls you will pay on the direct Calais– Marne-la-Vallée route.

If you take the Portsmouth–Le Havre ferry route, your journey from Le Havre will be around 240km (149 miles) via A13, the Paris Périphérique and the A4, and the tolls will be about €21.

BRIT TIP: The autoroute speed limit is 130kph (80mph), but this drops to 110kph (68mph) when it is wet. It is 110kph (68mph) on non-toll motorways and 90kph (56mph) on other roads, 80kph (50mph) when wet, plus 50kph (30mph) in towns.

Once in the Marne-la-Vallée area, your main route to and from the Theme Parks is likely to be the **A4**, a busy stretch of motorway at peak periods (especially into Paris itself) but otherwise an easy-to-use arterial. There are no toll booths along this section at all, hence you can use the A4 as frequently as you like at no extra cost. Once you turn off at Exit 14 for the Theme Parks, everything is well signposted to get you to the hotels or the main car parks. There

is a huge, circular ring road which completely encompasses the whole of the resort (plus Val d'Europe) called the Boulevard de l'Europe, which actually makes an interesting drive at some stage as you can get a series of unusual glimpses into the Theme Parks.

BRIT TIP: If a French driver flashes his lights at you, it means he intends to go NOT that he is giving you right of way.

Children under 10 are forbidden to travel in the front seat. On-the-spot fines, or deposits, (in cash – you should also get an official receipt) can be demanded for not wearing seat belts (compulsory front AND back), drink-driving, driving on a provisional licence and speeding offences (and French police are pretty hot on the latter). The use of mobile phones while driving is strictly prohibited in France.

BRIT TIP: If you exceed the speed limit by more than 40kph (25mph), the French police have the power to take your driving licence immediately, so you won't be able to drive. For serious offences they can confiscate your car.

Parking and rest zones are situated every 10–20km (6–12 miles) on motorways, with 24-hour petrol stations at about every 40km (25 miles). If you break down, pull up on the right hand lay-by, put on your hazard warning lights and place a red warning triangle 30m (33yds) behind your vehicle (compulsory for vans and cars with trailers).

Driving in France

There are no major differences in the traffic rules in France (other than driving on the right-hand side!), but driving with dipped headlights is compulsory in poor visibility – so don't leave home without a pair of headlight beam adjusters. It is also advisable to take a set of spare bulbs, while a red hazard warning triangle is compulsory in case of a breakdown. You should also take your vehicle registration document and insurance certificate, as well as your driving licence (it is a legal requirement to have your driving licence with you whenever you are behind the wheel). You should check with your insurance company to ensure you have full cover while driving in France. Green cards are no longer required, but some insurance companies issue them anyway as they are a sure way of convincing local police you are properly insured. Road signs are pretty much universal, but additional signs or warnings to watch for are:

Allumez vos phares/feux	Switch on your lights
Attention au feu	Fire hazard
Attention travaux	Beware roadworks
Cedée le passage	Give Way
Chaussée déformée	Uneven road surface
Essence sans plomb	Unleaded petrol
Fin d'interdiction de stationner	End of prohibited parking
Gazole	Diesel
Interdit aux piétons	Forbidden to pedestrians
Rappel	Remember (often on speed limit signs)
Route barrée	Road closed
Sens unique	One way
Sens interdit	No entry
Supercarburant	Lead replacement petrol
Verglas	Black ice

Emergency telephones (orange) are usually every 2km (just over a mile) apart on motorways. If you do break down and can't leave your vehicle, there are regular road patrols on all autoroutes. Additionally, you must not park on kerbs marked in yellow.

French motorway service areas (or *aires*) are generally 24-hour operations and offer a combination of facilities way beyond anything in the UK in terms of quality. There are two types of *aire*: one has full fuel, catering and shopping facilities, while the other is a picnic area with toilets. These are often pretty places to stop – but it is advisable to have your own toilet paper handy for some of the picnic area stops (for

some reason, it is not a standard French provision)!

Both AA and RAC members can take advantage of their organisation's European Breakdown Assistance service, which is highly

BRIT TIP: Buying petrol in French motorway service stations is as exorbitant as the equivalent in the UK. You can save 12–15% by filling up at the nearest hypermarket (*hypermarché*) in Calais or Le Havre. Savings on diesel can be even greater.

valuable when travelling on the Continent. Look up www.theaa.com (or phone 0870 600 0375) or www.rac.co.uk (08705 722 722).

For **maps**, the AA's France Series 7 (£3.99) covers the full route from Calais to Marne-la-Vallée, while you would need 2 and 7 to cover the journey from Le Havre.

All autoroutes have their own information radio stations. In northern France, there are English-language bulletins on 107.7FM on the hour and half-hour. Motorway info can also be found (in France only) on the premium-rate phone line 08 36 68 10 77. Calls cost €3.3 a minute.

By ferry

Of course, if you are taking the car, you need to decide which method of cross-Channel transport you prefer, the various ferry services from one of four south coast ports, or the Eurotunnel service from Folkestone. If you opt for the more traditional ferry route, you can go from Dover, Portsmouth and Newhaven (summer only). Here's how they break down.

Dover
To start with, Dover is an easy port to get to by road, either straight down the M2/A2 in north Kent or (my preferred route) via the M20/A20, both of which come off the M25 London orbital. It is about an hour-and-three-quarters drive from central London (given a relatively traffic-free run) and you need to head to the Eastern Docks for the main ferry operators, or the Western Docks for the hoverport, off Union Street, which caters for all Hoverspeed sailings. Dover is a thoroughly modern, well-organised port and should get you aboard your ferry with the minimum of fuss.

The main passenger terminal includes a bureau de change, bank and cashpoint, an AA shop, a cafe and newsagent, an information desk, telephones, toilets and baby-change facilities. Also, once you have passed into the terminal area itself in your car, there are two mini food villages offering another cafe, a Burger King, a bar, another bureau de change and cashpoint, a shop, plus the usual toilets, baby-change facilities and telephones. You should arrive at least 30 minutes before your sailing time and have your passports ready as you drive in.

If you have booked in advance (which is highly advisable), you proceed straight through to your ferry operator's check-in. If you haven't got a ticket, you can park up in the short-stay parking area at the main entrance to the passenger terminal and visit the Travel Centre.

Four main companies operate from this extremely busy cross-Channel hub:

P&O Ferries are Dover's biggest and most sophisticated operator, with up to 35 crossings to Calais a day, 364 days a year. They operate some of the newest and biggest ships on this route and, if you haven't travelled on a cross-Channel ferry for a while, you will probably be pleasantly surprised by the comfort and quality on offer these days. The crossing time from Dover is 75 minutes, although you mustn't forget to put your watches forward an hour on arrival in France.

Once through the Eastern Docks' main reception area, follow the signs for P&O Ferries, which will take you to the check-in booths (where you will usually need to show your passports – all British subjects MUST have a full, valid 10-year

> BRIT TIP: Look out for P&O Ferries' early booking discounts, which can often save you up to £100 on standard fares.

passport that will not expire for at least 3 months after you return. Non-British subjects should check their visa requirements in advance). At check-in, you are allocated a numbered embarkation lane to proceed to, from where you will be directed on to the ferry when it is ready to board. While waiting here, you can take advantage of the food villages and facilities.

Once settled aboard for a surprisingly brief crossing, you should have a good choice of bars, shops, lounges and cafes to while away the time. All P&O Ferries' ships now include an International Food Court (usually the busiest area on board, especially just after embarkation), a First Base fast-food counter, the Harbour Coffee Company, Silverstones Sports Bar and a shop selling sweets and other snacks (three ferries also include a NYC Deli, which adds to the food choice). Langan's Brasserie offers a more upmarket choice for a meal in mid-Channel, while, if you have opted for the Club Plus when you booked, you also get the benefit of the Club Lounge and its personalised service, as well as priority embarkation and unloading at the other end.

For young children (2–5s), there is an excellent (unsupervised) soft-play area where they can expend some energy, while there is also a good video games centre, the Coca-Cola Megadrome, to keep older children amused. For shoppers, P&O's onboard prices can be up to 50% cheaper than UK prices for beer, cigarettes and tobacco. For more info, visit www.poferries.com (there is an extra discount for booking online) or call 0870 600 0600.

SeaFrance is the other main operator from Dover, with up to 20 return crossings daily, 364 days of the year. The usual crossing time is around 90 minutes, except on the newest ship, the excellent SeaFrance *Rodin*, which is the largest and fastest ship on the Dover-Calais route and cuts the time down to just an hour. The SeaFrance fleet is a bit of a mixed bag, especially in high season when all their vessels are pretty much in operation, but they still all boast a reasonable range of mod cons and creature comforts and a second *Rodin*-class ferry is to be added (with the same short crossing time) by early 2005.

There is basically a four-way choice for food and drink: La Brasserie for full-service dining, Le

Join the Club

P&O Ferries offer three distinct extra services, which can be pre-booked or, in the case of the Club Lounge, booked on board (although it then costs more). The **Club Lounge** is a separate quiet lounge area, complete with comfy leather armchairs, where you are greeted with a complimentary glass of champagne, and offered tea and coffee, biscuits, fruit and newspapers to while away the time, all with its own waiter/waitress service.

The **Priorité** service is a pre-booked priority loading system, which allows you to be embarked early and unloaded first, which is highly worthwhile when speed is of the essence. The two can then be combined in a **Club Plus** service, which provides use of the Club Lounge and the priority loading/unloading as well. At the time of writing, the prices were: £8/person each way for the Club Lounge, if booked in advance (£10/person if booked on board); £10/vehicle each way for Priorité; if opting for Club Plus, £5/person each way plus £10/vehicle. For two people, Club Plus would be £30 return.

Relais self-service restaurant, Le Parisien coffee lounge and Le Pub, with a well-priced selection of beers and wines. The shopping opportunities are fairly standard, while the lounges are adequate. The *Rodin* adds a distinct element of extra style however, with a good children's play area, video games arcade and an enhanced onboard shop. For frequent travellers, SeaFrance's Carnet ticket offers some major savings (up to £130 across five standard return sailings), while they regularly feature significant discounts on early bookings. For more info, visit www.seafrance.com or call 08705 711 711.

Norfolkline provides an alternative to the occasionally hectic Calais crossings, with up to 10 sailings a day to Dunkerque, just over 40km (25 miles) further along the French coast from Calais. The crossing time is a slightly long (by Calais standards) 2 hours but the Dunkerque port facilities are well run, usually uncongested and easy to negotiate. Norfolkline operates two modern, well-equipped ferries on this route and, while there are fewer frills than elsewhere, they deliver great value for money. There is one self-service restaurant, a bar and a comfortable lounge with satellite TV and a good selection of recliner seats. The gift shop (at French duty-paid prices) offers fairly standard fare but is worth a visit especially on your return trip to grab a last-minute bargain or two.

Norfolkline advises checking in 1–2 hours before your departure time. From Dunkerque, Marne-la-Vallee is just over 300km (186 miles) away – follow the signs for the A16, then take the E42 to the A25 all the way to Lille and pick up the A1 to Paris. For more info visit www.norfolkline.com or call 0870 870 1020.

Hoverspeed is the other main Dover operator, with a couple of significant advantages over the others. With three Seacat fast ferries (two of 74m/243ft and one 81m/296ft) running up to 15 return trips a day, they make the crossing in just an hour with 88 vehicles and up to 450 passengers from their own terminal. With no freight or coach traffic, it's a more streamlined operation than any of the others and is especially suitable for those driving to destinations beyond Calais.

You can grab a snack at Upper Crust or Little Chef Express before boarding, while Hoverspeed also offers an excellent shopping service either on board, at the company's own dedicated store in Calais or even in advance on their website. Unlike the ferries, the Seacat is not a vessel loaded with restaurants, shops, etc. There is still space to wander around and some open deck space at the back, but it is more of an airline-type service, with airline seats (albeit with more leg room!) and cabin crew. You can also upgrade (at £15 a head) to their first class service, which has its own pre-departure lounge, private onboard seating area with at-seat service, priority embarkation and unloading, complimentary newspaper and refreshments. For reservations, call Hoverspeed on 0870 240 8070 or visit www.hoverspeed.com (with a 2% discount for booking online).

Newhaven

Between Brighton and Eastbourne on the Sussex coast is this small but busy ferry port operated by **Hoverspeed** on their Superseacat route to Dieppe (summer only). Newhaven is on the A259 coast road, but is best reached (from London) via the M23, A23, A27 (at Brighton) and A26. The 100m (328ft) monohull Superseacat takes up to 145 vehicles and 700 passengers and covers the Newhaven–Dieppe run in just 2 hours. Once again, the Hoverspeed

Thank you ferry much

I asked Britain's leading cruise and ferry website, **Seaview** (www.seaview.co.uk), to pass on their top tips for getting the most out of your cross-Channel journey – at the best price.

Here's what they said:

Don't leave your booking until the last minute. Prices rarely improve by waiting.

Make sure you receive a reference number when booking. Short crossings are often ticketless, so a booking reference is important – and have it ready when you reach the ferry terminal.

Booking directly with ferry operators doesn't necessarily save you money. Agents can often give you a cheaper deal.

If you want to sail with SeaFrance, try to get on the *Rodin*. She is by far the best ship in the fleet.

Don't try to pull a fast one by buying a daytrip ticket when you plan to stay longer. Ferry operators have a knack of finding out and take a very dim view.

Try to book a ferry you can make without having to dash. If you miss it, you might have to wait a long time for a space to become available on a later sailing. And there's nothing worse than racing against the clock.

If you travel with P&O Ferries and you can afford the extra, treat yourself to the Club Lounge. It's comfortable, usually quiet and soft drinks, coffee and tea, etc are complimentary.

Make sure you give the correct details when booking, such as names as they appear in passports, exact length of car, etc. It can save vital minutes at check-in.

If there is a person with disabilities in your party, then inquire about priority on and off arrangements.

When you receive your tickets, take time to read them carefully – twice! Mistakes have been known to happen.

Be aware that, should an emergency arise, Apex bargain tickets are non-refundable, while full-price tickets usually are.

And remember – you lose an hour on arrival in France, so take this into account when you are considering sailing times.

operation is similar to Dover's, with its own dedicated check-in and first class service upgrade option at £25 per person each way (although there is no departure lounge for the return trip from Dieppe). From Dieppe, it is some 257km (160 miles) to the *Disneyland Resort Paris*, and you need to follow the N27, A151, A150 and N15 before picking up the A13 and the route from Le Havre.

Portsmouth

For the closest port to Paris, head for Le Havre with **P&O Ferries**. The French capital is barely 2 hours from the Normandy port (see map on page 32) and Portsmouth is a lot more accessible from the Midlands and West Country than Dover or Newhaven. The down side is that it is a much longer ferry journey – around 5½ hours on day crossings and 7½ at night – but you can take advantage of an overnight sailing, arriving in Le Havre at 7am, and be in the heart of the Disney magic by 11am. There are usually three return sailings a day – leaving Portsmouth at 7.45am, 2.45pm and 10.15pm – and the port facilities are all new and well organised.

Portsmouth itself is also served by excellent road links, with the port situated at the base of the M275 with its own exit on to the motorway. It is actually closer to London than either Dover or the Channel Tunnel and is arguably Britain's best-connected ferry port. The new Newbury bypass on the A34 has also cut down the journey time from the Midlands, West and North.

The Le Havre terminal (open 6.30am–11pm) is equally well designed to provide a smooth return journey, with easy access and good facilities. You can also pre-order and pre-pay for your shopping for collection with P&O Ferries on your return journey.

The two ferries operating on this route are both modern and offer a good range of creature comforts, not unlike some cruise ships. There is a swimming pool and sauna, cinema (£4 for adults, £3 for children), games room, restaurants (including a new 175-seat Langan's Brasserie, with an excellent range of British specialities and extensive wine list, an elegant coffee bar and a self-service cafeteria), saloon bar, live entertainment and the Dolphin Club for youngsters (with face painting, colouring, quizzes and other games). There is even a small casino, plus a gift shop, bureau de change and the chance to buy your *Disneyland Resort Paris* tickets in advance.

For an extra supplement, you can travel **Club Class**, which adds the use of the VIP-treatment (non-smoking) lounge, with complimentary tea, coffee, juice and newspapers, as well as a bar and light meals service. Overnight passengers have a reserved recliner seat with a blanket. The ferries' en suite cabins ensure a decent night's sleep – if required – and there are even Club Class cabins, which include a nightcap in the Club lounge and a complimentary in-cabin continental breakfast. For more details or to book, visit their website (which has special deals from time to time) www.poportsmouth.com or call 08705 202020.

> **BRIT TIP:** There are two Auchan hypermarkets in Le Havre if you need to do that last-minute shopping before you return home.

For websites to help you with ferry crossings and road access after you arrive, the following are helpful, starting with the essential www.seaview.co.uk. Then there's www.ferrybooker.com (with lots of useful info on driving in France, the ports and working out your route), while www.doverport.com and www.portsmouth-port.co.uk give you the full story of these two main UK ferry ports. When it comes to driving, both www.autoroutes.fr and www.sytadin.tm.fr/ (for Paris traffic reports) are extremely useful and worth checking in advance.

By Eurotunnel

Need to get to Calais fast, conveniently and with a choice of services 24 hours a day? Well, Eurotunnel could well be the right service for you. This versatile 'train-ferry' operation from Folkestone in Kent has up to four departures an hour throughout the day, every day, with the crossing time just 35 minutes. In fact, from the time of loading to driving off at the other end can take just 45 minutes, making easily the quickest vehicle crossing times of any cross-Channel service. Finding Eurotunnel also couldn't be easier as the terminal is just off Junction 11A on the M20, usually just a 45-minute drive from its intersection with the M25 London orbital, and is well sign-posted.

BRIT TIP: For the latest travel, weather and road news for the area, call Eurotunnel's information line on 0800 0969 992.

After arriving at the Eurotunnel terminal, proceed straight to check-in and quote your booking reference number. You can just arrive on spec, but you will be allocated a space on the next available shuttle, and may have to wait a while. In busy periods, a booking is highly advisable to avoid a wait of up to an hour. You are requested to arrive at least 35 minutes before your booked departure time as at half an hour beforehand during busy periods your booking may be relegated to a later departure.

You can stop off in their extremely smart and spacious main terminal building, grab a bite to eat and do a bit of pre-trip shopping (pre-order your goods and they will be available for collection at the French terminal on your return). Once checked in, you drive through both British and French passport controls (there are no checks on arrival, as with the ferry arrivals procedure). Please note, LPG vehicles are NOT allowed to travel on Eurotunnel.

BRIT TIP: Don't forget the documentation for your vehicle, insurance and any breakdown cover you have for the journey!

For an even quicker and smoother passage, you can upgrade to the **Eurotunnel Club** service and benefit from a priority lane at check-in and a guaranteed space on the next available shuttle (and you can upgrade any Standard fare at check-in, if required, for a £45 fee per car one-way). There is a Club lounge (open 6am–10pm) to allow you to freshen up, enjoy a light meal, complimentary tea, coffee and newspapers, and use the phone/fax. There is even a takeaway service to have your free snack on the go. Call the dedicated Club booking line on 08705 388 388. From personal experience, the extra speed, convenience and service which this provides is highly worthwhile.

For direct access to the Club lounge, go straight to passport control, then follow the Club signs (in the UK, keep to the right hand lane, in France, keep to the left). Stay in the respective lane until you reach the Eurotunnel Club barrier, then use the token given to you at check-in to gain access to car parking for the Club lounge. You will also be given a hanger at check-in which you need to display on your mirror. From the lounge, you will be given priority boarding on the next available shuttle.

Once you're ready to board, you just drive straight on to the shuttle and the next 35 minutes are all taken care of. You have the choice of staying in your car or getting out to stretch your legs in the carriage (and there are toilets usually in every third carriage). There is even a dedicated Eurotunnel radio info link (on 95.6 or 99.8 FM) for news, music and info, while display screens keep you informed of the journey.

On arriving at the other end, you drive off (in Calais/Coquelles) practically straight on to the A16 autoroute. From there, you head for the A26 (sign-posted initially to Calais, and then to Saint-Omer, Arras, Reims and Paris) before picking up the A1 at Arras (see map on page 31).

On the return journey, you come off the A16 at Junction 13 (look for the signs for Tunnel Sous La Manche). If you have some time to spare here, you can visit the huge **Cité Europe** shopping mall, which has some 200 shops and offers the usual great deals on things like wine, beer, spirits and food, plus clothing at stores like Etam, Naf Naf, H&M, Sergio Tacchini, Zara and Quicksilver, and other well-known chains like Footlocker, Toys R Us and Pier Import.

BRIT TIP: Check out www.day-tripper.net for more details on Cité Europe, the bargains to be had and an excellent map of the area.

All in all, the Eurotunnel operation really is as simple as it

sounds, and the ease with which you are suddenly off and running in France comes as quite a surprise the first time, so don't forget to drive on the right! It is also a relatively cheap option, with Short Stay fares (2–5 days) from £173 per car (at 2003 prices), and Long Stay prices (more than 5 days) from £293, while the Club upgrade is an extra £90 (not available on promotional crossings).

The other great benefit of Eurotunnel v The Ferries (apart from it suiting more independent-minded travellers) is the fact the shuttle service is never affected by the weather, and you are certainly not likely to get seasick on their train! For more info, visit www.eurotunnel.com (which offers discounts of up to £6 if you book online and special promotional fares at off-peak times) or call reservations on 08705 35 35 35.

BRIT TIP: Eurotunnel's site at www.eurotunnel.com has an excellent route-planning facility. Just type in your route details from your home and, hey presto, you have easy-to-follow instructions to your destination. It even provides the total cost of the tolls on the way. Click on 'Passenger Travel' and then the 'Eurotunnel Journey' link to reach it.

Eurotunnel's standard cross-Channel service is not to be confused with their excellent Motoring Holidays division, which has a specialist *Disneyland Resort Paris* brochure (see page 55).

By Rail – Eurostar

The fastest direct route from London to Paris these days is via the smooth **Eurostar** operation from London's Waterloo station (and Ashford in Kent) to Gare du Nord in the French capital or, even better and highly recommended, direct to Marne-la-Vallée itself (which really does work out appreciably quicker than flying). This is literally the fast-track service to *Disneyland Resort Paris* (2 hours 50 minutes from London to Mickey!) a high-speed train link in great comfort, style – and massive convenience on the direct service.

Put aside any preconceptions (and real misgivings) of the British rail system, because this is how modern rail travel really *should* be. You are guaranteed a seat (no mean feat for some regional rail services), the trains are clean and comfortable and their time-keeping is second to none in the UK (okay, that latter is not saying a lot, but Eurostar really does have an excellent punctuality record). The opening of the first section of the new Channel Tunnel

Rail Link in September 2003 cut 15 minutes off the rather pedestrian journey from London to the tunnel itself, while the whizz through northern France remains a breathtaking experience.

Add to this the excellence of all the station terminal facilities – at Waterloo, Ashford, Gare du Nord and Marne-la-Vallée – and you have an operation of the highest order and user-friendliness. For anyone living within 2 hours' drive of Ashford, this is an extremely worthwhile alternative to Waterloo as the journey time is barely 2 hours in total to Paris or Marne-la-Vallée and the ease and efficiency with which you can park at Ashford International station and walk across to catch your train makes for a hassle-free journey, especially with children.

BRIT TIP: I recommend changing RER trains at Châtelet Les Halles, as you simply need to switch platforms rather than go up and down a potentially confusing set of escalators – the RER signposting takes a fair bit of getting used to.

BRIT TIP: If you haven't pre-purchased your RER ticket to get from Gare du Nord to Marne-la-Vallée (which you can do at any Eurostar station), avoid the main ticket offices on the Paris station concourse as these are often crowded. Instead, wait until you reach the last, smaller ticket office just before the entrance to the (Green) Line D of the RER as there is rarely much of a queue here.

Eurostar offers up to 15 services a day to Gare du Nord, and a daily service (departing Waterloo at 9.39am and Ashford at 10.31am) to Marne-la-Vallée (arriving 1.29pm), as well as links to Lille, Brussels, Holland and the French Alps (NB there are no direct Disney services in either direction on Christmas Day or Boxing Day, or on a handful of Saturdays in the spring).

If you choose the Gare du Nord route (or are unable to take advantage of the Disney direct service), you should find it relatively easy to transfer to Marne-la-Vallée

RER-ing to go

Using the **RER** system to get to and from *Disneyland Resort Paris* is a positive doddle. This largely overground train link takes about 35–40 minutes to get from the resort into central Paris and runs until after midnight every night. While the trains may not be the cleanest (the graffiti menace has been here with a vengeance!) they run at regular intervals every hour and scrupulously to time. The RER goes underground through central Paris, where it links up with the **Métro** underground system. You do not need to use the Métro – or the well-organised bus system, which links with both – unless you are on a serious sight-seeing tour of the city.

    Marne-la-Vallée is at the end of the (Red) Line A4, which runs basically east–west through Paris. **Gare du Nord** is at a junction of the (Green) Line D which runs largely north–south and (Blue) Line B, which bisects the city from northeast–southwest, and has the **Charles de Gaulle Airport** at the end of the B3 link (northwest). **Orly Airport** is on a branch of the (Yellow) Line C.

via the RER train link on Line D (although it can be a trial at rush hour, when the trains are seriously crowded). Just follow the (Green) signs to Melun.

From Gare du Nord, you can change trains either at Gare de Lyon or Châtelet Les Halles to switch from Line D to Line A for Marne-la-Vallée.

Another alternative (and a highly worthwhile tip if you miss the direct service) is to take one of the Eurostar trains to **Lille** and change there for a TGV train to Marne-la-Vallée (about 65 minutes). You do not even have to change platforms at Lille, just wait (usually no more than half an hour) for the French high-speed train and you're off straight to the heart of the Magic once more.

Of course, the high-speed nature and regularity of the Eurostar service also means you can opt for just a **day trip** to *Disneyland Resort Paris*. Taking the 5.34am from London Waterloo would put you in Paris by 9.23am. The direct return service is usually at 7.35pm, but if that does not suit you, the last train from Paris to London is usually around 9pm, which means you could still have until 7.30pm in the Theme Parks before leaving.

Eurostar services: With the Eurostar service to Paris and Lille (or any of their other regular destinations), you have the choice of **Standard** or **First Class**. If you are used to your local train service, Standard will feel like travelling first class (the individual seats are comfortable with decent elbow room, carriages are roomy and there is easy access to the two buffet cars), while Eurostar's First is a genuine high-quality, business-level service.

First Class (at £66–97 extra, depending on ticket type) provides for a 10-minute check-in and offers a 3-course meal at your (extra-width,

BRIT TIP: A special fare applies for both wheelchair users and a travelling companion on Eurostar – less than the Standard price – and there are toilets and an area especially for wheelchair-users in First Class accommodation. Blind people travelling with companions also benefit from preferential rates.

reclining) seat, a trolley service and complimentary newspapers. There is plenty of space if you need to work en route (or keep the kids amused with board games, etc), and uniformed staff are on hand. Baby-changing facilities and bottle-warming is available, along with activity packs for children if you ask at the terminals. Plenty of ramps, passenger conveyors and lifts are provided as well.

> BRIT TIP: At Ashford International, as you enter the departure lounge, there are two cafes. Pass through to the second one and there will be less congestion.

On the direct Waterloo – Marne-la-Vallée route, there is Standard and Castle Service (for about £35–50 extra, depending on ticket type), with the latter offering the same carriages and spaciousness as First Class but only a boxed meal. There are still two buffet cars per train and a trolley service (with priority given to Castle Service passengers). A smattering of Disney fun whets your appetite along the way, with a jazz band playing prior to departure, Disney Cast Members on board to assist with your hotel arrangements and to provide some entertainment for the children and (occasionally) a character welcome at Marne-la-Vallée to get your visit off to a flying start.

When it comes to the main Eurostar **terminals**, you should find everything efficient and easy to use. At London's **Waterloo** mainline station, the Eurostar services operate from the lower level at the front of the concourse. Here you will find their purpose-built facilities offer a good range of shops, cafes, bars, currency exchange and a left luggage area. At **Ashford International**, the main concourse offers a pleasant cafe, plus shops, currency exchange and left luggage, while passing into the departure lounge gives you more chances to grab a drink or bite to eat, another shop and currency exchange, plus a Eurostar information desk. The multi-storey car park here holds 2,000 cars and parking is £8 a day (an alternative, open-air car park is available nearby at half the price, although it involves about a 100-m/100-yd walk to the station).

If you are returning from **Gare du Nord**, the Eurostar service can be found upstairs on the first level (it's surprising how many people don't notice this when they arrive), where there is again a good range of cafes and shops once you pass into the departure area.

You are advised to check in a good 30 minutes before your departure time or 20 minutes if you are travelling on a Premium First ticket with hand luggage only (sadly, security screening is now an important part of all European travel).

Ticket types: at first glance, the Eurostar ticket options are a little bewildering with Business, Leisure, Apex, Weekender and other fares. But, for our purposes it is possible to simplify things somewhat. Business Fares are the most expensive and offer complete flexibility for travel

> BRIT TIP: With Leisure Apex and Weekend Day Return fares, it is possible to travel one way in First Class and the other in Standard. It is worth travelling in First on the way home to give yourself room to wind down after all that exhausting fun!

any day of the week from London to Paris. However, if you are interested solely in getting to *Disneyland Resort Paris*, your choice really boils down to the London–Paris Leisure fares or the three main direct fares. With the London–Paris Leisure variety, all trips (except the Weekend Day Return) must include a Saturday night stay. Best value is the Leisure Apex 14, which must be booked at least 14 days in advance and include a Saturday night OR a minimum 2-night stay.

For the direct *Disneyland Resort Paris* service, there are three ticket types – a **Normal fare** (with complete flexibility for travel any day of the week); a **Leisure fare** (which must include a minimum 1-night stay); and the excellent value **Leisure Apex** 7 fare (which must be booked at least 7 days in advance and include at least 1 night's stay, and can save as much as £85 on the Normal fare). Youth fares cover those from 12–25, while children's fares are for under 12s.

Eurostar fares compare extremely favourably with airline prices (even the low-cost carriers) and, for the extra convenience of arriving absolutely right in the heart of the Disney fun, they take some beating. **Marne-la-Vallée** is the least exciting of all the main Eurostar terminals (but then it can afford to be with its situation). You arrive at the lowest level of the station and need to take the escalator or lift up to the main concourse. If you are heading straight for the Theme Parks, there should be a Disney Cast Member (or even a character or two!) to direct you to the nearest exit. If you are heading for your hotel first, go out of the main doors straight ahead of you, and the bus stop for all the Disney hotels (with the exception of *Disney's Davy Crockett Ranch®*, which has no bus service) and those of the three Selected Hotels (the Explorers, Holiday Inn and Kyriad) is

BRIT TIP: To find the Disney Express baggage service office at Waterloo, turn right immediately after check-in and it is located by escalator 23A. The Marne-la-Vallée trains usually leave from platform 23 or 24.

immediately in front of the station.

The Eurostar service includes the considerable bonus of the **Disney Express** baggage arrangement, which enables you to go straight to the Theme Parks on arrival while your bags are taken to your hotel. This has to be organised before you travel either through your tour operator or at the Waterloo terminal if you have booked Disney accommodation independently (you need to be able to show confirmation of your hotel booking to do this at Waterloo).

Once you have the correct baggage tags (and Disney Cast Members will be on the direct service to assist you and provide the right tags if you have not been sent them with your tickets), you simply attach them to your luggage and take them to the first floor Disney Express baggage office when you arrive at Marne-la-Vallée.

For my money, this is the most efficient and stress-free form of travel I have encountered, especially

BRIT TIP: Unless you are going First or Castle class, it is worth taking a packed lunch with you on Eurostar to circumvent the relative lack of child-friendly food on board.

in Europe. And, when travelling with children, it provides a fair degree of parental ease of mind (as well as the bonus of the seemingly eternal child-like fascination with trains). The only downside that occurs to me (apart from the fact it is primarily of benefit to those living in the South East) is the late departure time of the Sunday return service if you have young children. With the train not leaving until 7.35pm, you are not back at Waterloo until 9.30pm, and that can result in tired, irritable children on the final part of your journey home. The onboard buffet food could be better (especially for children – we found there was little to tempt our two for either breakfast or an early lunch) and smokers will not be happy to know Eurostar is a completely non-smoking service but those are extremely minor quibbles.

By Air

If the Eurostar route is the most time-efficient way of getting to the heart of the Magic, where does that leave air travel? Well, if you live anywhere outside the South East, it provides the best alternative,

> **BRIT TIP:** Beware the low-cost carriers who use Beauvais as their 'Paris' airport. Beauvais is more than 60km (37 miles) north of Paris and there is NO way to get people to Marne-la-Vallée other than a hired car. The one exception is Ryanair, who provide a shuttle bus to Porte Maillot RER and Métro station in west Paris for €10/person.

especially using the two main Paris airports of Charles de Gaulle and Orly. The proliferation of the low-cost airlines in recent years has broadened your choice here quite considerably (although Air France still takes some beating for its service and Disney 'extras').

The many regional airports around the UK all have at least one service daily to the French capital and, with the likes of EasyJet, KLM and bmi (and bmi baby) all offering variations on the low-cost alternative, it means your choice of flights has never been greater. Add in the scheduled services of Air France (from no less than eight UK airports) and British Airways (who use 10) and you have a total of 22 regional flight gateways to Paris, including Southend, Jersey, Nottingham, Belfast, Bristol and Aberdeen.

Charles de Gaulle Airport (CDG) is by far the bigger (and more complex) of the two Paris air terminals (it is the main international terminus, whereas Orly is more for domestic flights). Situated some 23km (14 miles) to the northeast of the city centre, it actually consists of no less than three main terminals, CDG 1, CDG 2 and the smaller satellite arm CDG T9. The CDG 2 terminal is sub-divided into Halls A, B, C, D and F, with the RER and TGV stations situated between A–D and F.

> **BRIT TIP:** It is a long walk from the RER station to the Air France departure gates in Hall F at CDG 2 and from the station to Halls A and B.

Both CDG 1 and CDG 2 have their own RER stations, while the T9 terminal is linked to CDG 1. There is also a free shuttle link between CDG

1 and 2 that runs every 7 minutes or so (at CDG 1 on the shopping level, at CDG 2 at Exit 10 of Hall A, Exit 12 of Hall D and Exit 2.08 – departure level – of Hall F).

The **VEA Navette** shuttle offers a direct service from CDG (all terminals) to the hotels of *Disneyland Resort Paris* from 8.30am–7.45pm daily (until 10pm Fridays and Sundays). It is a fairly plodding coach service, taking a good 45 minutes to reach the first stop, but it does have the great benefit of being door to door as far as the hotels are concerned and runs at 20–40-minute intervals throughout the main part of the day. It costs €14 for adults and €11.50 for children 3–11 (under 3s free). To phone the VEA service in advance, call 00 33 1 64 30 66 56. Using CDG 2, you pick up the VEA shuttle at Gate A11 from Hall A; Gate C1 from Hall C; Gate D12 from Halls B and D; and Gate 0.05 from Hall F.

BRIT TIP: The VEA Navette shuttles will take credit card payment, so don't worry if you don't have any euros to hand yet.

Alternatively, you can take the **RER** service on Line B all the way in to Châtelet Les Halles (about 40 minutes), then change there for Line D to Marne-la-Vallée (another 35–40). It is a simple enough route at off-peak times but much harder to negotiate with luggage in the morning or evening rush hour. For RER info (in English), call 00 33 1 36 68 41 14.

Another alternative is to take the **TGV** train from the airport to Marne-la-Vallée, which can work out slightly cheaper than the VEA shuttle (although the services are fewer). There are 10 trains between 6.51 and 11.19am, then basically one an hour

from 1–6pm and another 12 up to 9.34pm. At off-peak times, the ticket is €12.90 one way but it rises to €19.90 at peak times. The big benefit though, is that it takes just 15 minutes and you can walk out of the station to pick up the shuttle bus to any Disney hotel right outside. For the return journey to the airport, there are 13 services between 8.12am and 12.45pm, then another 12 from 3.01–10.16pm. (Be warned – if you miss the Charles de Gaulle stop, you will end up in Lille or even Brussels!) You can also get **taxis** outside all the terminals, although it will cost around €40 one way to any Disney hotel.

At **Orly Airport**, 15km (9 miles) to the south of the city centre, it is divided more simply into South and West terminals, and there is a free shuttle service operating every 5 minutes or so over the 2-minute journey between the two (from the South terminal, look for Exit K, and from the West terminal, go to the departure level and Exit W). With good direct links into the city, Orly makes a reasonable alternative to Charles de Gaulle, although it lacks the handy option of the TGV service to Marne-la-Vallée and the **RER** route is a little more complicated (take the airport link to Antony, on Line B, then go to Châtelet Les Halles and change to Line A for Marne-la-Vallée). At Orly South, take Exit G on the ground floor (platform 1 to Paris), and at Orly West, take Exit G also.

Much the better choice though, is

BRIT TIP: For all information on both Charles de Gaulle and Orly airports – including terminal maps, flight times and services – visit www.adp.fr and click on the Welcome link for the English version.

to use the direct **VEA Navette** shuttle bus service to all the Disney hotels (8.30am–7.30pm daily, until 9.30pm on Fridays, journey time 45–50 minutes) for €14/adult, €11.50 for children 3–11 (under 3s free). At Orly South, take Gate H for the VEA bus and at Orly West, take Gate C. A taxi from Orly to any of the Disney hotels will be about €30–35.

When it comes to the airlines themselves, **Air France** is not, surprisingly, the biggest carrier in terms of daily flights, using both main airports. At Charles de Gaulle, they fly into CDG 1 and CDG 2 (Halls A, B, C, D, F). **British Airways** flies to CDG 1, as does **bmi** (from Belfast, Edinburgh, Glasgow, Leeds/Bradford, Heathrow, Manchester and Teesside) and **bmi baby** (from Cardiff and East Midlands). **British European** operates to CDG 2 (Halls D and F), plus occasionally to Orly South. **EasyJet** (from Liverpool, Luton and Newcastle) flies into CDG T9 and **KLM** (from Stansted) operates at CDG 1. There are few direct flights to Orly from the UK – Egyptair and Royal Jordanian Airlines fly there from London, along with the occasional charter and at the time of writing EasyJet was looking at it as a destination.

Destination Magic

Of all the airlines offering a UK–Paris service, Air France offers the most family-friendly option thanks to their **Destination Magic** programme from Heathrow, Manchester, Birmingham and Newcastle. Apart from the fact their 55 daily flights to Charles de Gaulle make them the main carrier to Paris, their choice of 10 UK departure points – Aberdeen, Bristol, London Heathrow, London City, Manchester, Birmingham, Edinburgh, Glasgow, Newcastle and

Southampton – means they offer a comprehensive flight coverage for just about the whole country. And, from four of those airports, the bonus of Destination Magic is a strong one.

For this programme, one flight a day is chosen as the special 'Disney' service (outbound only), which means enhanced in-flight service to include well-designed Disney activity packs for the kids and a surprise gift (especially valuable on the longer flights from the likes of Manchester and Newcastle); free VEA shuttle buses to and from the resort, free children's lunches at *Disney Village* (with one child eating free with a paying adult at either The Steakhouse or Annette's Diner), discount coupons for some of the shops and restaurants in both the *Disneyland Park* and *Disney Village*, plus La Vallée outlet shopping village and that extra smattering of 'pixie dust' to start your holiday off on just the right note.

The best thing about it? There is no extra charge. No supplement has been added to the price of any of the four flights in question – just choose either the AF 1171 from Heathrow, the AF1669 from Manchester, the AF 3005 from Birmingham or the AF 3023 from Newcastle – and you get all the exclusive benefits of Destination Magic as part of the package, available with six of the main tour operators, plus Disney's direct booking facility. Call 08705 030 303 or look up the brochures of Cresta Holidays, Bridge Travel, Osprey, Thomson, Thomas Cook Signature or Sovereign.

Choosing a tour operator

While it is perfectly possible – and sometimes cheaper – to book a DIY holiday by putting together your own hotel and travel arrangements, the tour operators to *Disneyland Resort Paris* have developed an extremely sophisticated, not to mention exceptionally good value, raft of packages that make booking with them (especially if you book direct) highly worthwhile. Add in the number of internet travel companies like ebookers.com and lastminute.com, plus new specialists like themeparkholidays.com (see page 56), and there is again a bewildering variety on offer.

The best thing to do is to shop around and get an idea of the prices for the different types of packages. Most of the tour operators in this market are the big well-known chains, who all feature some of the keenest pricing thanks to their ability to deal in bulk (Cresta, Paris Travel Service and Leger Holidays are all part of the MyTravel – formerly Airtours – group), but there are several out-and-out Paris specialists, and these are worth considering as well.

BRIT TIP: For all the up-to-date *Disneyland Resort Paris* issues go to the UK Discussion Boards on the No 1 Disney-related website, the DIS (www.wdwinfo.com). Either click on DISboards, or go to www.disboards.com and visit the Disneyland Parks section. I may even be there to offer some advice myself!

When it comes to simple price comparisons, it is more the method of travel which makes the main difference, hence a coach-based trip is usually the cheapest on offer, followed by Eurotunnel or ferry self-drive, then Eurostar and finally flying. But, as I say, there are often special deals on offer – particularly at off-peak times – and it definitely pays to keep your wits about you

when looking for a bargain. So you need to know what the general going rate is before you plunge in!

Here is a look at the main dozen or so tour operators on the Disneyland beat (and their Disney accommodation comes complete with unlimited entry Theme Park passes for the duration of your visit):

Cresta Holidays: One of the biggest of the mainstream operators who offer the full range of options, Cresta has been voted the Top Short Break Specialist by the UK travel trade for the past 10 years, so they have a good idea of what they're about. They also aim to be one of the most flexible outfits in the business, hence they can combine just about any aspect of the resort, hotels and travel arrangements to suit customers' requirements. Their brochures are also among the clearest and most readable on offer.

Cresta features the full range of Disney accommodation and 22 off-site hotels, of which 21 offer 'free night' bonuses, and many of which are deliberately chosen for their proximity to the RER line into Marne-la-Vallée. They also boast a few neat little extras, like a pre-bookable Planet Hollywood meal deal, which includes kids' discounts, a privilege card for a free beer or soft drink with every meal purchased, and a free gift with any purchase at the merchandise store, plus special kids' fares if flying with British Midland.

The smart new Explorers Hotel (see page 73) is heavily featured in Cresta's 2004 programme and their lead-in price for the excellent value hotel (based on a 2-night stay) is an eye-catching £199 per adult and £69 per child, self-drive via Hoverspeed, inclusive of breakfast and unlimited Theme Park entry. Free activity packs are given to all children (3–11) staying at the Explorers Hotel and plenty of Kids Go Free offers are available in the first quarter of the year. Contact Cresta on 0870 161 0910 or visit www.crestaholidays.co.uk.

Transport: Self-drive via Eurotunnel, P&O Ferries, SeaFrance, Hoverspeed; Eurostar; flights (Air France, British Airways, bmi).

Leger Holidays: The biggest coach-tour operator to *Disneyland Resort Paris*, Leger has a countrywide network of coach and feeder coach routes, with more than 400 pick-up points, taking their customers to Dover or Folkestone, crossing the Channel for what is then a 4-hour drive to the resort (with one refreshment stop en route). They operate a mixture of their own branded coaches plus those of well-known coach companies from all over the country, usually with modern, comfortable vehicles which all feature onboard toilets and drinks facilities. There is also a dedicated programme from Scotland and Northern Ireland.

It is largely Disney on a budget (although they do also feature Eurostar departures) and they package it all extremely well using the new Explorers Hotel (see page 73) as their base price accommodation (which comes in slightly cheaper than Disney's most budget-orientated offering, the *Hotel Santa Fe*). They feature primarily 2-, 3- and 4-night packages, with the option to upgrade to *Disney's Hotel Cheyenne* or *Disney's Sequoia Lodge* (and some free upgrade offers for early bookers). A self-drive alternative also uses the exciting Explorers Hotel.

Another new feature in 2003 was Leger's first flight programme, using low-cost carriers from either East Midlands or Cardiff airports. Transfers are provided from Charles de Gaulle.

Once in the resort, the coach is often used to take Leger customers on excursions into Paris (a worthwhile little extra). For their off-site hotels (they use Ibis, Campanile and Novotel chains on the Paris outskirts), the coach stays with you for the duration and acts as your transport to and from the Theme Parks. They obviously operate year-round, but the summer is their busiest period (although the Kids Go Free season from January to March is also hugely popular), and the 4-night stay has really caught on well since the opening of the *Walt Disney Studios Park*. The addition of the Explorers Hotel has given them an extra boost in the value-for-money stakes and has proved extremely popular in its first year.

Leger has 10 main departures over the 6 weeks of the summer holidays and aims to get you to the resort on the first day between 8 and 10 in the evening. The return journey usually leaves after breakfast on the last day.

The majority also uses P&O Ferries crossings from Dover but some dates are served via Eurotunnel. I have highlighted a typical Leger 4-night break in Chapter 2 (see page 16) and will not be surprised to see them introduce a 5-night getaway before too long, as it is still hard to fit everything into 4 days! Their brochures also highlight the Disney special events like Bonfire Night, Halloween and Christmas extremely well. Call Leger Holidays on 0845 130 7007 or visit www.leger.co.uk.

Transport: Coach via P&O Ferries or Eurotunnel; Eurostar; self-drive; flights (various, from Cardiff or East Midlands).

Paris Travel Service: Under the umbrella of Bridge Travel (and ultimately part of the MyTravel group), Paris TS was the first British tour operator to sell *Disneyland Resort Paris*, hence they have had more than 11 years to hone their offering. They have some of the most knowledgeable staff and arguably the most comprehensive brochure, with every possible combination of travel (including fly-drives) and every accommodation option – all seven Disney properties, the three neighbouring Selected Hotels and a good selection of nearby off-site options. For those looking for something a bit different to the regular packages and the greatest flexibility, this could be the place to look, as the Bridge brand also covers a huge variety of short breaks, tours and special events throughout Western Europe.

Their documentation and ticketing is first class, and there are some useful 'extras', like a free kids' autograph book (a really neat touch) and an array of special offers (like Kids Eat Free with P&O Ferries, Free Kids' Character Breakfast, free kids' entry to Sea Life and a privilege card for Planet Hollywood). Paris TS offers an optional free upgrade to transfer by taxi from Charles de Gaulle Airport for parties of five or six.

You can pre-book virtually every show and character experience, while the new Manchester United Soccer School (for 7–14s) is also bookable through Paris TS. A third or fourth night free is offered on selected dates, as are price reductions for travel on Eurostar. The Kids Go Free season is again a big part of their programme from January to April. Contact Paris TS on 0870 010 2456 (brochure request) or 0870 191 7200 (reservations), or visit www.paris-travel.co.uk.

Transport: Coach (Eurolines); Eurostar; flights (bmi, Air France, British Airways); self-drive via Eurotunnel, P&O Ferries, Hoverspeed.

Thomson: Formerly Thomson Breakaway, this member of the TUI travel group (which also includes travel agent Lunn Poly) now trades on the good name of its main parent company Thomson Holidays, hence the operation is large scale, well organised and extremely knowledgable (especially for Near the Magic hotels). There are some useful special offers, such as Single Parents (£50 off the second child fare) and Kids Go Free all year in nearly all of their Near the Magic hotels (inclusive of breakfast). Free Night offers are available periodically at Disney resorts.

An immensely readable brochure contains all the Disney hotels and the full range of travel options (with Kids Eat Free deals on P&O Ferries), including Eurolines coaches from London Victoria (a direct day service, departing at 10.30am and leaving Disney at 9.45pm). They offer meal vouchers as an optional extra, which helps with your pre-holiday budgeting and you can pre-book character meals. They stress that early bookers will get the best deals with the increasing popularity of the resort since the *Walt Disney Studios Park* opened in March 2002. A good number of their Near the Magic hotels are close to the RER line into Marne-la-Vallée, so you can still take advantage of the Eurostar direct service. Call Thomson direct on 0870 606 1496 or visit www.thomson-holidays.com.

Transport: Coach (Eurolines); Eurostar; flights (bmi, Air France, British Airways, bmibaby, EasyJet); self-drive via Eurotunnel, P&O Ferries, Hoverspeed.

BRIT TIP: One travel agent said to me: 'Please let people know that this is truly a resort experience now. It is not just a day at a theme park any more.'

Thomas Cook Signature: This famous name in the travel agency business operates an extremely well-run *Disneyland Resort Paris* programme. From the clarity of their brochure to the quality of their ticketing material – which includes a huge leather wallet with all the necessary documentation, baggage tags etc, plus a 36-page information booklet – Thomas Cook Signature lives up to its reputation as one of the originators and innovators in the tour operating business. Their free kids' pack – for all children aged 3–11 (but not on accommodation-only bookings) – is one of the best I've seen, with a J-bag containing a disposable camera, poncho, water bottle, ripper wallet, mini playing cards, activity book with crayons and a pen, refresher bar, sunglasses and autograph book.

Their booking staff are extremely switched on when it comes to advising guests with disabilities. You can again pre-buy meal vouchers to use in the hotels, parks and *Disney Village*, and book character meals in advance (advisable during peak periods), which can help with your budgeting. They also offer free nights at Disney resorts periodically, some Kids Go Free deals, and a free kids' character breakfast and Buffalo Bill's show ticket with every adult booking (for children under 12). Additionally, there are exclusive offers such as free Sea Life Centre tickets and Earlybird Money Savers.

Thomas Cook features the full range of Disney hotels and the usual off-site options (these tend to vary very little between operators). The latter are designed either for self-drive customers (or fly-drives, with Cook's using Avis Car Hire) or with hotels close to the RER line, and there are also some 'free night' deals to be had at various times of the year. On P&O Ferries, kids eat free with a paying adult in the International Food Court.

The flight options are extremely well detailed, from no less than 17 UK airports (although Aberdeen and Belfast flights go via either Gatwick, Heathrow or East Midlands). For more info, call Thomas Cook Signature on 0870 443 4452 or visit www.tcsignature.com.

Transport: Eurostar; flights (bmi, Air France, British Airways, EasyJet, bmibaby); self-drive via Eurotunnel, P&O Ferries, Hoverspeed.

Sovereign: The direct booking arm of First Choice is an extremely quality-conscious operation, from their ticketing material to the extras such as kids' packs, hence you do pay a slight premium for their service. The excellent kids' packs are actually different for those aged 3–7 and 8–11 and will contain even more from March 2004 – both groups get a special pen, a Sovereign-logo plastic poncho (handy for any showers), a disposable camera and a rucksack, while the younger set get an autograph book and the older ones a Filofax (with a section for photos and autographs) and a French phrase book. You can pre-book meal vouchers, character meals and Buffalo Bill's, while there are free kids' deals for character breakfasts and the Wild West Show.

BRIT TIP: The main Disney tour operators advise: 1. Book early (essential for high season); 2. Use Disney's FastPass system in the Theme Parks (see page 87); 3. Plan your day with the aid of park maps (and this book, they forgot to add!), which give you all the show times, parades, etc; 4. Book your meals on arrival.

A full range of accommodation is available – both on and off-site – and Sovereign features the new Kyriad and Holiday Inn hotels right next to the resort quite prominently. Their off-site hotels have free child places year-round, while periodically they also offer free nights at Disney hotels. The seasonal Kids Go Free offer at all Disney hotels and the Hotel l'Elysée can also be combined with the free night offers. In all, they provide 17 different departure points (including Aberdeen, Bristol, Newcastle, Leeds-Bradford, plus the obvious ones of Ashford, Waterloo, Folkestone and Dover). Call Sovereign on 08705 768 373 or visit www.sovereign.com.

Transport: Eurostar; flights (bmi, Air France, British Airways); self-drive via Eurotunnel, P&O Ferries, Hoverspeed.

Osprey Holidays: This Disney specialist is designed especially for those who live in Scotland. With the choice of either Eurostar or flights, plus any of the Disney hotels and a small selection of central Paris ones, Osprey also gives free night offers at resort hotels, while like the other operators you can pre-book for things like meal vouchers, character meals and Buffalo Bill's show. The free hotel nights at certain times of the year also apply to this company. Call 08705 605 605 for Osprey reservations, or visit www.osprey-holidays.co.uk.

Transport: Eurostar; flights (bmi, Air France, British Airways, Buzz).

Newmarket: Mainly a coach operator, you won't notice Newmarket in any travel agent, but you will find their Magical Breaks packages in many local and national newspapers. From Aberdeen to Plymouth, you are likely to see their newspaper-endorsed reader offers, and usually at extremely eye-catching prices (even for Eurostar

packages). They offer mainly off-site hotels (hence the budget-orientated nature of the operation) with good, reliable coach services (most of which cross the channel via P&O Ferries from Dover).

Their Paris expertise dates back to the opening of the *Disneyland Park*, hence they have a thoroughly knowledgable staff (including their own in-resort reps), and they also do big business in affinity groups and schools' Study Experiences (for students of information and communications technology, plus many other curriculum driven subjects for schools and colleges).

With their coach tours (which are the vast majority), they have some 500 pick-up points all over the country and the coach acts as your transport throughout the trip at the off-site hotels, which tend to be in the Greater Paris area (usually of the Campanile, Ibis, Novotel standard – a basic but comfortable 2- and 3-star). The only drawback is you are restricted to the coach's one trip to and from the hotel each day (you would need to make your own way back to the hotel if you wanted to return earlier, for any reason).

All are on a bed and breakfast (of the continental variety) basis, and they feature either 3- or 4-day trips (with the latter growing increasingly popular). On coach tours, the 3-day trips feature two 1-Day Passports for the Theme Parks (you arrive mid-evening on the first day, have one full day there, then return in early afternoon on the third day), while the 4-day version has a 3-Day Passport included (as you have 2 full days for the Theme Parks, plus part of the final day before an afternoon return; Scottish departures leave earlier on the final day).

Going by Eurostar, Newmarket offers 2- and 3-day trips, arriving in the early afternoon on day one and departing in the evening on day two or three (although both versions give you two 1-Day Passports on the 3-day trip you are not provided with park access on the afternoon of your arrival). For more information, call 020 8335 3030 or visit www.newmarket-group.co.uk.

Transport: Coach via P&O Ferries or Eurotunnel; Eurostar.

Harry Shaw: Another popular and busy coach-tour operator, this company's speciality is 1-, 2- and 3-day trips, with the possibility of overnight travel on some to give you extra time in the Theme Parks. The basic option is between off-site accommodation (usually a 2-star hotel in the Ile de France region), where the coach takes you to and from the Theme Park, and four of the Disney hotels *(Disney's Hotel Cheyenne, Disney's Hotel Santa Fe, Disney's Newport Bay Club* and *Disney's Sequoia Lodge).* However, the one drawback with off-site hotels is that you are tied to the coach's return times. Call 024 7654 5544 or visit www.harryshaw.co.uk.

Transport: Coach via P&O Ferries or Eurotunnel.

Eurotunnel Motoring Holidays: In conjunction with Cresta, Eurotunnel has its own holidays division offering fairly loose-knit packages all with, naturally, self-drive travel via the Channel Tunnel. The full range of Disney accommodation is offered including one of the most extensive choices of off-site hotels in the area. The packages can also be combined with skiing holidays and any of their other excellent self-drive breaks in northern France (including an even wider choice of places to stay in and around Paris).

The Cresta tie-up means they can also offer the new Explorers Hotel (see page 73). All the usual character meals and shows can be pre-booked and they have the same 'free night' deals at certain times plus the benefit

of Cresta's reliable reservations and bookings staff. My one reservation is that they still charge a supplement for the Eurotunnel crossing at various times, which can be up to £62 at peak school holiday times. For more info, call 0870 333 2001 or e-mail ethols@crestaholidays.co.uk.

Transport: Self-drive via Eurotunnel.

Travelscene: This specialist short-break company has more than 35 years' experience of the European holiday business and, although their Cities brochure includes only a couple of pages on *Disneyland Resort Paris,* their Paris section is extensive and extremely polished. Their Disney packages feature a small range of off-site hotels, all close to the RER line, in conjunction with Eurostar travel, and with a 'Sunday night free' option if you stay Friday and Saturday as well. All bookings come with a free guidebook and their own Cities For Kids info. For more information, call 0870 777 4445 or visit www.travelscene.co.uk.

Transport: Eurostar.

Harris Holidays: The last of the main coach-tour operators, Harris keep things simple and operates coaches via Eurotunnel, using *Disney's Hotel Santa Fe* with upgrade options to *Disney's Hotel Cheyenne* and *Disney's Sequoia Lodge.* However, they can also arrange independent travel for you with Eurostar or self-drive. Their stock-in-trade is a 3-day coach trip, arriving on the evening of the first day, having a full day in one park on the second, and departing late afternoon on the third, with two 1-Day Passports provided for access to the Theme Parks (some summer itineraries arrive in time to visit the Theme Park on the first day; in this case, a 3-Day Passport is provided). They even offer a 1-day trip, travelling overnight on a Friday, having nearly all Saturday in the *Disneyland Park* and returning Saturday evening. For more details, call 01375 396688 or visit www.harris-travel.com.

Transport: Coach via Eurotunnel; Eurostar; self-drive.

Finally, for a company with a difference that is designed to help both the more independent-minded traveller, who knows how to get there but wants some good advice on tickets etc, and those who need to be assisted all along the way, the new **www.themeparkholidays.com** is an ideal website. Full of great info, practical advice and a wealth of detail on the Theme Parks and hotels (both on- and off-site), not to mention some great Disney photos, the site offers all the benefits of a travel agent at the click of a mouse. Call up the site, go to Destinations, then Europe and France, and just follow the easy-to-use instructions for whatever you need to know. You can also talk to the site's highly knowledgeable team (not surprising, since it's the brainchild of a former senior Disney marketing manager) on 0870 247 1000. Well worth looking into.

Book direct

Of course, you can always book directly with **Disney** if you have an idea of what you want to do. The resort offers a full range of packages with all the usual methods of

transport and they even have a good range of off-site accommodation, both nearby and in Paris itself. Their brochure is worth getting just for all the lavish photography and large-scale maps and they highlight all the extras, 'free nights' and Kids Go Free deals which you find elsewhere. The pricing system and dizzying array of supplements for each of the different forms of transport can take some deciphering (if you studied calculus at school you'll have an advantage!), but you basically have every possible permutation open to you. The way their brochure is designed, you first choose your accommodation, then how long you want to visit (from 1–4 nights), select any additional features (like character meals and shows), and finally decide upon the mode of transport. For details, call their hotline on 08705 03 03 03 or simply visit their website at www.disneylandparis.com.

Transport: Eurostar; flights (Air France, British Airways, bmi); self-drive via Eurotunnel, P&O Ferries, SeaFrance, Hoverspeed.

But wait, before you can make a fully informed choice, you need to have a good idea of the array of accommodation that awaits you, both in the form of the Disney resorts themselves and the usually cheaper alternatives for staying off-site. So, read on, and I will reveal all about how to choose your hotel…

Staying There
(or, How to Play the Hotel Game)

When it comes to your choice of places to stay in and around *Disneyland Resort Paris*, you will not be surprised to know there is a bewildering variety. Disney alone has six highly contrasting and entertaining hotels on site, while *Disney's Davy Crockett Ranch®*, about a 15-minute drive away, offers an alternative for those with a car. There are then another five hotels 'near the Magic', which benefit from being close to the resort and several dozen more within a 15–25 minute drive.

The key is the combination of location and price. All the Disney resorts offer the huge convenience of being just minutes from the essential Theme Park magic, but their hotels do tend to be on the expensive side. If you are staying on-site, the chances are you won't need any other form of transport. But a car is also not always necessary if you stay off-site, as the wonderful ease of use of the RER rail line makes staying in somewhere like Bussy-St-Georges, Noisiel or even Bercy, towards the centre of Paris, a perfectly viable proposition.

The section on the various tour operators in the previous chapter reveals the great range of packages on offer. Virtually every operator also features off-site hotels as the demand for the Disney ones is pretty high –

UK visitor numbers were up by more than 5% in 2002 on 2001. The area along the RER corridor still makes a handy base for tackling Disney (and Paris, for that matter), and the general standard of hotels is sound if unspectacular. Their star-rating system is pretty accurate and virtually every hotel works on a bed-and-breakfast basis (a continental breakfast with cereal, pastries, cold meats, cheese and tea/coffee). More people choose to stay off-site in summer as Disney's prices are at their highest then, while the price difference between on- and off-site properties is less in the winter months.

> **BRIT TIP:** The quoted price rates of hotels in France are always per room and not per person.

Staying **off-site** can actually provide more flexibility for your holiday if you want to use the hotel just as a base and not part of the holiday itself (the Disney hotels certainly play an important role in the holiday experience). You'll have more incentive to get out and about if you stay off-site and it's convenient for seeing more of Paris, while many hotels offer 'extra night free' deals which make their value that bit more wallet-friendly.

You should certainly check in advance, however, whether or not you'll need a car. If you are not close to an RER station – or the hotel does not have a shuttle service to the nearest station – you will struggle without your own transport. However, many of the tour operators (notably Thomson, see page 52) now offer travel to the resort by Eurostar with off-site hotels along the RER line and this option is worth seeking out.

Disney Hotels

When it comes to getting the maximum out of your trip, you can't beat the full and all-encompassing experience of staying **on-site**, as the majority of Brits do (curiously, only a small percentage of other nationalities choose this option, which means Disney hotels are often significantly British in their guest ratio). Just the simple fact of being able to walk into the Theme Parks in the morning, through *Disney Village*, is one of the great pleasures of visiting here. Even from *Disney's*

Hotel Santa Fe, which is the furthest away of the six on-site resorts, it is no more than a 20-minute stroll and, on a sunny morning, it is a true delight. The old estate agent's adage of 'location, location, location' is just as true here!

There are also other significant benefits to staying *chez* Mickey for the duration of your visit, most notably the excellent **character interaction** you get at all six hotels, in the morning and evening. At least one character will always be 'on parade' in the hotel foyer and kids are virtually guaranteed to get their autograph books off to a flying start in this way. Disney's **service and hospitality** adds significantly to everyone's enjoyment, while all resort guests get their own **Identification Card** that can be used as a charge card in both parks and at *Disney Village* (apart from the Rainforest Café, Planet Hollywood, McDonald's and the Gaumont Cinema complex).

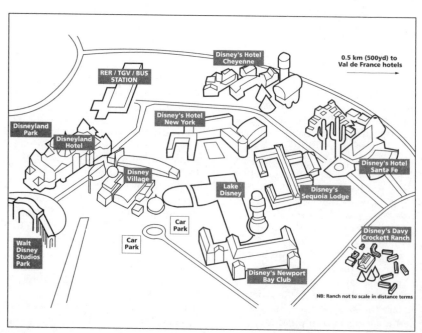

Resort guests also benefit from **free parking** at the hotels, theme parks and *Disney Village*, the **free shuttle bus service, free entry to Hurricanes disco** in *Disney Village*, along with a whole range of **recreational activities,** depending on which hotel you choose, from swimming pools and tennis courts to outdoor playgrounds, video games and even ice-skating (outside *Disney's Hotel New York*, but open to all hotel guests, for a small fee). There is a **shopping service** for hotel guests, whereby you can have anything you buy in one of the Theme Parks delivered to the Disney shop in your hotel, for collection from 8pm that day. Each hotel also organises regular **children's activities** and all have Disney TV, and an interactive computer games console in their play area.

> BRIT TIP: The character breakfast options can be booked through your hotel concierge in the foyer (see page 61), and it is advisable to do this as soon as you check in.

Finally, and highly important for those with children, there is the option to have a **character breakfast** at one of three locations – the *Disneyland Hotel*, for guests there, Café Mickey in *Disney Village*, or Walt's – An American Restaurant in the *Disneyland Park* (there is, as you would expect, an additional charge for this). These feature an American buffet breakfast with a wide variety of breads, pastries, scrambled eggs, ham, sausages, cereals, fruit juices and hot drinks, and are priced at €16 per adult and €12 per child (3–11).

The two outdoor **tennis courts** at *Disney's Hotel New York* are also available to all Disney resort guests (for a small fee for ball and racket hire), on production of your ID card.

An additional (non-character) feature at peak times for guests at *Disney's Newport Bay Club*, *Disney's Sequoia Lodge*, *Disney's Hotel Cheyenne* and *Disney's Hotel Santa Fe* is the **Good Morning Fantasyland breakfast**, whereby hotel guests can opt to enter the *Disneyland Park* an hour early and board the Disneyland Railroad train (or just walk) to Fantasyland, where a continental buffet breakfast is served for you in one of the restaurants, usually Au Chalet de la Marionette. You will then be in pole position to ride the likes of Dumbo and Peter Pan at the stroke of 9am.

> BRIT TIP: Although there is no extra charge for the Good Morning Fantasyland breakfast, you need to specify where you would like to have it – either in the hotel or the *Disneyland Park* – when you book.

In nearly all cases, when booking a Disney hotel you are obliged to accept the Unlimited Access Pass as part of the package (or a 3-Day Passport if you opt for the minimum 2-night/3-day package), which obviously suits most people as it keeps you up and running in the Theme Parks from the first minute to the last. However, it may not be suitable if you plan on doing some non-Disney sightseeing as well, hence you need to weigh up whether an off-site hotel might be the better option. The main exception to the Disney hotel rule is if you are an Annual Passport holder, in which case you can book just bed-and-breakfast packages through the central reservations office on 00 33 1 60 30 60 30 from the UK.

Most **room sizes** will accommodate a family of four comfortably, but you are limited for choice with five or more (although some rooms can also accommodate a cot if required). Basically, you have only three choices in this instance: *Disney's Davy Crockett Ranch®*, where the cabins can house up to six people (but you must have your own transport); two connecting rooms in one of the six hotels; or one of the 15 family rooms, which can accommodate up to six at *Disney's Newport Bay Club*, although these rooms are more expensive and are at a premium, so you would need to book early. (Looking outside the resort, the new Pierre & Vacances Residence Val d'Europe is an ultra-smart apartment block in the town which can accommodate up to seven, while the Explorers Hotel can take family groups of up to 10.) Rooms for guests with disabilities are available in all six hotels, apart from *Disney's Davy Crockett Ranch®*.

All rooms feature a telephone, international TV channels and radio and a shower/bath. *Disney's Hotel Cheyenne, Disney's Hotel Santa Fe* and *Disney's Davy Crockett Ranch®* do NOT have air-conditioning (although the former two have ceiling fans), while only the *Disneyland Hotel* and *Disney's Hotel New York* have hairdryers fitted as standard in the bathrooms (the others have hairdryers available on request). *Hotel Disneyland, Disney's Hotel New York* and *Disney's Newport Bay Club* all have mini-bars, as does *Disney's Sequoia Lodge* in its Montana rooms only, while the former trio also have room safes. All but *Disney's Davy Crockett Ranch®* offer non-smoking rooms and a left-luggage service.

When checking in, you will be given your park tickets, any vouchers for various options you might have booked (for meals or Buffalo Bill's Wild West Show), park maps, an information guide to the hotel (these are well written and highly collectable), a *Disney Village* programme and your Resort ID card, while children also get their own name badge to wear all the time (if they want!).

BRIT TIP: If you arrive at the hotel between midday and 2pm, have lunch there before heading off to the Theme Parks. You will get served much quicker.

Each resort hotel should be able to supply a cot on request and all feature **children's menus** in their main restaurants. **Room service** is available only at the *Disneyland Hotel* and *Disney's Hotel New York*, and the Admiral's Floor of *Disney's Newport Bay Club*. In all cases, check-in time is 3pm (although rooms are occasionally available from 1pm, but the left-luggage provision means you can head straight for the Theme Parks) and check-out is 11am. However, there is no official in-house **baby-sitting** service for any of the hotels, although there is a private firm who can arrange in-room baby-sitting for you via the front desk.

BRIT TIP: If you have booked Eurostar's Disney Express service (see page 46), you simply leave your bags, cases, etc, in the left-luggage office at your hotel when you check out, and they will be transferred for you to collect at the Disney Express office at the station. Whether or not you've booked, Disney Express labels are available for your return journey for a few extra euros at the check-in.

Disney's six hotels (amounting to 5,200 rooms, plus the 535 cabins and 60 caravan sites of *Disney's Davy Crockett Ranch®*) come with a range of prices to suit most pockets, from the more budget-priced style of *Disney's Hotel Santa Fe* to the opulent 4-star *Disneyland Hotel* itself. We at *A Brit's Guide* have our own ratings system for the hotels, too, allocating €s in the following price ranges:

€€€€€ = More than €150/night
€€€€ = €100–150/night
€€€ = €75–100/night
€€ = €50–75/night
€ = Less than €50/night

We also award CCCs out of five for the extra facilities at each property. Hence you can be sure a CCCCC hotel should have all the creature comforts you can think of, including a swimming pool and a choice of restaurants, while a CC would be of the more basic, motel-type. Here are Disney's magnificent seven in detail:

Disneyland Hotel

The resort's signature hotel, right at the entrance to the *Disneyland Park* and otherwise known as the Pink Palace, is a massive mock-Victorian edifice featuring the most comfortable and spacious rooms, sumptuous decor and one of the best restaurants in the whole area. The Disney theming is at its most discreet here (you have to look closely at the wallpaper to realise the in-built Mickey subtlety) and there is some elegant furniture sprinkled around (witness the four classic grandfather clocks along one corridor which display the times at each of the Disney resorts around the world – they also play Disney tunes on the hour and half-hour!). Standard rooms feature either a king-size bed and a fold-out or two doubles, plus a very elaborate

TV/video cabinet with mini-bar, and all have the high ceilings reminiscent of Victorian buildings.

The top two floors feature the exclusive **Castle Club,** with a private lift (straight to the Theme Park!) and reception desk, a lounge bar for breakfast, afternoon tea and light refreshments, plus a fabulous view out over the *Disneyland Park*. There are then even more spacious Junior Suites (58sq m/624sq ft as opposed to the 34sq m/366sq ft of standard rooms), plus four Tinker Bell Suites (69sq metres/743sq ft) with a lounge and a separate walk-in shower as well as a bath and three one-off suites of truly exceptional order – Walt's Apartment, the Vice-Presidential Suite (Cinderella) and the Presidential Suite (Sleeping Beauty).

BRIT TIP: Each Disney hotel has a concierge desk in the foyer specially for booking meals and shows in any of the hotels, parks or *Disney Village*. Try to plan day by day and visit the concierge desk first thing in the morning to make your bookings – especially at peak times of the year.

From the 3-storey lobby right through to the sauna, the period theming is impressive but not overwhelming. There is a **Galerie Mickey** selling souvenirs and a few travel essentials, the main bar area **Café Fantasia** (with smart, inventive decor geared to the film of the same name) as well as two restaurants. **Inventions** is themed on the great technical inventions of the 20th century and offers an excellent international dinner buffet with Disney characters in attendance, in addition to the character breakfasts.

The **California Grill** is the hotel's fine dining establishment and the quality on offer here is truly 5-star, with a conservatory-style motif and a show kitchen at one end. At the other end, a lounge affords more great views of the Theme Park.

The indoor pool area is equally smart, with a medium-sized pool, a large, semi-circular Jacuzzi, a gymnasium and massage treatment rooms, as well as the sauna, steam room and solarium. The inevitable video games room – the Mad Hatter's Arcade – is fully geared up for kids of the requisite age, while the Minnie Club children's activity centre includes TV, video, computer games and various play areas. The only thing it doesn't have is an outdoor play area, but then you can argue that the *Disneyland Park* is pretty much its own playground! However, there is a supplement for a standard room with a park view. In all there are 496 rooms, plus 18 suites, and it really is the pinnacle of all the on-site accommodation. **Official rating ****; our rating €€€€€, CCCCC.**

Disney's Hotel New York

Welcome to the Big Apple! It is not the fact this is a Disney hotel so much as it is wonderfully themed, with an art deco, 1930s' view of New York that extends from the massive 'tower block' façade to individual touches in the rooms and the background jazz throughout the lobby and bar area. There is very little overt Mickey-ness about it, but lots of grand style and clever imagery, with the bonus for some rooms of a fabulous view over Lake Disney. It also has, for my money, the most amazing suite of them all, the 2-storey Roosevelt Presidential Suite, with floor-to-ceiling windows, wonderful furniture, a living room complete with piano and a dining room for up to eight guests. The upstairs double

bedroom has a separate lounge and a relaxing Jacuzzi.

Most standard rooms (31sq m/334sq ft), which have some lovely rosewood cabinets, sleep four comfortably, while others offer just one king-size bed. The Resort Suites (56sq m/603sq ft, one on each corner of each floor) have masses of space for a family of four, with a separate bedroom and living room. There is a beautiful Honeymoon Suite (62sq m/667sq ft) as well.

With 565 rooms in all (including 27 spacious suites), the hotel features two restaurants (the intimate, formal atmosphere of the **Manhattan Restaurant** and the more relaxed cosmopolitan style of the **Parkside Diner**), a delightfully elegant bar, a hair salon (the only one on-site), boutique and gift shop, two outdoor tennis courts (small fee for racket and ball hire) and an ice-skating rink (a real eye-catching facility in winter).

For kids, there is the Roger Rabbit corner, with differently themed activities at different times of the day, and the ubiquitous video games room. The one drawback here is that the hotel is also a big convention facility, and it can draw a sizeable business/conference crowd at times.

BRIT TIP: If you find the *Disney Village* a touch too frenetic in the evening, head for the City Bar at *Disney's Hotel New York* and you will find the perfect surroundings for a relaxing and enjoyable beverage or two.

A bonus with *Disney's Hotel New York* is the swimming pool complex, which is easily the best of the on-site hotels. The extremely large pool has both an indoor and outdoor aspect, depending on the weather, while there is also a Jacuzzi, sauna, steam room and a good-sized gymnasium, plus an extremely pleasant outdoor terrace. After the *Disneyland Hotel*, it is also the closest to the Theme Parks, situated right at the opposite end of *Disney Village*, and is barely a 10-minute stroll from the gates of the *Disneyland Park*, slightly less for the *Walt Disney Studios Park*.

> BRIT TIP: *Disney's Hotel New York* is a product of American architect Michael Graves, who also designed the Swan and Dolphin Hotels in *Walt Disney World Resort in Florida*. So, if you enjoy the fun-style architecture of those two, *Disney's Hotel New York* is bound to appeal.

While it may be a touch too formal for some tastes (mainly as a result of the conference aspect), *Disney's Hotel New York* does have a terrifically exciting feel, especially for young adults and teenagers, and is possibly in the perfect situation looking out over Lake Disney but still within an easy stroll of *Disney Village*. **Official rating ****; our rating €€€€, CCCCC.**

Disney's Newport Bay Club

Keeping with the American theme, *Disney's Newport Bay Club* has a New England seaside resort feel, with the largest spread of rooms of any of the on-site hotels (or any hotel in Europe, come to that). It may not appeal quite so much to children (it has possibly the most 'grown-up' style of all six hotels), but it is well equipped to cater for all the family, with two excellent pools (a large outdoor one and an elaborate indoor pool, with a pirate ship centrepiece), an outdoor play area, the usual video games arcade and a Children's Corner play area with organised activities on particular days, under parental supervision. There is also a convention centre here, but it is more detached than *Disney's Hotel New York*, hence the business aspect is not so intrusive.

The two restaurants are semi-formal – the **Cape Cod** serves European cuisine with a touch of Mediterranean flair, while the similar **Yacht Club** specialises in fish, seafood and grilled meats (try the clam chowder for a true taste of New England) – and you are allocated either one for breakfast when you check in if the hotel is full (the Cape Cod is used otherwise). There are two fine bars, **Fisherman's Wharf,** which opens from the foyer, and the more intensely nautical-themed **Captain's Quarters** piano bar and both look out over Lake Disney. In addition to the pool, there is a Jacuzzi, steam bath and fitness room. The large Bay Boutique offers a good selection of Disney merchandise and other travel essentials.

> BRIT TIP: Hairdryers and irons are available on request, free of charge, from the front desk of most of the Disney hotels, subject to availability and sometimes a deposit, except for the *Disneyland Hotel* and *Disney's Hotel New York* where they are provided in the rooms.

The sheer size of the hotel (1,080 rooms, plus 13 suites) means the foyer area can get terribly congested, especially from 9–10am when people are checking out. There is a separate reception desk for the **Admiral's Club**, which covers the lake side of the top two floors (hence wonderful views), and offers a more personal level of service, plus room service, and a quieter, more relaxed atmosphere (quite a bonus when the hotel is full). The majority of the spacious, 2-room suites (55sq m/ 592sq ft) are at this level too, with the unusual octagonal Honeymoon Suite (45sq m/484sq ft) being quite stunningly romantic.

The main suites also feature some lovely colonial-style furniture and extra nautical touches. Standard rooms (27sq m/290sq ft) continue the refreshing blue-and-white colour scheme of the rest of the hotel, and all include mini-bars and room safes, but I feel there are quite a few in need of some gentle refurbishment to maintain the upscale feel elsewhere. *Disney's Newport Bay Club* is also at the furthest end of Lake Disney, hence it is a good 15-minute walk to the Theme Parks. But, on a pleasant morning, there is not a more delightful walk anywhere in the Ile de France. **Official rating ***; our rating €€€, CCCC.**

Disney's Sequoia Lodge

If you like to be surrounded by gardens and greenery, head straight for *Disney's Sequoia Lodge*, as here you will be transported to one of the great American national parks. The main aspect of the hotel is a touch flat and monolithic but the interior and landscaping detail are quite breathtaking, with a fabulous use of stone and hundreds of imported trees and bushes for a truly authentic feel.

If you want the ideal winter retreat, there is no better place to while away some time than the **Redwood Bar and Lounge,** which has a massive open fireplace and cosy

furniture. The low, sloping, beamed ceiling and flagstone floor of the lobby set the scene for an outdoors adventure with all the comforts of a luxury resort (well above it's 3-star rating, in my opinion). The judicious use of dark woods adds to the rugged feel and, when the weather is good, there is a lovely outdoor terrace where you can sit with a drink and survey Lake Disney.

BRIT TIP: Not sure of where to stay at Christmas? Look no further – *Disney's Sequoia Lodge* is the perfect choice during the winter generally, but takes on a positively enchanted atmosphere with all the festive decorations.

The gift shop, **The Northwest Passage**, also sells a standard range of toiletries, snacks, drinks and souvenirs, while the Little Prairie is the kids' corner, with a TV and video, games station and an elaborate character photo area (available 5 days a week to either take your own snaps or use the official Disney photographer). Then there is the usual video games room, plus an outdoor play area with slides and a sandpit, set among some beautiful gardens, full of unique (for western Europe!) foliage, a waterfall and even a mock beaver dam. Stroll the paths along the 'Rio Grande' and you come to the hotel's pool lodge, an indoor/outdoor facility that features a water-slide, freeform leisure pool (great for kids), large Jacuzzi, sauna, steam room and gymnasium. There is a solarium that may be pre-booked at €6 for 10 minutes, as well as massages (€45 per half-hour).

The 1,011 rooms (including 16 suites) are split between the huge main building and five lodges spread

Frontierland

Left: Phantom Manor
Above left: Riverboat Cruise
Top: Frontierland cabin
Above: Big Thunder Mountain
Below: Disney characters in Frontierland

Adventureland

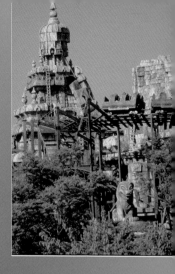

Above: Adventure Isle
Top right: Indiana Jones™
  and the Temple of
  Peril: Backwards!
Right: La Cabane des
  Robinsons
Below: Captain Hook's
  Galley and
  Skull Rock

FANTASYLAND

Left: Alice's Curious Labyrinth
Top left: The Sword in the Stone outside Sleeping Beauty Castle
Top right: Mad Hatter's Tea Cups
Above: Carrousel de Lancelot
Below: Meeting Mickey Mouse

DISCOVERYLAND

Left: Videopolis
Top left: Space Mountain
Above: Star Tours
Below right: Orbitron
Below: Les Mystères du Nautilus

throughout the gardens. Standard rooms (22sq m/237sq ft) have either a Lake Disney or gardens/car park view, large windows and a few extra touches like rocking chairs and rustic light fittings, which combine well with the dark wood furniture and the dark green bedspreads and curtains to provide that American backwoods ambience.

The cabin lodges offer exactly the same room space and facilities as the main building (Montana) rooms, apart from a mini-bar (hence they are slightly cheaper). A lake view carries a supplement but is well worthwhile (and should be requested when you make your booking). The spacious 2-room suites (55sq m/ 592sq ft) all have a lake view and the Honeymoon Suite features an open-plan arrangement with no separating door between the bedroom and living room.

Disney's Sequoia Lodge has two mouth-watering diners, the **Beaver Creek Tavern** and **Hunter's Grill**. The former is the more family-orientated option, with a varied menu to suit those with a big appetite that includes their speciality of an extra large brochette of skewered lamb with a stuffed baked potato and mushroom garnish. The dessert buffet is outstanding and there is a set menu for €20, with salad, choice of three main courses

---

BRIT TIP: My suggestion for the Hunter's Grill at *Disney's Sequoia Lodge* is the Ranger's Rotisserie – an endive salad, followed by a marinated roast chicken thigh, a herb sausage and spiced pork fillet, and then prime roast rump steak, sliced at your table, plus dessert. Outstanding!

---

and dessert. Within the restaurant is a kids' area with a TV showing Disney cartoons.

The Hunter's Grill continues the hotel's outdoors theme in magnificent style, with a huntin', shootin', fishin' motif that boasts a feature kitchen serving up delicious rotisserie dishes. There are three main, set options, including an excellent vegetarian menu, with a choice of desserts, all for €26 (without drinks). For both restaurants there is a separate children's menu (€10) and there is even a takeaway pizza facility. Neither of the restaurants are open for lunch.

At first view, *Disney's Sequoia Lodge* may seem more of an adult environment, but children usually love the 'outdoorsy' feel and the great extras of the pool, gardens and play area, hence it makes a great family base, and you may have trouble persuading the kids to leave when the characters are in residence! It takes 10–15 minutes to walk into the Theme Parks, or you can take the 5-minute free shuttle bus ride. **Official rating ***; our rating €€€, CCCC½.**

Disney's Hotel Cheyenne

Howdy partners, welcome to the Wild West – or Disney's version of it at least (actually far safer and a lot more comfortable!). This wonderfully imaginative hotel is usually a huge hit with children and is therefore a popular family choice (although it can be a little raucous at times when the kids re-enact Custer's Last Stand at regular intervals, armed to the teeth with rifles and bows and arrows from the hotel shop!). The theming is comprehensive and convincing, from the wonderful period-style entrance lobby (complete with two striking bronze horse-and-rider statues) to the individual rooms and their rustic-style, kid-friendly bunk beds. It is

4

also quite an extensive property, as all the rooms are low-rise (no more than 2 storeys) to maintain the Wild West cowboy illusion.

The level of creature comforts is not quite the same as elsewhere (no swimming pool or air-conditioning, no luggage delivery to the rooms and only a self-service restaurant), but there are some significant extras aimed at the kids, with optional pony and covered-wagon rides (spring and summer only, for a small fee) and a Fort Apache outdoor play area.

The lobby is themed like a Goldrush-era claims office, with a Land Claims desk instead of a reception area, a huge stone fireplace and a mock hotel entrance at the opposite end of the vaulted-ceiling foyer, which also has a kiddie corner (with organised activities like colouring, face painting and drawing on certain days) that has mini-saddles instead of chairs! The **General Store** is the standard gift shop and there is also a video games room next door.

Western paraphernalia abounds, and the cowboy theme continues into the bar and restaurant areas, with saloon-style doors, wooden tables, chairs, balustrades and ceiling beams. The **Red Garter Saloon** features live country music of an evening, with an outdoor terrace from which to enjoy your drinks overlooking the main street when the weather is fine.

The 750-seat **Chuck Wagon,** which also has its own **Saddle Bar** and wagon play area, is a cafeteria-style eaterie dressed up like a Texan pioneer market place and serves a good mixture of international dishes, from BBQ-smoked chicken and beef to salads, pasta, risottos and fresh wok-fried Chinese specialities, as well as a children's menu (€10).

Step out of the main building and you are in a true cowboy town, with raised, boarded sidewalks, dirt streets and blocks of hotel rooms all disguised as various buildings, such as the Guest House, Blacksmith and Sheriff's Office. The 14 blocks are each named after a famous character like Doc Holliday, Jesse James, Calamity Jane and Running Bear. Blocks 17–19 (they are actually numbered from 10–25, omitting 13!), Sitting Bull, Wyatt Earp and Billy The Kid, are closest to the main building and the bus stop for the free shuttle to the Theme Parks and *Disney Village.* There are 1,000 identical rooms (all of 21sq m/226sq ft) spread out through the 14 blocks, all of which have internal access only and most of which feature a double bed and two bunks. The two guest launderettes are free to use, although you need to buy washing powder from the General Store.

The in-room theming is more limited here and the bathrooms slightly more Spartan compared to the other resorts, but then it is designed for more budget-minded visitors (hence no air-conditioning either, just ceiling fans). The regular shuttle bus to the Theme Parks, *Disney Village* and RER station takes about 5 minutes, but you can walk it along a pleasant pathway that runs under the main road and up alongside *Disney's Hotel New York* in about 15. **Official rating **; our rating €€, CCC½.**

Disney's Hotel Santa Fe

Right at the budget end of the six-hotel spectrum is this extensive pueblo-style resort decked out in best American South West fashion, with Native American, Spanish and Mexican cultures providing the decorative motif, with a giant Clint Eastwood billboard (like a drive-in movie screen) welcoming you 'into town'. In truth, this is a glorified motel, but that doesn't stop it being quite fun for kids, excellent value for money and still well situated to enjoy all the Disney magic. It gets extremely busy in high season (breakfast sittings are pre-allocated from 7am) and is popular with coach operators, hence it gets congested in the morning with large numbers of guests arriving and departing at the same time.

At first appearance, *Disney's Hotel Santa Fe* looks rather stark with its collection of square, concrete accommodation blocks up to five storeys high, but the Imagineers have still been at work here, even if the fanciful 'volcano' is now a derelict grey hulk. There are four different 'trails' through the resort (corresponding to the four different room sections – Artefacts, Water, Monuments and Legends) each with their own symbols and numerous icons scattered around – from rusting desert 'vehicles' to outlandish meteorites, water trails, a geyser and even a crashed flying saucer! The smattering of desert scenery is also convincing and quite eye catching.

> BRIT TIP: As at *Disney's Hotel Cheyenne*, breakfast at *Disney's Hotel Santa Fe* is of the most basic continental kind – cereal, croissants, pastries, juice, tea and coffee – but you can pay a supplement to add bacon, eggs and fresh fruit.

The main facilities are housed in the reception building, while the 1,000 rooms are spread out over 41 blocks, surrounded by small car parks, hence, if you are driving, this is the only hotel where you can park more or less outside your room. The 700-seat **La Cantina** serves up Tex-Mex food in a food court-style servery, where you can make up your own meals (salads, tapas, fajitas, chilli burgers, nachos, roast pork,

chicken, beef, spaghetti and meatballs) or choose one of the set meals (€20 for adults and €10 for children) and there is an ice cream and coffee bar.

The imaginative touches here have food being served from the back of a flat-bed truck and drinks dispensed from 'petrol pumps'. These are worth highlighting as so many people actually miss them in their rush to get through and out to the Theme Parks! The children's corner with organised colouring and drawing activities (in the evenings) is also located here, with a computer console and Disney TV.

Next door to La Cantina is the **Rio Grande Bar,** with live entertainment and karaoke on selected evenings. The **Trading Post** is the Disney gift shop, with a good range of souvenir merchandise, snacks, drinks and basic toiletries. A video games room is available for the kids, plus an outdoor playground, the Totem Circle, which is handy if they have any energy left at the end of the day! Back in the lobby, characters meet 'n' greet in the morning, which is the ideal way to start the day if you have any young autograph hunters.

The identical rooms (21sq m/226sq ft) are cheerfully decorated, if a little spartan by comparison with the more upmarket hotels, but many also come with bunk beds instead of two

> BRIT TIP: You need to request a room with bunk beds when booking accommodation at *Disney's Hotel Santa Fe* if that is what your children will require (and which is usually a lot more comfortable for children aged 6 plus).

double beds. As with all Disney accommodation, they can house a family of four (or four plus one in a cot), although the rooms are a little short of drawer space.

Like *Disney's Hotel Cheyenne*, there is no in-room air-conditioning, just a ceiling fan, hence it can get a bit warm in the summer. The two hotels are next door to each other, so it is perfectly permissible to pop 'next door' to enjoy some of the facilities there too, notably, the Fort Apache play area for kids, the pony rides and the Red Garter Saloon. The hotel is a good 20–25-minute walk from the Theme Parks, but once again, if the weather is clement, it is a lovely way to start the day as you stroll alongside the 'Rio Grande' and up by *Disney's Hotel New York*, around Lake Disney and through *Disney Village*. Alternatively, the shuttle bus takes about 10 minutes and, while there is usually quite a queue for it in the morning around park opening times, they run several buses at once on this route (as they do at all the bigger hotels). **Official rating **; our rating €€, CCC.**

> BRIT TIP: The Esso petrol station next door to *Disney's Hotel Santa Fe* is one of the few places on-site where you can buy fresh milk – invaluable if you have children who drink a lot of it!

Disney's Davy Crockett Ranch®

If you are driving down to *Disneyland Resort Paris* and are happy to use your car to get to the Theme Parks every day, staying at *Disney's Davy Crockett Ranch®* is the best-value way to enjoy all the fun and

> BRIT TIP: The camping sites are particularly popular with the Brits and the Dutch, and they sell out well in advance at peak season, so you need to book EARLY for these in summer.

still have a taste of Disney imagination with your accommodation. Here, in 'trapper country', are 535 cabins with 1- or 2-bedrooms accommodating up to six, plus 60 caravan and camper van sites, which all have water supply and connections for electricity and water drainage, plus their own picnic bench and open-air barbecue.

Set in 57 hectares (140 acres) of pretty woodland about a 10-minute drive from the Theme Parks (where parking is free with your resort ID card), you do get the feeling of being out in the cowboy wilds here (see map on page 71). The woods are dotted with imaginative touches such as Native American tepees, while all the main services and facilities are located in a wonderfully fun cowboy 'village' at the heart of the ranch. Here you will find a host of great activities and amenities, from the **Alamo Trading Post** (the gift shop and grocery store, open 8am–11pm) to the great children's play area and even a farmyard and mini menagerie featuring reindeer and wolves.

> BRIT TIP: It is advisable, especially in summer, when the resort can hold around 4,000 people, to book a table for dinner at Crockett's Tavern. Lunch is rarely over-subscribed.

The 'village' is actually a fully-fledged resort in its own right, centred around the Trading Post and **Crockett's Tavern,** a log-cabin restaurant serving lunch (12.30–2.30pm) and dinner (6–10.30pm), with a takeaway service too.

The buffet-style servery offers up a good variety of dishes, from salad, fish and chips, roast chicken and pasta to entrecote steak and even a vegetarian meal, while there is a choice of four kids' meals (€10). Across the street is the authentic (if a little small) **Saloon** (open 5pm–midnight) serving beer, wine and cocktails, with live entertainment and karaoke at peak times, plus outdoor seating and a large-screen TV in the summer.

Bowie's Bike Barn (8am–6, 8 or 10pm seasonally), also the information centre, houses the children's activity corner, with a computer play station, video console and organised face-painting and colouring, all set up around a large table with clever mini-saddles to sit on.

Disney characters make an appearance every evening, while there is grown-up entertainment too, with themed evenings, line dancing and discos, plus organised sports, from jogging and aerobics to *petanque* and archery. The Lucky Raccoon video games room adds that essential amenity for kids, while they are then spoiled for choice with the likes of horse and pony rides (4–11 only; from €6–14), Davy's Farm (a petting zoo with goats, sheep, rabbits, birds and ducks), an

BRIT TIP: The reindeer actually 'work' in Disney's Christmas Parade at the *Disneyland Park*, but they get 10 months of the year off, which they spend at the ranch!

outdoor play and climbing area, table tennis, volleyball, basketball, archery and mini-golf (the latter for €6 for nine holes). There are two free-to-use indoor tennis courts (in winter, one of which is used alternately for archery, table tennis and volleyball) and a nature park with the Indian Meadows village and trails to see the reindeer park and wolf enclosure.

Bike hire is another opportunity for children and adults, with a huge range of bikes, scooters and quadracycles, which rent from €3–15 for an hour, and you can use them on the cycle trails throughout the resort and woods. The final outstanding element of the resort is the **Blue Springs Pool,** an extensive indoor water park (8.30am–10pm) with a semi-circular paddling pool for toddlers, a large, free-form leisure pool, subdivided with a waterfall and long water-slide, fountains and squirt pond, and a huge Jacuzzi. You can rent towels for a small fee. Under 12s must also be accompanied by an adult at all times in the pool area. It is an exceptional facility and you may struggle to get the kids out of here, even with the lure of the Theme Parks!

Eight circular 'trails' house all the accommodation. Each trail has its own takeaway cottage, where breakfast is served each morning (7–11am) and you simply pick it up and take it back to your cabin, caravan or tent. The 1-bedroom cabins (all 36sq m/388sq ft) each feature a spacious lounge with TV, a kitchen complete with two hot-plates, dishwasher, fridge, microwave, kettle, coffee machine and all the necessary cutlery, crockery and cooking utensils. There is also a breakfast bar area.

The bathroom (fully stocked with towels) includes the toilet but the two are separate in the 2-bedroom version. Some have a pull-down double bed in the lounge, others a

> BRIT TIP: The ranch's 60 two-bedroom cabins are all newer than the one-bed ones, and come at a slight premium. They also go quickly (although more are due to be built), so you need to book early to grab one.

convertible sofa, while the bedroom has a double bed and two bunks. Many of the 1-bedroom cabins do look their age (more than 12 years old), hence it is a basic 2-star property. Outside, they all have their own brick-built barbecue and picnic bench, plus room to park the car.

The 2-bedroom version (39sq m/ 420sq ft) has the two bunk beds in their own room, ensuring Mum and Dad a little peace and quiet! The living quarters are arranged slightly differently and the general fixtures and fittings are that bit smarter, but the difference in price is minimal, hence these are definitely the better ones to go for.

The caravan and camp sites are all located on Moccasin Trail (the others are named after similar Davy Crockett imagery – Wagon Wheel, Big Bear, Tomahawk, etc) and you will find toilets, showers and a launderette at the centre of this area. At peak times, a mini train/tram runs around all the trails, ferrying people between the accommodation units and the village area.

The site is completely secured against non-visitor traffic. You check in at the reception area at the main entrance, much as you would for a hotel, and they provide you with your keys, the all-important Disney resort ID cards and the security code to access the site, which you punch in at the gate just past reception. Then, when you depart, you can just drop the keys off in a deposit box, so you don't need to go back into the reception area.

The parks and *Disney Village* are about a 15-minute drive from the ranch, which is located about 3km (2 miles) off Exit 13 of the A4 autoroute. To get to the Theme Parks from the ranch, simply come out of the property, take the second exit from the roundabout (signposted A4 Reims), and continue along the A4 to Exit 14 for 'Les Parcs Disneyland'. **Official rating **; our rating €€, CCCC.**

Beyond Disney

Once you move beyond Disney for your choice of accommodation, things become much simpler to a large extent. There are no grand theme hotels (with the exceptions of the new Holiday Inn and the Explorers Hotel) and no great variation in style or facilities (almost all are 2- or 3-star). Rooms tend to be small but comfortable and the majority will provide a good, basic continental breakfast. I have toured the Seine-et-Marne region extensively and looked at most of the hotels on offer and have been impressed by the generally high standard of cleanliness and friendliness.

A lot of hotels in the immediate vicinity of Marne-la-Vallée are relatively new, hence they are still quite smart and pleasant, while all hotels are inspected regularly to ensure they conform to their star rating. Quite a few have swimming pools, but you need to decide if you are likely to make use of this kind of facility after a long day at the Theme Parks to make it worthwhile paying that bit extra.

It is also possible to subdivide the off-site hotels into those which are Near The Magic, and those which are a Short Drive away, and hotel chains which have accommodation

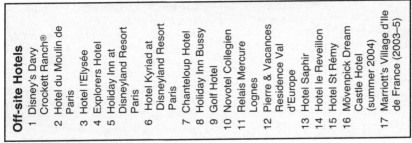

Off-site Hotels
1 Disney's Davy Crockett Ranch®
2 Hotel du Moulin de Paris
3 Hotel l'Elysée
4 Explorers Hotel
5 Holiday Inn at Disneyland Resort Paris
6 Hotel Kyriad at Disneyland Resort Paris
7 Chanteloup Hotel
8 Holiday Inn Bussy
9 Golf Hotel
10 Novotel Collegien
11 Relais Mercure Lognes
12 Pierre & Vacances Residence Val d'Europe
13 Hotel Saphir
14 Hotel le Reveillon
15 Hotel St Rémy
16 Mövenpick Dream Castle Hotel (summer 2004)
17 Marriott's Village d'Ile de France (2003–5)

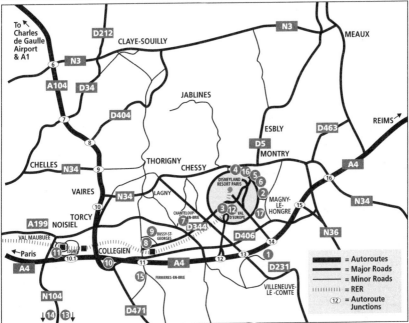

4

in Paris itself (which is not necessarily a bad idea if you want to see a lot of the city, as it is only 35–40 minutes to *Disneyland Resort Paris* by RER).

Near the Magic

When it comes to hotels that are within a figurative stone's throw of the Theme Parks, there are six contrasting choices in the Val d'Europe area. These include three brand new hotels (four by summer 2004) in an associated development just off the main ring road (which

Disney refers to as its Selected Hotels). One of these, the Explorers Hotel, is primarily for the UK market, while all usually host a high percentage of British guests. Looking at them in detail, they are:

Hotel du Moulin de Paris: Built in 2001, this smart, well-run hotel in Magny-le-Hongre (a 5–10-minute drive from the Theme Parks) has already been extensively refurbished, with all the 82 identikit bright, clean rooms getting a fresh, new look. They comfortably accommodate four, with a double bed, a single and a pull-out, or a double and two bunks (you need to request a room with bunks in advance). Cots are also available on request but maximum occupancy for each room is four. The bathrooms feature a shower only, no bath. Breakfast is served from 7–10am in their airy conservatory-style restaurant, with dinner from 7–10pm (and sandwiches available 7am–midnight at the bar) and, in summer, an outdoor patio makes a lovely place to sit with a drink. A heated outdoor pool (open May to September), a sauna and a small fitness room, are all available free to hotel guests.

If you arrive early and want to head to the Theme Parks, you can leave your bags in a luggage room. A daily shuttle runs to and from the Theme Parks (returning half an hour after closing time) for €1.50 per person, while there is also a public bus to Marne-la-Vallée station. The hotel is on the Rue du Moulin á Vent, just off the Boulevard de l'Europe, the long highway that encircles *Disneyland Resort Paris*. More importantly, most packages here include your Theme Park tickets. Call 00 33 1 60 43 77 77 from the UK or look up their website at www.moulindeparis.com. **Official rating ***; our rating €€€, CCC.**

Hotel l'Elysée: At the heart of the Val d'Europe development, and therefore just a 5-minute RER ride to the Theme Parks, this brand new, ultra-smart 3-star property opened in July 2002. The Hotel l'Elysée features a grand reception lobby, underground parking and an extremely quiet ambience (a nice contrast after the hectic hurly-burly of the Disney resort). The 152 rooms all accommodate four in a double and two single sofa beds (which are made up ready for your arrival), while there are four spacious junior suites and five rooms adapted for the disabled (two persons maximum). The rooms all have a mini-bar and safe and the marbled bathrooms are extremely smart. Cots are available on request, but they can't add up to a fifth person. However, there are inter-connecting rooms for larger families.

The hotel has a left-luggage room, a video games room for kids, an elegant bar and a high-quality restaurant (breakfast €10 for adults, €6 for children), while 24-hour room service is also available. Most packages here include park tickets and either a free parking pass or daily RER tickets (which are €1.35 each way). The last train from Marne-la-Vallée back to Val d'Europe is at 12 minutes past midnight each day. Call 00 33 1 64 63 33 33 for more details. **Official rating ***; our rating €€€€, CCC.**

Pierre & Vacances Residence Val d'Europe: New in 2003, this stylish apartment complex from the French chain of holiday residences has a good array of flexible accommodation which makes an ideal base for a longer stay in the region. With 292 apartments and studios, sleeping from two to nine (at a squeeze), this is a modern and well-furnished offering. All feature a fully-equipped kitchenette (cooking hob, fridge, microwave and dishwasher) with a living room and either a one- or two-bedroom option, plus what they call a 'cabin' that has additional bunk beds. The studios offer living/sleeping space for up to three, while the largest apartments can sleep three in the living room, four in the two bedrooms and two in the cabin. All have a bathroom and the larger ones have a shower room too.

BRIT TIP: Towels are only provided in Pierre & Vacances properties for a fee, so it is advisable to bring your own. You are also required to pay a €200 deposit when checking in.

The resort-style set-up offers a launderette, indoor car park, luggage room, small gym and an outdoor heated swimming pool open year-round. A separate charge (on check-in) is made for TV and phone use. Continental breakfast is served daily (€8.50 for adults, €7.50 for children) in a corner of the big reception area. Call 00 33 1 60 42 82 00 or visit www.pierre-vacances.com. **Official rating *****, our rating €€€, CC.

Selected Hotels, Val-de-France

This sub-section of new properties (all of which opened in spring/ summer 2003) is well worth looking out for. Disney refers to them as its Selected Hotels, tour operators call them Near The Magic and they can be found just off the Boulevard de l'Europe in an area officially known as Val-de-France. A lot more development is due here in the next few years, with the fourth hotel opening in June 2004.

BRIT TIP: The shuttle bus to the RER station serves all of the Selected Hotels and runs like clockwork every 15 minutes (every 10 minutes at park opening and closing times). It operates from 6.30am–11.30pm September to June and 6.30am–1am in July and August.

Explorers Hotel: This highly imaginative 390-room hotel was built for tour operator MyTravel and its affiliate companies (Cresta, Paris Travel Service and Leger Holidays) but caters for some European guests as well. It is designed primarily with the British visitor in mind however, hence there are some particularly smart touches for families. It is the first fully-themed off-site hotel (closely followed by the Holiday Inn – see page 75), and offers both extra-spacious rooms (with families of six to 10 in mind) and some superb children's facilities. It is pretty much the same price to eat and drink here as in the parks or *Disney Village*, however and their fine dining restaurant can be an expensive experience.

Designed like a grand French manor – the preserve of mythical explorer Sir Archibald de Bacle and his various 'discoveries' – it is a fun and spacious creation, from the huge lobby area (complete with a Kids Corner with TV and a novel fountain) to the buffet-style restaurant with its outdoor terrace (wonderful on a sunny morning). Walk through the lobby and you have a startling view over the **Tropical Atrium** at the heart of the hotel, which is also home to the **Secret Lagoon Swimming Pool,** a 20m (66ft) heated indoor pool with a separate toddlers' area. The wreck of the Seven Seas Raider pirate ship is beached at one end of the lagoon, allowing kids the chance to explore the decks and passageways or take to the water-slide.

BRIT TIP: Surprisingly, there is a €1 charge for a pool towel at the Explorers, which seems a bit penny-pinching. So take your own towels. The pool also gets VERY busy in late afternoon.

The **Plantation Restaurant** is the main diner, a market-style emporium offering breakfast

(7–10.30am) and dinner (6–10pm). The excellent continental-style buffet breakfast offers a good selection for all the family (or you can choose a cooked breakfast for a few extra euros), while dinner is again a buffet option with a set menu €20 for adults, €10 for children 3–11) or a good range of individual items (especially their salads and desserts).

BRIT TIP: Like the Disney hotels, you are given a time 'slot' for breakfast each day. You can collect these from reception when you check in and it is advisable to pick your times for your whole stay as the best ones go quickly.

For more informal dining, there is **Marco's Pizza Parlour** (noon–11pm) where you can order a take-away if you prefer and **Traders Café Bar** (noon–11pm) for snacks and a drink or two. The **Far Horizon Terrace** (5–11pm) offers an elevated view of the Atrium and the chance to sip a speciality tea or coffee, or a glass of wine or beer. The **Captain's Library** (6.30–10pm) is a themed full-service restaurant, once again offering children's meals, and with a small play area to keep the kids amused while Mum and Dad finish their dinner. While I feel it is a touch expensive for an off-site restaurant, the food here is outstanding for what is, in theory, a 2-star hotel. Finally, **Smugglers Tavern** (5pm–1am) is the hotel's main bar, with a corner given over to a large-screen TV for sports events. Snacks are available here too. Traders Café is also brilliantly designed for parents to be able to sit back and watch their offspring expend some energy in the activity areas. **Scally Wagg's Jungle**

Adventures is the big indoor soft-play area (in two sections, for 2–4s and 5–12s), with all the requisite ladders, ropes, slides and ball pools, while the **Seven Seas Raider** is also nearby and the inevitable video arcade is provided by **Harry's Action Zone**.

The room choice is definitely a cut above usual hotel accommodation. Standard rooms, called 'Crew rooms', feature one double bed and two singles, with a bath, shower and separate toilet (a useful idea), plus interactive satellite TV with video games, internet access and pay-per-view programmes and films, room safe, hairdryer and ceiling fan (there is no air-conditioning). Each Crew room can be connected to a 'bunk cabin' for two children. Extended families or groups of friends can take two interconnecting Crew rooms with the bunk cabin in between and sleep up to 10 people (bunk cabin doors can be closed).

The upgraded 'Officer's rooms' add tea and coffee-making facilities, special toiletries, a suprise gift for children and a top-floor location with great views of the surrounding countryside. These can again accommodate four, six or ten.

Finally the 10 suites or 'Captain's Quarters' sleep up to six in two bedrooms and all have a lake view and the vital addition of air-conditioning for the hot summer months. Some rooms are suitable for guests with disabilities.

Additional features include free parking both at the hotel and at the parks and *Disney Village*, picnic lunches, currency exchange facilities, a Disney store, a concierge and information desk. However, the hotel is non-smoking, apart from areas such as Smugglers Tavern.

The hotel is situated just across the resort-encircling Boulevard de l'Europe from *Disney's Hotel Santa Fe*. It is a walkable distance from the parks (about 25 minutes), but the free shuttle will get you there in less than 10 minutes. Call 00 33 1 60 42 60 00 or look up www.explorershotel.com. **Official rating: **; our rating: €€€€, CCCC½.**

Holiday Inn at Disneyland Paris Resort: If you are looking for that more upmarket touch, look no further than the newest Holiday Inn in the Seine-et-Marne region. Designed in French manorial style with a circus-themed flavour throughout (and quite stylishly done too), this is a cut above the usual tourist fare and it scores high marks for families too. At once both chic and cheerful, the hotel comes as a refreshing change from the usual identikit styling. It will appeal to all ages, having those extra service touches expected of a 4-star property, such as 24-hour room service and a business centre.

The 325 standard rooms (many inter-connecting) feature a double bed and a curtained off section (like a circus big-top) with bunk beds and a separate TV/games console for the kids. The 23 Kidsuites rooms have children's areas built into them in a more elaborate fashion. All rooms come with a main TV with international channels and internet access, plus room safe, hairdryer and tea- and coffee-making facilities. They are also fully air-conditioned.

BRIT TIP: Don't overlook the value of the Holiday Inn's family rooms and Kidsuites. If my boys are anything to go by, you'll have difficulty getting your offspring out of the room because of 'their' area!

The hotel offers a sophisticated indoor leisure pool (with toddler area), smart fitness club and an extensive outdoor playground in the park-like gardens for the young 'uns, where they can burn off any excess energy. The main restaurant, **L'Etoile,** serves a pleasing mix of traditional French and international cuisine, plus a children's menu, while their all-inclusive buffet breakfast (with an extensive array of cereals plus hot and cold dishes) is possibly the best in the area – including Disney's hotels. The inner courtyard features an adjoining terrace to the restaurant and, for breakfast, this makes a wonderful start to the day if the weather permits. There is the inevitable Disney Store and an excellent bar/lounge, **Bar des Artistes,** which features a unique computer-generated circus 'show' on the double-height ceiling every evening. The hotel has its own Bureau de Change, and the overall value for money here is top notch. Call 00 33 1 64 63 37 37. **Official rating: ****; our rating: €€€€, CCCC.**

Hotel Kyriad at Disneyland Resort Paris: Right next door to the Holiday Inn is the new flagship hotel of the budget Envergure group. With a lovely country house style, it is an excellent option for those who want to watch the pennies but still get a taste of the Magic. The 300 airy and spotlessly clean rooms are all air-conditioned, which is a bonus at this end of the scale, and come with tea- and coffee-making facilities, hairdryer and room safe. The standard room features a double bed and two bunks, while the twin room can be either two singles or a double bed. No room can accommodate more than four, but there are various connecting rooms bringing the number up to six or eight. The rest of the hotel is equally straightforward, with one restaurant (for breakfast, which costs €19 for adults and €6 for children, and dinner) and two bars in a friendly, relaxing ambience. The small

4

children's play area in the lobby can get quite crowded in the morning. Although it is fully French owned and run, up to 60 per cent of guests can be British at peak times, and the overall feel is pleasingly fresh and cosmopolitan. Call 00 33 1 60 43 61 61 for more details. **Official rating: **; our rating: €€€, CC½.**

Mövenpick Dream Castle Hotel: This is due to open in August 2004 and is another upscale property of the big Swiss hotel group, aimed primarily at the German market. Next door to the Explorers Hotel and similarly on the free shuttle bus route to the parks, the 400-room property will have two restaurants and an outdoor terrace grill – and, as Mövenpick set great store by the quality of their cuisine, the choice should be quite mouthwatering. There will also be a lobby bar, conference rooms, children's facilities, fun swimming pool, fitness/health facilities and a garden overlooking the lake which backs on to the other hotels in Val-de-France. The whole hotel will have a Middle Ages/European castle motif, adding to the fun theming of this happening area. **Expected rating: ****; our rating: €€€€€, CCCC.**

A short drive from the Magic

Chanteloup Hotel: Tucked away in the pretty little village of Chanteloup-en-Brie, just to the west of Val d'Europe, is this small, family-run hotel. With just 64 small but smart rooms, each with a double bed and two fold-up bunks, plus a neat fitness centre, Jacuzzi and sauna, this is an ideal retreat after a day of frenetic theme-parking. It has a pleasant restaurant and a little foyer bar, and that's about it for the creature comforts, although there is a daily shuttle bus to Disney for €9/person return. To reach the

hotel, turn off the A4 at Exit 13 and take the D231 past Val d'Europe for 4.5km (3 miles), then turn left into Chanteloup-en-Brie. For more info, call 00 33 1 64 30 00 00. **Official rating **; our rating €€€, CC.**

Holiday Inn Bussy: One of the few 4-star hotels in the area, this Holiday Inn is situated at the entrance to the modern town of Bussy-St-Georges, handy for both road and RER links to Marne-la-Vallée. It is a quiet, rather unprepossessing property, but it hides real charm and style, a long way removed from the usual rather brash image of the Holiday Inn group. The light airy foyer opens up to reveal a smart restaurant with a conservatory annexe and a small, intimate bar, with a couple of video games and a pool table. The outdoor (unheated) swimming pool is open until the end of September (or sooner if it turns cold), and has a lovely patio area that allows guests to have breakfast or dinner outside when the weather permits.

The 120 rooms are extremely comfortable, even for four, with the choice of a double, triple and quad (two doubles) configuration, plenty of cupboard space, and a marbled bathroom with hairdryer. There is also satellite TV, a trouser press and a kettle (although you need to buy tea and coffee sachets from reception), and a lot of the rooms interconnect for larger family accommodation.

It does host a lot of business conferences, hence it can be quite busy during the week, but it is only a 5-minute walk to the RER station (which is then 10 minutes to Marne-la-Vallée) and 10 minutes to the Theme Parks by car, so it is well situated. To get to the hotel, take Exit 11 off the A4 and follow the signposts to Bussy-St-Georges, go straight across two roundabouts, and the Holiday Inn is immediately on your right. Call 00 33 1 64 66 35 65 or visit www.hi-marnelavallee.com for more info. **Official rating ****; our rating €€€€, CCC.**

Golf Hotel: On the other side of Bussy-St-Georges is this distinctly countrified hotel, with a genuinely welcoming aspect, set on the edge of a golf course and with obvious benefits for the sporting fraternity. However, you don't need to be a golfer to stay here as the 93 light, airy rooms cater for everyone, with double, triple, twin and family rooms, the latter with one double bed and two fold-down or fixed bunks. Mini-bars and hairdryers are standard in all rooms and, if the bathrooms are rather ordinary, there is plenty of storage space.

The large restaurant has big picture windows and an outdoor terrace for good weather, while there is a children's play area to the side and a large green for kids to expend any remaining energy on. The outdoor heated pool is open from May to mid-September and there is also a small lobby bar for a quiet drink, plus two private tennis courts available for hotel guests. Given the surrounding greenery, you could easily think you were a million miles from the hectic Disney whirl, but you are only 10–15 minutes' walk from the RER station or 5 minutes on their free shuttle bus (on request). To get to the hotel, carry on past the Holiday Inn, cross the Place du Close St Georges, then turn right at Boulevard du Golf and the hotel is along on the left. Call 00 33 1 64 66 30 30 or visit the parent company website at www.ahmi.com. **Official rating ***; our rating €€€, CCC.**

Novotel Collégien: Slightly off the beaten track lies this smart hotel of the business-like Novotel chain (see page 81). Just south of the A4 and the town of Collégien, it is tucked away on a mini-industrial estate and has some surprisingly family-friendly touches, with a free welcome gift for children and a free character dining set at the restaurant. There is table football in the lobby, a heated outdoor pool (mid-April to end of September), and an extremely pleasant bar area (open until midnight). The 146 rooms (with one floor designated non-smoking) are all brightly furnished and feature a double bed and a fold-out sofa which will sleep two (smallish) children. Each room also has a mini-bar and TV with English channels and pay-per-view films, while there are two pairs of connecting rooms and six adapted for guests with disabilities. Usefully, the toilet is separate from the bathroom.

A busy convention hotel for much of the year, it is given over completely to the tourism business in July and at weekends. It is located just past the junction of the A104 and A4, heading south (to Croissy-Beaubourg), turn left off the D471, straight over at the traffic lights, and it is on the right. There is a free, secure parking area and you really do need to have a car here as it is 3km (2 miles) from the nearest RER station. Call 00 33 1 64 80 53 53 or visit www.novotel.com. **Official rating ***; our rating €€€€, CCC.**

Relais Mercure Lognes: Conveniently located just off the A4 (but far enough away not to be bothered by traffic buzz), this neat, modern offering of the budget Mercure group (see page 81) is in a quiet residential area in the new town of Lognes, not far from the RER station (about 10 minutes' walk). It offers 85 comfortable, modern rooms with satellite TV, safe, well-designed bathroom and hair dryer. Family rooms for two or three children are in split-level duplexes, while the restaurant also caters well for kids (and offers a good buffet breakfast). There is a pleasant wine bar and outdoor terrace and a small fitness room and sauna.

The staff are unfailingly cheerful and helpful, and there is an internet terminal in the lobby to check e-mail and news from back home (works with a France Telecom Telecarte, available from reception). Barely a 15-minute drive from the Theme Parks, the hotel is located just off Exit 10.1 of the A4 (Val Maubuée Sud). Turn left at the first roundabout then right on to the Boulevard de Mandinet and it is on the next roundabout on the left. Call 00 33 1 64 80 02 50 or visit www.mercure.com. **Official rating ***; our rating €€€, CC½.**

Hotel Saphir: A one-off property, just to the south in Pontault-Combault, this has 179 exceedingly smart rooms for two to four people, with the family rooms consisting of a double bed plus a single or a double sofa bed. While not the prettiest of hotels, it maintains a high standard of interior decor and service, and the heated indoor pool is an excellent (and rare) amenity, along with a sauna, fitness centre and tennis court (for an additional charge). The family-friendly restaurant is also well priced (set meals from €14 for adults and €8 for children) and there is also a pleasant bar. Call 00 33 1 64 43 45 47 for more info. It can be found just off the N104 travelling south at Exit 15. **Official rating ***; our rating €€€, CCC.**

Hotel le Reveillon: Further south, in the older confines of the town of Lesigny, this former monastery has been tastefully converted to hold 48 immaculate rooms on the edge of a beautiful golf course. Dating back to the 12th century, it also boasts a wonderful restaurant, and yet is still under half an hour from the Theme Parks. It makes a great base for investigating some of the other villages of this area, although you would need a car anyway as it is some way off the RER routes. Family rooms offer an extra bed or bunks for children, and all feature satellite TV, mini-bar and hairdryer, while the superb

traditional-style restaurant still has a children's menu. Take Exit 18 off the N104, continue south on the Avenue des Hyveneaux, then turn left after 1km (about ½ mile) at the signpost for Golf du Reveillon. Call 00 33 1 60 02 25 26. **Official rating ***; our rating €€€, CC½.**

Hotel St Rémy: Finally, a hotel to suit couples, as this is a touch more detached and romantic than most, set in the picturesque hamlet of Ferrières-en-Brie, but only 7km (4 miles) from Disney. Originally built in the 19th century, but tastefully restored and reopened in 2000, it has just 25 rooms (all en suite, with satellite TV and hairdryer) with some wonderfully elegant individual touches and style, wooden floors and antique furniture. Its fabulous restaurant still offers a children's menu (not Saturday lunchtime or Sunday evening), but there is not a lot else to keep kids amused in this quiet location. A car is advisable, although Bussy-St-Georges is only 2km (about 1 mile) away. The hotel is just off Exit 11 from the A4 – follow the signs to Ferrières-en-Brie and pick up the main Rue Jean Jaurés. Call 00 33 1 64 76 74 00 or visit www.hotel-st-remy.fr. **Official rating ***; our rating €€€, CC½.**

Camping

With the ease in which you can drive down to this region of France, it makes sense for people to look at camping alternatives, and one new campsite near the village of Touquin (13km/8 miles south of the town of Coulommiers) is worth highlighting in particular. **Camping Les Etangs Fleuris** is a wonderfully rural and secluded site with 170 pitches and a host of clean, modern facilities, including an excellent pool with childrens' pool, a games room, bar and takeaway, in addition to showers, toilets and a laundrette.

Their sporting activities include table tennis, mini-golf, *petanque* and fishing, plus horse-riding and nature walks nearby. The site also boasts two kinds of 2-bedroom mobile homes, all extremely well furnished and maintained. It is about 20 minutes from *Disneyland Resort Paris* and an easy drive along the D231. The site is packaged with either a Channel crossing or flights to Beauvais or Charles de Gaulle, plus Theme Park tickets, by British tour operator Canvas Holidays. Call 01383 629000 or look up www.canvasholidays.com for more details.

Hotel chains

A number of French hotel chains offer good, cheap, basic accommodation for those on a budget both in Paris itself and in the Marne-la-Vallée area. Most are in the 1- and 2-star categories but a few offer a greater level of creature comforts. Here is a rundown of the most notable ones:

Formule 1: This is a basic, motel-type chain which keeps things pretty much cheap and cheerful (okay, forget about the cheerful bit). Built in boxy, prefab units, they are accommodation only, hence you need to find meals elsewhere (apart from an extremely simple continental buffet breakfast for a €3.50 supplement per person) but they are almost invariably the cheapest in any location with around 60 in the Ile de France region) and they are surprisingly high-tech, with automated check-in and clean, functional but small rooms. However, the rooms do not have a shower or w/c, there are only communal facilities on each floor. Part of the huge **Accor** hotel group, this is not the ideal place to go with a family because their service is so limited (and most rooms sleep only three) but for couples on a strict

budget, they might be worth considering. For more details, call 0870 609 0961 in the UK or visit www.hotelformule1.com. **Our rating €, C.**

Etap: Similar to Formule 1 (and with 55 hotels in the region), but with the advantage of an in-room shower and w/c. Non-smoking rooms are also available. Call 0870 609 0961 in the UK or visit www.etaphotel.com. **Our rating €, C.**

Campanile: Another motel-style group, they also don't have meals or bar service (although there is usually a restaurant attached to the property). Again, their hotels are all pretty uniform and stylised, but they are ideal for those on a budget, offer plenty of rooms for guests with disabilities and usually serve a great buffet breakfast. The rooms themselves are small but clean and comfortable. Part of the **Envergure** group (the second largest in Europe), the hotels rate officially as 2-star in France but provide a few extra, more thoughtful touches, such as in-room tea- and coffee-making facilities, which make them a highly worthwhile place to stay. Again however, rooms usually sleep only three and you need to reserve a child's fold-out bed in advance. Breakfast is an extra €4/person at the associated restaurant and there are children's menus, too. To book, call 020 7519 5045 in the UK or visit their website www.campanile.fr. **Our rating €, CC.**

Kyriad: There are a lot more variations within this generally 2-star chain (which is also part of Envergure and a half-step up from Campanile) but it is still a basic family-orientated hotel, with decent rooms that comfortably sleep three and some that accommodate four (one double bed, two singles). Some hotels include mini-bars and hairdryers, and there are some pleasant individual touches such as a welcome snack tray. Their excellent-

Holiday ownership

Inevitably, the explosion in hotel accommodation and tourist interest in the resort area has created the opportunity to 'buy' a piece of the holiday dream and there are several timeshare companies who would love you to sign on the dotted line. However, the only one that I believe carries the right seal of approval is the extensive **Marriott's Village d'Ile de France** property, less than 2km (1 mile) from Disney. The first phase opened in June 2003 (with additional elements scheduled for 2004/5), and consists of 190 two bed/two-bath townhouses with around 105sq m (1,260sq ft) of living space. The Marriott Vacation Club International has genuine international bona fides and strong Disney ties, hence you can be sure of getting a quality product, with excellent back-up at a good price.

The Village will have access to Disney's 27-hole golf course, plus its own dazzling array of facilities, including two swimming pools (one indoor lap pool and one outdoors), children's pool, whirlpool, health club (featuring a gym and aerobics room, sauna and steam room), children's facilities (games room, activity centre and outdoor playground), a bar/restaurant featuring local cuisine, a lobby lounge, a convenience store and deli (the Market Place, with a full array of fresh produce, wines and spirits, plus other essentials and even branded apparel). There are also 24-hour security and full reception services and a regular shuttle bus to the Theme Parks.

The two-storey townhouses themselves offer possibly the most luxurious accommodation in the region, with a king-size bed in the main bedroom, fully-equipped kitchen (including microwave and dishwasher), a spacious living room (with satellite colour TV, DVD player and stereo, an additional TV in each bedroom), a utility room with washer/dryer and an individual terrace.

With Marriott Vacation Club, you purchase weeks within a particular season and you are free to reserve weeks within that season, while you may change dates within your purchased time period from year to year (and there are then more than 50 Vacation Club resorts worldwide you can exchange weeks for). For more details, contact Marriott on 0800 004477, by e-mail at mvciparis.owners@vacationclub.com or visit www.vacationclub.com.

value restaurants all have children's menus. To book, call 020 7519 5045 or visit www.envergure.fr/kyriadfr.html. **Our rating €–€€, CC.**

Comfort Inn: A similar quality and style to the Kyriad and Campanile chains, the Comfort Inn hotels (part of the **Choice Hotels International** group) are mainly found in central Paris and offer an excellent-value selection. Their city location means there is quite a wide variety between the different style of each property but the basic standard remains sound. To book, call 0800 44 44 44 (in the UK) or 0800 91 24 24 in France, or visit www.choicehotels.com. **Our rating €€, CC.**

There are some 22 Paris Comfort Inns, and the closest one to *Disneyland Resort Paris* claims to be the **Comfort Inn Marne-la-Vallée**, but don't be fooled into thinking it is on the parks' doorstep – it is actually at Noisy-le-Grand, 1km (about ½ mile) from the Noisy-Champs RER station and six stops (about 15 minutes and 15km/9 miles) from Disney. However, it is still a good choice, just off Exit 10 of the A4 (the exit for Champs), a pleasant, new property, with well-equipped family rooms for three, four and five people (children 12 and under stay free with their parents). There are also non-smoking rooms and rooms for the disabled, plus a surprisingly good restaurant, where the buffet breakfast costs €7. Call 00 33 1 64 68 33 36.

The Choice Hotels group also includes six of their more upmarket **Quality Hotel** properties in central Paris, with an official 3-star rating and some elegant touches.

Ibis: A more upmarket 2-star choice (in the Accor group), this chain is generally functionally comfortable, with standard rooms (international satellite TV is a bonus) that sleep three (with an extra fold-out bed) and compact bathrooms. All have a restaurant, bar and snacks available 24 hours a day (part of their commitment to a more personal service), with an outstanding self-service breakfast buffet from 6.30–10am, and a drinks and pastries service from 4–6am and 10–midday. The restaurant choice varies from hotel to hotel. There are 42 Ibis hotels in the Paris region, including three in Marne-la-Vallée. To book, call 0870 609 0961 in the UK or visit www.ibishotel.com. **Our rating €€–€€€, CC.**

Mercure: This member of the Accor group has a 3-tier quality system, the basic Relais/Inn Mercure, the genuinely 3-star Hotel Mercure and the more upmarket Grande Hotel Mercure, with enhanced levels of service and comfort. Most rooms accommodate three, while they also have some family rooms for four, all with mini-bars and hairdryers. Non-smoking and rooms adapted for the disabled are also available.

The **Libertel** chain is also a Mercure affiliate, with a similar 3-star-plus style to the Grande Hotels. All have a decent restaurant (with a range of regional specialities), bar and a full-service continental breakfast. Their wine list is usually outstanding. The lobbies all feature a reading room, with a choice of international newspapers and magazines. They also specialise in weekend breaks and most of their 52 hotels are in central Paris. To book, call 0870 609 0961 in the UK or visit www.mercure.com. **Our rating €€€–€€€€, CCC.**

Novotel: More of a businessman's hotel (and another member of the Accor group), but full of mod cons to suit tourist tastes as well, this fully modern chain offers fresh, spacious and comfortable rooms (sleeping up to four), chic restaurants and bars, and extras like satellite TV, mini-bars and room service. Most feature outdoor swimming pools (although they close from the early autumn to the end of spring) and conference/meeting facilities. Conversely, while they can be busy during the week, they often offer some great weekend breaks when they are quieter. Children stay free with their parents, but breakfast is usually an extra €10–11. For more info, call 0870 609 0961 in the UK or visit www.novotel.com. **Our rating: €€€€, CCC.**

Sofitel: The premium brand in the Accor group, each hotel is an individual, but all boast a de luxe style in both the sumptuous rooms and the excellent restaurants, with the latter featuring some of the best cuisine in Paris. The full range of mod cons and facilities are accompanied by efficient, courteous service. However, the handful of Sofitel hotels (17 of them) in the Ile de France are either in central Paris or by Charles de Gaulle Airport, hence their price reflects both their location and upmarket nature. To book, call 0870 609 0961 in the UK or visit www.sofitel.com. **Our rating €€€€€, CCCC.**

Well, that's about all the essential accommodation info I think you need for now. Having dealt with all the preliminaries, it is finally time to… hit the Theme Parks!

Welcome to the Parks

(or, Here's Where The Fun Really Starts!)

Okay, it's finally time to deal with the main business of being in the *Disneyland Resort Paris* – the Theme Parks themselves and there is a lot to take on board here. The *Disneyland Park* alone boasts some 45 attractions on its 57 hectares (140 acres), and there is something for all tastes and all ages. The new *Walt Disney Studios Park* adds a wealth of film and TV-orientated fun, although there is probably less to captivate the youngest visitors.

In all, there is at least 3 days' worth of pure adventure-mania spread between the two parks, and you need to have a pretty good idea of what's in store to get the most out of it and ensure you don't waste too much energy in the process! It is easy to get side-tracked by some of the clever detail or minor attractions and miss out on some big-time thrills, while equally there is a genuine treasure trove of small-scale Disneyana which would be a tragedy to overlook. Therefore, the following chapters will provide all you need to know to draw up your own plan of campaign for visiting each one.

If you have never visited a Disney theme park before, it is probably fair to start by reminding you that this is NOT a comparable experience to a day at any other European park. That is not to denigrate the likes of Alton Towers (which is actually on a similar scale), Thorpe Park or Chessington World of Adventures. All three possess some wonderful rides and offer good value for money. It is just that Disney builds and creates with a thoroughness, a detail and a sense of wonder and fantasy that no one else can match.

It truly is a magical world you enter when you pass under the gates reading 'Le Parc Disneyland' in 1m (3ft) high lettering and, for the duration of your stay, you will be surrounded and beguiled by a realm which offers the most enchanting – and thrilling – range of attractions anywhere on earth.

Anyone who has already been to the *Magic Kingdom Park* in Orlando or *Disneyland* in Anaheim, Los Angeles, will have a good idea of what to expect. However, while the *Disneyland Park* bears a strong resemblance to both of those, a lot of the essential detail and a good number of the attractions are completely different. When the Walt Disney Company set out to build a new resort experience on the European mainland, they did not want a mere copy of existing ideas. Rather, they wanted to update, enhance and improve, go back to the Imagineering drawing board if you like, cherry-picking some of the best features of all their parks and re-inventing them in a dramatic, new setting.

The Paris version also is, to my mind, a more refined and artistic interpretation of the American examples. The Imagineers were well aware they were building for a European market and have deliberately tried to tailor their designs in a less overtly American way. Of course, much of the fundamental magic inherent in their parks is quintessentially American, hence they do maintain a strong essence of Uncle Sam much of the time.

But there is also a greater awareness of Disney's European heritage (Walt Disney himself spent a good deal of time in France as a young man and his family traced their lineage back to French antecedents) and of the need to tell the stories in a way that makes sense to an audience consisting primarily of French, British, Germans, Dutch, Belgians, Spanish and Italians (and they are never just plain 'rides' or 'attractions' in a Disney park – everything has to tell a story and add to the overall theme).

The multi-lingual nature of the resort is therefore a key component to the overall feel and style of what's in store, and some of the design influences of those various nations are also evident in the Theme Parks themselves (the Sleeping Beauty Castle in the *Disneyland Park* is modelled on Mont St Michel in Normandy, for example).

The language challenge

It is also true to say that the need to think in several languages provided the Imagineers with an additional range of challenges which they had to meet in different ways, using subtitles, translations and extra soundtracks. While this adds a unique feel to familiar attractions ('it's a small world' or The Adventures of Snow White, for example), it does irk a small minority of English-speaking visitors – although I have yet to meet any children who didn't enjoy Pinocchio's Fantastic Journey simply because the commentary was in French!

To my mind, the answer is always to remember that this is, after all, another country where we Brits are usually just visiting and it pays to try to remember those few words of French (or German, or Spanish) we might have picked up at school. At the end of the day, the resort is trying to appeal to the widest possible audience and, by and large, they succeed with an extraordinarily cosmopolitan ability.

BRIT TIP: It pays to arrive a little early for the opening time at each park to put yourself in pole position ahead of the crowds for the first couple of hours, giving you the opportunity to enjoy some of the rides which attract serious queues later on.

Set menus

An additional point worth highlighting for anyone unfamiliar with French restaurant culture is the provision in most cases throughout the resort of a fixed-price menu (*prix fixe*, in French terminology) in addition to the à la carte choice. Even at the standard counter-service burger-and-chips type diners, there is a Menu Mickey, consisting of a main course (burger, salad, pizza or pasta), a choice of dessert and a soft drink. At the full-service restaurants, the set menus also offer a cheaper alternative to straight à la carte choice, although the menu selection (starter, main course and dessert) is obviously more limited.

For both parks, I have provided an At-A-Glance guide (on pages 91 and

120) which gives you some idea of what to expect to pay for food and souvenirs along the way, and it is worth pointing out that your costs can quickly mount up if you buy numerous snacks – a 50cl bottle of mineral water costs €1.85, a 25cl beer is €3.45, soft drinks variously €2, €2.60 and €3.40, a simple doughnut €1.70 and a large portion of chips €2.45. Kids meals, which consist of a main course, like chicken nuggets or pizza, chips, a yoghurt or ice cream, a small drink and a 'surprise' toy, are all €5. Even if you are totally unfamiliar with euros, you should be able to work out the kind of real cost you are looking at for a day in the Theme Parks.

> **BRIT TIP:** If you fancy a beer at one of the counter-service restaurants around the Theme Parks, the best value is to choose the set meal option with beer instead of soft drink and you pay just €0.90 extra.

Vegetarians are usually well catered for however, as many of the outlets can provide something for the veggie appetite. The full-service restaurants all offer at least one vegetarian main course and good salads are not hard to find. They will also do what they can to accommodate requests from guests who have particular dietary requirements: don't be afraid to ask.

Unlike the versions of the *Magic Kingdom* park in other Disney resorts, this one does serve alcohol, but it is not cheap. A beer in one of the full-service restaurants is usually around €5, while a bottle of wine varies from around €16.50 to €44.

Ticket types

Moving along to more practical matters, you need to work out what type of ticket you should have to make the most of your stay. With many packages that provide your accommodation, a length-of-stay pass is included. That means you can enjoy both parks from the minute you arrive until the time set for your departure. It obviously provides the peace of mind and convenience of knowing this part of your visit is fully taken care of and you do not need to worry about the mechanics of which park to visit when, as you have the benefit of being able to hop between parks at any time.

> **BRIT TIP:** Whenever you leave either park, intending to return later, you need to get a hand-stamp at the designated exit gate and show both the stamp (which shows up only under ultra-violet light) and your entrance ticket for re-admittance.

However, there is a range of ticket types, including annual ones, which are worth considering if you are staying off-site or if you might be a regular visitor. Prices also vary according to the time of year, whether it is 'high' or 'low' season. Here is your choice:

1-Day Passport: This provides admission to either the *Disneyland Park* or the *Walt Disney Studios Park* for a full day's fun (which can be up to 11pm at peak periods). You may exit and re-enter that same park as many times as you wish during the day. If you spend the day in *Walt Disney Studios Park*, your 1-day ticket also entitles you to the *Disneyland Park* 'Evening Access' from 5pm each day.

A new **1-Day Park Hopper** ticket was being tried out in summer 2003, allowing access to both parks for one full day and at only a small premium on the cost of a 1-Day Passport. This is due to continue in 2004 (at €49 for adults and €39 for 3–11s), when it will be re-evaluated.

3/4/5-Day Passport: This great-value ticket provides 3, 4 or 5 full days at the two parks, offering total freedom of movement between them on each day. The days do NOT need to be consecutive either, which is invaluable if you are staying off-site and visiting other attractions in the Paris region over, say, a 1-week stay. Passport tickets are also valid for 3 years from the date of purchase (but not if tickets are part of a package).

Classic Annual Passport: For 345 days a year, this provides entry to both parks, plus a few useful extras like free parking, a free annual magazine, access to the official website with special offers and invitations to special occasions (like new attraction previews). However, there are various blackout days at both parks when the Passport is not valid for admission. In 2004, these are: 1 January; 28 March; 11, 25 April; 8, 21, 30 May; 26 June; 14 July; 14 August; 1, 13 November; 27 and 30 December.

Fantasia Annual Passport: This version offers unlimited year-round access to both parks, plus a number of exclusive advantages, discounts and events especially organised for Fantasia Passport holders, including preferential rates on Disney hotel rooms. These bonuses include 10% off in most shops, restaurants and bars throughout the resort, 10% off up to eight tickets for Buffalo Bill's Wild West Show, free admission to Hurricanes nightclub in *Disney Village* for the passport holder and one guest, 10% discount in the boutiques of La Vallée Outlet Shopping Village, free parking for the Theme Parks or *Disney Village*, free pushchair and wheelchair hire in the Theme Parks, free luggage

storage, 10% off *Golf Disneyland* fees, free annual magazine, priority information and reservation hotline, access to the official website with special offers and information and invitations to special occasions at the resort. You can also choose one day in advance when your discount at the shops, restaurants and bars is increased to 20%.

> **BRIT TIP:** You can save money if you are tempted to buy an Annual Passport after a 1-day visit to one of the Theme Parks, as the price of your 1-day ticket will be deducted from the price. Visit the Annual Passport office at either Theme Park before you leave the resort.

There is a substantial difference in price between the two Annual Passports (see At-A-Glance guides on pages 91 and 120), but you can save a good deal over the course of a year if you plan on visiting the resort at least twice, and the possible savings against the multi-day Passports should also be obvious.

> **BRIT TIP:** If just one family member buys the Fantasia Annual Passport, the whole party would still benefit from the many discounts at the shops and restaurants.

Finally, for all Disney hotel guests, an **Unlimited Access Pass** for both parks is built in to the price of your package and this is valid for the duration of your stay. So if you book a Disney hotel stay, either independently or through a tour operator, you will not need to buy any further park tickets.

Now, I would like to be able to say you can find outlets that discount Disney tickets (as sometimes happens in America) but that just does not happen here. With the exception of the annual Kids Go Free promotion, usually from January to March (which is still a fairly sizeable 'discount'), there are no sources for cheap tickets, apart from occasional special promotions through Disney's business partners such as Esso and Air France. In quiet periods, there may be discounts to be found at the Disney hotel concierge desks for events like Buffalo Bill's, but that's about as far as it goes.

BRIT TIP: Fancy a dabble on the stockmarket? All shareholders of Euro Disney SCA (the holding company which actually runs the resort) benefit from a range of hotel, park, shop and restaurant discounts similar to those of the Fantasia Annual Passport holders.

Where to buy tickets

So, if that's the reality, where can you buy your tickets, apart from joining the usually long early-morning queues at the ticket booths at the entrance to both parks? Well, you can call the UK booking centre on 08705 030303 or the 7-day-a-week French version on 00 33 1 60 30 60 30; visit any Disney Store in Britain or on the Champs Elysées in Paris; call in at FNAC or Carrefour stores, Virgin Megastore or Auchan supermarket; find the ticket office in either of the two main Paris airports or the Paris Tourism Office, plus many RATP ticket windows on the Métro or RER; go to the Travelex Foreign Exchange Bureau at the Eurotunnel terminal in Folkestone, at Portsmouth ferry terminal or on board P&O Ferries; stop by the special ticket office at the Eurostar terminal in London Waterloo or Ashford stations; or call Keith Prowse ticket agency on 02890 23 24 25 (highly recommended, as they run occasional 'extras' with their tickets, like a free child's meal voucher with every 3-Day Passport – summer 2003). Keith Prowse also offers a whole range of Paris city excursions, dinner shows, sight-seeing visits and cruises, and it is well worth getting hold of a copy of their brochure, visiting their website at www.keithprowsetickets.co.uk, or e-mailing them at attractiontickets@keithprowse.com. Another useful ticket source is www.themeparkholidays.com or 0870 0621022.

Once you have your tickets arranged in advance, you can circumvent the first bugbear of visiting either park – the ticket booths. These are located prominently outside both parks, but, however many windows are open, there is nearly always a slow-moving queue to endure. If you can avoid the booths, you will get a significant jump on quite a few people.

The final thing to remember before we get to the Theme Parks proper – especially the *Walt Disney Studios Park* – is you can always

BRIT TIP: It is usually worthwhile buying your tickets as far in advance as possible, to avoid any price increase, which usually happens annually.

escape the madding crowds during the day by stepping out into *Disney Village* for a while. The great accessibility and convenience of the whole resort means that, if the Theme Parks are heaving, the *Disney Village* and the hotels are probably a lot quieter, hence it IS possible to find places without queues to enjoy a meal, a drink or just somewhere to recharge the batteries (and, at peak periods, you WILL feel the need to find some breathing space at times) before you charge back into the hectic whirl of it all.

Ratings

All the rides and shows in the Theme Parks are judged on a unique *Brit's Guide* rating system that splits them into the Thrill rides and Scenic ones. Thrill rides earn T ratings out of five (hence a TTTTT is as exciting as they get) and scenic rides get A ratings out of five (an AA ride is likely to be over-cute and missable). Obviously it is a matter of opinion to a certain extent but you can be sure a T or A ride is not worth your time, a TT or AA is worth seeing only if there is no queue, a TTT or AAA should be seen if you have time, but you won't miss much if you don't, a TTTT or AAAA ride is a big-time attraction that should be high on your list of things to do, and finally a TTTTT or AAAAA attraction should not be missed! The latter will have the longest queues and so you should plan your visit around these rides.

FastPass

Disney has introduced a unique FastPass (FP) system for some of the most popular shows and rides throughout their parks worldwide and it is worth taking advantage of it when possible.

BRIT TIP: Some rides DO run out of FastPasses before the end of the day, so it is advisable to grab one for the likes of Peter Pan's Flight and Big Thunder Mountain BEFORE mid-afternoon.

Here's how the FastPass works: at all attractions with the FastPass service (which is FREE remember – many people don't realise this), there are a series of kiosks next to the main entrance where you insert your park entrance ticket. The kiosk immediately spits your ticket out, followed by a separate slip with a time 'window' during which you should return to the separate FastPass queue (usually at least an hour later, or sometimes even 3 or 4 hours). When your 'window' is open, simply return to the FastPass queue and enjoy the attraction with only a minimal wait. However, you can hold only ONE FastPass ticket at a time, hence you need to weigh up the pros and cons of, say, doing Peter Pan in 3 hours' time, or Space Mountain in 1 hour. You also need FastPass tickets for *every* member of your party.

BRIT TIP: Although you can hold only one FastPass at a time, once your 'window' is open you CAN get another. So, if your FP time for Big Thunder is 11.05–11.35am, you could go over to the Indiana Jones ride at 11.10 and grab a FP there, then return to Big Thunder for your ride.

5

Top 10 attractions

Here, purely for fun, is what we rate as our Top 10 attractions, first for the *Disneyland Park*:

1 Space Mountain
2 Pirates of the Caribbean
3 Big Thunder Mountain Railroad
4 Disney's Fantillusion Parade
5 Phantom Manor
6 Princess Parade
7 Tarzan Encounter
8 Star Tours
9 La Tanière due Dragon
10 Peter Pan's Flight

And for the *Walt Disney Studios*:

1 Moteurs…Action! Stunt Spectacular
2 Cinémagique
3 Rock 'n' Roller Coaster starring Aerosmith
4 Disney's Cinema Parade
5 Rhythmo Technico
6 Studio Tram Tour
7 Dining on first floor terrace of Restaurant En Coulisse
8 Animagique
9 Flying Carpets over Agrabah
10 Disney Animation Gallery

Some rides are restricted to children over a certain height and are not advisable for people with back, neck or heart problems or for pregnant women. Where this is the case, I have noted 'Restrictions: 1.32m (4ft 3in)' and so on. Height restrictions (strictly enforced) are based on the average 5-year-old being 1.02m (3ft 3in) tall, 6s being 1.1m (3ft 6in) and 9s being 1.32m (4ft 3in).

The 'baby switch'

If you have small children, but don't want to leave them while you have a ride, you DON'T have to queue twice. When you get to the front of the queue, tell the operator you want to do a 'baby switch.' This means that Mum can go on the ride while Dad looks after junior and, on her return, Dad can ride while Mum does the babysitting.

Many children also get a big thrill from collecting autographs from the various Disney characters they meet, and nearly all the hotels and shops sell some great **autograph books** for that purpose.

If you have children of wide-ranging ages, check out the special section at the end of the chapter to see which rides and attractions appeal most to which age groups. It is important in a park of this size to concentrate on those areas which have most appeal for YOU and, while it is not possible to be 100% accurate, the advice here is fairly tried and tested, and you can get a pretty good idea of what is most likely to be popular with your offspring!

There is a full **Baby Care Centre** in the *Disneyland Park* next door to the Plaza Gardens Restaurant at the top of Main Street USA on the right, where there are nappy-changing facilities and a feeding room, with baby food (and nappies) on sale. The

BRIT TIP: If you have young children, it is a good idea to put a note in their pocket with details of their name, your mobile phone number, hotel, etc. That way much of the stress of a child possibly going astray is relieved. Cast Members are trained to take lost children to the Meeting Place and the provision of a note makes their job easier too.

BRIT TIP: Kids, try to find the thickest pen you can for collecting autographs. Most of the characters find it a struggle to write with the usual thin ballpoint in their great big hands.

Meeting Place for Lost Children is also to be found here, with its own Disney staff. At the *Walt Disney Studios Park* the Baby Care Centre is behind the Studio Services just inside the entrance on the right-hand side and you can find your lost children there, too.

Park etiquette

One final word of warning. Picnics are NOT allowed in the Theme Parks (although it is permissible to take a bottle of water with you), but there is an area set aside for picnics outside at the exit of the moving walkway from the main car park.

Appropriate clothing must be worn – which means shirt and shoes – at all times. No bare chests – even for women! Smoking, eating, drinking, flash photography and video lighting are not permitted on the rides, during shows or while queuing. So what *are* we waiting for? First stop the *Disneyland Park*...

5

Pin trading

In addition to collecting souvenirs, you will probably also encounter the pin-trading phenomenon at some stage of your Disney adventure. This is hard to explain to the uninitiated as it has no real parallel in modern British culture. It is a particularly American idea and involves collecting – and trading – the many dozens of different enamel pins which you can buy in almost every shop. They vary in price from around €8 to €15 and serious collectors carry them on lanyards around their neck, eagerly looking to barter and swap with other members of this not-so-secret society. Various Disney Cast Members also join in by displaying lanyards with pins to swap, and they are duty-bound to swap for anything they may be displaying.

I must admit, pin trading is something which rather baffles me, but those who get hooked on it will attest to having great fun looking for potential swaps with fellow devotees (as well as spending a small fortune on their collections!). For more info, log on to the UK-orientated discussion boards of www.disboards.com and ask one of the regulars to explain how you get suitably enthused!

6

The Disneyland Park
(or, To All Who Come To This Happy Place, Welcome!)

It makes sense to start by taking an in-depth look at the original development here at *Disneyland Resort Paris*, the first Disney park in Europe, which opened its gates in April 1992. Although it is comparable to the *Magic Kingdom* in the *Walt Disney World Resort in Florida* (America's biggest tourist attraction with some 14 million visitors annually), be prepared for some surprises in both scale and content from the US version. The *Disneyland Park* is bigger by some 17 hectares (42 acres) than its Orlando counterpart and, while it has fewer 'lands', the Paris version is distinctly more elaborate and involving.

The attractions range from the twee and fairly ordinary (Mad Hatter's Tea Cups and Autopia) to the wonderfully inventive (Phantom Manor and Pirates of the Caribbean) and on to the downright thrilling (Space Mountain and Indiana Jones™ and the Temple of Peril: Backwards!). The all-encompassing theming covers the Wild West (Frontierland), dark jungles and mysterious caverns (Adventureland), film and storybook fantasy (Fantasyland) and a kind of retro future world (Discoveryland), possibly the most imaginative of the lot. There is at least one (depending on the time of year) unmissable daily parade and a range of other live theatrical productions which all carry the Disney hallmark of imaginative family entertainment. In fact, plenty to make you go 'Wow!' and also a whole variety of attractions which will raise a big smile or two.

Prepare to be immersed completely in a convincing world of make-believe, where every tiny detail, from the uniforms of the Cast Members to the clever signage and even the rubbish bins, conforms to that land's theme, but be aware of some fairly blatant attempts to lighten your wallet along the way, notably at the many gift shops, especially after a number of the rides. By Disney's own reckoning, 16,513 different types of merchandise are on sale and, although 90% of it costs less than

BRIT TIP: Take advantage of Disney's free package pick-up service if you do a lot of shopping. When you pay for any item, ask for it to be made available in the *Disney Village* for collection later. Then pick it up at The Disney Store in the village after 6pm. If you are staying in a Disney hotel, you can have gifts delivered to The Disney Store there for collection after 8pm.

The Disneyland Park at a glance

See full-colour map opposite page 96.

Location	Off Exit 14 of the A4 autoroute, proceed to the clearly signed car park; or turn right out of the Marne-la-Vallée RER and TGV station; or through the *Disney Village* if staying at a resort hotel
Size	57 hectares (140 acres) in five 'lands'
Hours	10am–8pm autumn and winter weekdays; 9am–8pm spring, plus autumn and winter weekends, Christmas and New Year; 9am–11pm summer holidays
Admission	**Under 3**, free; **3–11s** €25 (1-Day Passport, low season), €29 (1-Day Passport, high season), €69 (3-Day Passport, low season), €80 (3-Day Passport, high season), €129 (Classic Annual Passport) and €199 (Fantasia Annual Passport); **adults** (12+) €29 (1-Day Passport, low season), €39 (1-Day Passport, high season), €79 (3-Day Passport, low season), €107 (3-Day Passport, high season), €149 (Classic Annual Passport) and €229 (Fantasia Annual Passport)
Parking	€7.50
Pushchairs	€6.50 (Pushchair shop to right of main entrance, just under railway arch)
Wheelchairs	€6.50 (Pushchair shop)
Top Attractions	Space Mountain, Star Tours, Peter Pan's Flight, Dumbo the Flying Elephant, Big Thunder Mountain
Don't Miss	The Princess Parade; Fantillusion Parade and Tinker Bell's Fantasy in the Sky fireworks (summer and Christmas seasons only); The Tarzan™ Encounter; 'it's a small world'
Hidden Costs	**Meals** Burger, chips and coke €5.90 3-course meal €26 (Blue Lagoon) **Kids' meal** €5 (at all counter-service restaurants) **T-shirts** €10.50–30 **Souvenirs** €1.50–80 **Sundries** Kids' autograph book €4.50 Space Mountain photo €12

6

€15, it can quickly add up if you have children of the large-eyed variety!

The counter-service diners are not terribly imaginative in their fare (apart from a few, which I will highlight along the way), while the full-service restaurants offer some fabulous food – but at a price (a family of four can easily spend €80 or more on lunch or dinner). A cheaper alternative is to keep going with snacks from the many hot-dog, popcorn, doughnut and drinks wagons around the Theme Park, and have your main meal back in *Disney Village* or the hotel in the evening.

You actually enter the Theme Park underneath the *Disneyland Hotel*, the rather fanciful conglomeration of buildings otherwise known as the Pink Palace. You pass some extremely pleasant gardens (the whimsical Fantasia Gardens, with a number of topiaries in the shape of characters from the film) and the inevitable fountains and ponds (good photo spot, this) before entering the main entrance plaza. The ticket booths are just to the right of the entrance passageway, but hopefully you already have ticket in hand and can head straight through to the turnstiles. If you need Guest Relations or Left Luggage, bear to the right of the main hotel building and they are right in front of you.

Main Street USA

Once through the turnstiles, you enter a plaza in front of the main Disneyland Railroad station. Walk under the station and you are suddenly in **Town Square**, the main entrance to *Disneyland Park* proper, and the lower portion of the first 'land', Main Street USA. This is a grand, turn-of-the-century version of small-town America, with a truly eye-catching array of shop and office facades all built in epic detail. It is not so much a thoroughfare as a living museum to generations of genuine Americana and it offers a fabulous glimpse into an idealised past of the United States.

Here you will get your first look at the most-photographed edifice in the whole resort – the Sleeping Beauty Castle (or Le Château de la Belle au Bois Dormant, to use its full French title). To your left is **Disneyland City Hall**, basically another guest relations office where you can pick up park maps (if you haven't already got one at your hotel or in the many cubicles underneath the Railroad Station), book meals at any of the restaurants or just ask any park-related questions.

BRIT TIP: Can't find the characters? Check in at City Hall first and they will be able to tell you exactly where they can be found. In fact, City Hall is your best friend for a variety of queries, from the location of baby facilities to meal bookings (there are NO baby facilities at City Hall).

To your right is the **Main Street Transportation Company**, which consists of several vintage and horse-drawn vehicles that take you the length of Main Street USA to the Central Plaza, the Theme Park's hub, from which radiate the other four 'lands'. If you have time (or children), it is quite fun to take one of the horse-drawn trams or vintage cars (including a police paddy-wagon), but it usually works out quicker to walk straight to the Central Plaza yourself (especially if you use either of the two covered arcades which run alongside Main Street USA).

One of the most eye-catching

features, though, is the **Disneyland Railroad**, with a station (it has four; Adventureland is the only section without a railroad stop) well positioned here to catch the unsuspecting visitor. The Victorian-style station provides an elevated view down Main Street USA, but the signature steam train ride, which circles the whole park and includes a clever 'Grand Canyon' scene en route to Frontierland and a neat glimpse inside Pirates of the Caribbean, quickly draws long, slow-moving queues for much of the day. AAA.

BRIT TIP: The Disneyland Railroad is a relaxing ride when many of the others are showing long queues but DON'T join it at Main Street where few people actually get off. Instead, try the stations at Frontierland or Fantasyland for the shortest wait.

Main Street USA is basically the Theme Park's principal shopping opportunity, with a whole range of stores (including the gargantuan **Emporium**, which stocks just about every kind of souvenir known to mouse-kind!) and cafes. Also here is **Dapper Dan's Hair Cuts**, a wonderfully atmospheric vintage barber's with the kind of furnishings you would usually find only in an antique shop (or an apothecary's), where you can stop for a haircut and/or shave if the mood takes you (€18 each or €30 for both!). If you need any film or photographic equipment, **Town Square Photography**, hosted by Kodak, should be able to help you out (although beware the prices here – it is much cheaper to bring basics like film with you). In all, there are 12 cunningly arranged shops along

this 100m (109yd) boulevard and it is worthwhile returning in the afternoon when the rides are busiest to check out some of the amazing detail both inside and out.

BRIT TIP: Video camera battery running down? Don't fret – you can visit City Hall and they will be able to recharge the battery for you there and then.

You can also find 10 different snack bars and restaurants to provide everything from breakfast, to a gourmet lunch, afternoon tea and evening dessert. Pick of the bunch is **Walt's – An American Restaurant**, which offers Disney character breakfasts from 8–10.30am, plus lunch 12–3pm (set menu €22 or €30, €10 for children). This fabulously elegant diner, designed like a 1900s' hotel, is a tribute to Walt himself, his ideas and creations, and features a wealth of personal detail, photos and memorabilia which are well worth a look. The character breakfast, which is an all-you-can-eat affair served at your table, is €25 for adults and €17 for kids (3–11) if you are not staying at a Disney hotel, or €16 and €12 if you are (it actually counts as a supplement because your hotel stay automatically includes breakfast).

BRIT TIP: Celebrate your birthday in style at Walt's. Order a cake at the start of your meal and it will be brought to your table at the end with a great fanfare. It costs €22 and serves 4–8.

Elsewhere in Main Street USA, the **Plaza Gardens Restaurant** offers an excellent all-you-can-eat buffet for lunch or dinner (€25 for adults, €10.55 for kids) in a plush, conservatory-style setting. Your food choice ranges from a huge cold spread – salads, meats, bread and fruit – to a whole array of hot dishes – casseroles, pasta, roast beef, sausages, hot dogs and several types of vegetable and rice – and a mouth-watering selection of desserts. There is also an excellent **character tea-time** (3–4.30pm) every day, featuring all the Disney favourites, with a mouth-watering spread of cakes, pastries and desserts, plus one hot and one cold drink each (€13 per person). For an extra €5 a head, you can enjoy the even more fun-filled character Birthday Party for that special occasion.

Otherwise, your eateries are mainly of the counter snack kind, with the **Market House Deli** (sandwiches, salads and pasta), **Casey's Corner** (all manner of hot dogs and soft drinks), **Victoria's Home-Style Restaurant** (pasta, quiche, pizza and salads), **The Coffee Grinder** (coffee, tea and cakes), **The Ice Cream Company** (hosted by Nestlé), **The Cookie Kitchen** and **Cable Car Bake Shop** (two sides of the same breakfast-orientated servery, with some delicious pastries and cookies) and the **Gibson Girl Ice Cream Parlour** (a full range of ice cream delights). Bear in mind that not all of these are likely to be open at any one time (apart from weekends in high season).

BRIT TIP: As an example of the Imagineers' art, listen carefully outside Victoria's Home-Style Restaurant and you will catch the distinct sounds of someone using the bathroom in the 'guesthouse' above!

For shopping, you should definitely check out the Emporium, as well as **The Storybook Store** (books, stationery, CD and audio cassettes), **Harrington's Fine China & Porcelain** (some lovely china, crystal and glass giftware), **Disney Clothiers Ltd** (for a more upmarket selection of apparel) and **Main Street Motors** (dedicated to Winnie the Pooh and friends), while **Disneyana Collectibles** is a must for Disney collectors with its range of original books, film cels, lithographs and ceramic figures.

As an alternative to walking up Main Street USA itself, pick one of the two arcades at either side (the **Liberty Arcade** to the left, and the **Discovery Arcade** to the right) and wander right through away from most of the crowds. The Liberty Arcade also features a clever tableau

BRIT TIP: Need to stay dry? Both Liberty and Discovery Arcades are fully covered and provide back-door access to most of the shops and cafes along Main Street USA. In the depths of winter, these are very popular places!

about immigrants arriving in New York (admittedly in French), while the Discovery Arcade is also decorated with some clever period historical detail, which is worth perusing at your leisure later in the day.

At the top of Main Street USA on the right-hand side (just after the Gibson Girl Ice Cream Parlour) is a handy **Information Board** which displays the waiting times at the various attractions. Late arrivals should take note of this to get an idea of where to head first (and where to avoid for a while).

Main Street USA is also one of

the prime locations to meet various **Disney characters**. Most days start with the official character 'opening ceremony', an early-morning cavalcade featuring Mickey, Pluto and various other chums. Many of them stop to sign autographs in three locations – on a platform outside the Liberty Arcade (just past Casey's Corner on the left as you come up the street), in the Central Plaza area and on the Théâtre du Château stage just to the right in front of the castle. For Halloween 2003, Main Street USA was transformed into **Spooky Street**, with a major pumpkin-inspired makeover and it is hoped that this wonderfully fun transformation continues in 2004.

Rope drop

If you arrive prior to the official opening time (either 9 or 10am), Main Street USA is not the place to linger as most of the crowds will be flocking to the **Central Plaza** in front of the castle. This is REALLY where the action starts for a full day in the Theme Park, so don't be fooled into thinking they have opened early by letting you into Main Street USA. This is where you need to have planned your campaign to get a head start on the masses. Depending on which of the 'lands' in front of you appeal most, head in one of the four directions and wait

> BRIT TIP: If you are among the first to reach Central Plaza and if you seek out the main rides first, you will enjoy the Theme Park at its very best – with short or non-existent queues at the most popular attractions.

for the opening hour 'rope drop' by the Cast Members at each entrance.

If you fancy the appeal of cowboy country and the lure of a great thrill ride like Big Thunder Mountain or the scary fun of Phantom Manor, head up Liberty Arcade and, right at the top, wait to turn left into Frontierland. For the mysteries of Adventureland (including the wonderful Pirates of the Caribbean ride), move into Central Plaza and wait at the land's main entrance on the left.

Those with children in tow, who will demand rides in the company of all their favourite characters like Dumbo, Peter Pan and the Mad Hatter, wait in front of the castle for the chance to get into Fantasyland first. Or, if the appeal of big thrill rides like Space Mountain (an interior, looping roller-coaster) and Star Tours (a brilliant simulator space ride) is highest on your 'To Do' list, then turn right in the middle of Central Plaza and await rope drop there.

6

> BRIT TIP: Park too busy? Don't forget it is relatively easy to head back out to *Disney Village* and grab a bite to eat at places like Planet Hollywood and Annette's Diner.

Once the ropes go down, the early-morning crowds will move (quickly!) in one of the four directions, so keep your wits about you. Study the Theme Park map for where you want to go – and benefit from a first hour or so without lengthy queuing for the popular rides. It also pays (and royally so in peak periods) to avoid the main meal times if you want to eat without considerable queuing and frenzy. It is a notable fact of *Disneyland Resort Paris* that people tend to pack out the counter-service cafes rather than the handful of full-service, sit-down restaurants. This means 12–2.30pm is a seriously bad time (unless it is an extremely quiet period of the year) to head for places like the Fuente Del Oro Restaurant, Pizzeria Bella Notta, the Cowboy Cookout Barbecue or any of the other 14 counter-service diners in the park. Try to have a snack prior to midday or look to eat in mid-afternoon and you will also benefit from slightly shorter ride queues during the main lunch period. Alternatively, you could book lunch at the start of the day at one of the five main restaurants – especially with children – to guarantee a pleasant sit-down and some rest.

Pace yourself

When it comes to eating, be aware that inclement weather quickly causes long queues to mount up in the restaurants, even in *Disney Village*. If you can pre-empt that sudden rain squall by getting to a café first, you will be well placed to watch the rush come in when the deluge starts. Equally, if you have brought some good **rain gear** with you, it is a great time to enjoy some of the rides while the majority seek shelter.

The final piece of advice before I send you off on the great *Disneyland Park* adventure is to pace yourself. It is easy to get caught up in all the fun and imagination and end up a frazzled wreck by mid-afternoon! Especially in summer months, when the crowds are at their peak and the temperature can top 30°C, it can be a tough business negotiating the queues, the long periods standing in line and the demands of tramping from one side of the Theme Park to the other in the name of entertainment. This is when you will most feel the benefit of a **solid plan**, booking your mealtimes in advance and giving yourselves a rest at

Key to Disneyland Park Map

Main Street, USA
1　Main Street USA Railroad Station
2　Town Square
3　Disneyland City Hall
4　Main Street Transportation Company Vehicles
5　Liberty Arcade
6　Discovery Arcade
7　Central Plaza

Frontierland
8　Fort Comstock
9　Phantom Manor
10　Thunder Mesa Riverboat Landing
11　Rustler Roundup Shootin' Gallery
12　Big Thunder Mountain
13　Pocahontas Indian Village
14　Critter Corral
15　Chaparral Theatre
16　Frontierland Railroad Station

Adventureland
17　Indiana Jones™ and the Temple of Peril: Backwards!
18　Adventure Isle
19　La Cabane des Robinsons
20　Skull Rock
21　Pirates Beach
22　Pirates of the Caribbean

23　Agrabah Bazaar

Fantasyland
24　Sleeping Beauty Castle
25　Le Carrousel de Lancelot
26　Blanche-Neige et les Sept Nains
27　Pinocchio's Fantastic Journey
28　Dumbo the Flying Elephant
29　Peter Pan's Flight
30　Fantasy Festival Stage
31　Fantasyland Railroad Station
32　Alice's Curious Labyrinth
33　Le Pays des Contes de Fées
34　Casey Jr – le Petit Train du Cirque
35　Mad Hatter's Tea Cups
36　'it's a small world'
37　Le Théâtre du Château

Discoveryland
38　Space Mountain
39　Les Mystères du Nautilus
40　Orbitron – Machines Volantes
41　Star Tours
42　Discoveryland Railroad Station
43　Honey, I Shrunk the Audience
44　Autopia
45　Le Visionarium
46　Videopolis
47　Arcade Omega

DISNEYLAND PARK

Top: Backlot Express
   Restaurant
Above centre: Rainforest Café
Above: Billy Bob's
Right: Agrabah Café
Below: Annette's Diner
Below right: Café Mickey

WALT DISNEY STUDIOS

Above left: Rock 'n' Roller Coaster
Top left: Studio Tram Tour
Above: Bug's Life Photo Spot
Below: Streetmosphere
Below left: Armageddon: Special Effects

WALT DISNEY STUDIOS

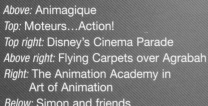

Above: Animagique
Top: Moteurs…Action!
Top right: Disney's Cinema Parade
Above right: Flying Carpets over Agrabah
Right: The Animation Academy in
   Art of Animation
Below: Simon and friends

strategic moments, whether it be finding a quiet corner for a drink or visiting one of the shows that provides a welcome sit-down, preferably in the air-conditioned cool.

You will also need to drink a lot of **water** during the summer. The physical demands of the parks will quickly creep up on you unless you remember to rehydrate at regular intervals. It is, sadly, an all-too-common feature in mid-afternoon to see or hear grizzly children, often being berated by parents for not enjoying themselves (!), when all everyone needs is just to sit down for a few minutes, recharge the batteries and drink some water.

Most children (mine included) get a huge energy charge from being in the Theme Parks and the adrenalin keeps them going long after they should have keeled over. But that

> BRIT TIP: Save €s by taking a bottle of water with you and refilling it from the many drinking fountains throughout the Theme Parks.

excited state can run out at a moment's notice and turn to angst if they are not regularly fed and watered – and it is easy to overlook the latter with all the fun that greets you at every turn.

In summer, it is also advisable to carry a good **sunscreen** and use it liberally while you are queuing in order to prevent everyone from getting an unhealthy dose of the sun, which also exacerbates the tiredness factor – your biggest enemy.

Frontierland

Okay, enough of the warnings – let's get to the fun! Fair enough, there is masses in store, so let me take you on a full tour of the remaining four

'lands' in the *Disneyland Park*. Starting immediately to your left from the Central Plaza brings you to Frontierland, a true rootin', tootin' cowboy town that oozes child appeal and has plenty of visual creativity and stimulation for grown-ups too. It is a realm of pioneers and gold diggers, the Wild West in vivid 3-D, with a generous helping of some of the epic scenery which the real-life version possesses in places like Nevada and Arizona.

Like virtually all areas of the Theme Park, Frontierland rewards the casual wanderer with some neat little paths and alleyways leading nowhere in particular but which throw up some interesting details or amusing scenery, like the Indian village encampment or the hot springs (complete with Old Faithful geyser).

Once again, the faithful re-creation of the era can be seen in every building and façade, none better than the main entrance through **Fort Comstock**, which is an attraction in itself with its Legends of the Wild West historical scenes. Here, you can climb the wooden stairs to the ramparts, visit the US Marshall's office, check out the Fort Jail and peer into various offices (see if you can spot Buffalo Bill) and stables. Kids will want to roam the ramparts and scrutinise other areas of the Theme Park through the telescopes provided for just that purpose. It is a handy place to let youngsters explore on their own for a while too. AAA.

Phantom Manor: Turn left after coming through Fort Comstock and head along the plaza past the Silver Spur Steakhouse for one of the most clever and amusing rides in the Disney repertoire. This elaborate haunted mansion is a variation on the theme firmly established in Anaheim and Orlando, with a ghoulish entryway leading to an underground ride of wonderfully creepy proportions. Unfortunately,

6

BRIT TIP: Queues build up at Phantom Manor from mid-morning onwards, and, although they rarely top half an hour, this is a good one to do early on, or during one of the parades which tend to trim waiting times down a bit. Late evening is your best bet otherwise.

the introductory spiel and commentary throughout are all in French, but it needs little real explanation as the gloomy entrance parlour (watch for a remarkable trick here) takes you down to this spook-tastic world.

Under 5s may find the mock-horror elements a bit too convincing but otherwise the whole experience is more fun than frightening. The story of an elaborate socialite wedding that went tragically wrong, leaving the bride as one of the 999 ghosts, is a bit hard to follow, but the ride takes you right through the manor and into a realistic haunted town in best graveyard fashion.

Take some time during queuing to appreciate the elaborate terraces and gardens outside the manor, while you exit into Boot Hill and some more pun-laced scenery that includes various graves – such as 'Here lies Shotgun Gus, holier now than all of us'. The more attentive will also notice the sounds of knocking coming from the largest of the mausoleums in the graveyard here. This can be a great source of amusement when people notice it for the first time on wild and windy nights! AAAA (TTTTT for youngsters).

Thunder Mesa Riverboat Landing: Backtrack slightly along the plaza and you can hop on a boat, offering a slow-paced and picturesque ride around much of Frontierland, including several sections which can be seen only from the water. The commentary is bi-lingual and it is quite a capacious ride, so there is rarely much of a queue here. The two boats, the Molly Brown and Mark Twain, both provide an enjoyably authentic experience. This is a good ride to save for later in the day when both Phantom Manor and Big Thunder are busiest. AAA.

Fans of the old-style arcade shooting ranges can get a quick 'fix' at the **Rustler Roundup Shootin' Gallery**, where €2 (the only additional charge for any attraction in the Theme Park) will give you 10 shots at various audio-animatronic targets. TT.

Big Thunder Mountain: This is one of Disney's trademark roller-coasters. While others may thrill (or terrify!) you with their topsy-turvy antics, Big Thunder sticks firmly to the straight and narrow and is as fun and inventive as most people desire, with this abandoned 'gold mine' showing it still has some life in it in the shape of its runaway train. Again, you get a different version from other Disney parks, this one starts straight away with a dive into the dark under the lake before whizzing around the mock sandstone monoliths and mine shafts in a terrifying fashion.

With three different ascents (and

BRIT TIP: If you head to Frontierland first, Big Thunder should be your opening ride, followed by Phantom Manor. Then return to the mine-train coaster and grab a FastPass for another go later!

plunges), the proliferation of clever scenery all around you is never less than spectacular, so it usually needs two or three rides to take in all the detail (it looks great at night, too). This is one of the five FastPass (FP) rides, so it is well worth taking advantage of, as the queues often reach an hour during peak periods. Afterwards, you can buy the souvenir photo of your ride for €9 or €11. Restrictions: 1.02m (3ft 3in). TTTT.

Pocahontas Indian Village: If the youngsters are too short (or apprehensive!) to ride Big Thunder, they will probably want to head for this straightforward play area with a mixture of slides, swings and climbs geared towards under-6s. Sadly, this is one area that is affected by the weather as it closes when wet, but when dry it is a valuable place to allow the young 'uns to let off some steam. TTT (for the right age group!).

Critter Corral: Continuing the tour of Frontierland brings you next to this fairly standard petting zoo aimed primarily, once again, at younger children. Here, they can pet rabbits, donkeys, sheep and goats, dodge the chickens and enjoy the other paraphernalia of this farmyard set-up. AAA (under 8s).

Chaparral Theatre: Opposite Critter Corral, this is one of the Theme Park's four main live entertainment venues. The attractions here are seasonal and Disney does tend to change them for something new at regular intervals but, at the time of writing, the two offerings were: **The Tarzan™ Encounter**, a sensational 25-minute song, dance and acrobatic extravaganza showcasing the music from the animated film, with a cast of energetic 'apes' who find all manner of ways of leaping off, around and over the clever stage scenery. Tarzan and Jane (inevitably) make an appearance and, while it can be a bit loud for very young ears, the whole spectacle is a riot of colour

and movement. There is also an audience participation section for children that is worth being ready for. AAAA (plus TTT).

Mickey's Winter Wonderland takes over in the theatre from mid-November to early March, with an equally clever ice-skating show featuring Mickey and all the gang (including a suitably hapless Donald Duck) that will keep youngsters enchanted for the full 25-minute duration. It is a fairly straightforward song-and-dance pastiche, but once again the staging and lighting are impressive and its bi-lingual style ensures English speakers are not left out. AAAA.

Next door is the **Frontierland Railroad Station**, which is often the best place to catch the Theme Park's steam train and take the slow chug all the way around.

Your dining options feature two more outstanding opportunities here. The **Silver Spur Steakhouse** is a truly de luxe establishment, designed like a classic Western hotel, using rich, dark woods and plush upholstery. The subdued lighting provides quite an intimate dining style and there is a display kitchen at

6

BRIT TIP: If there is no queue, take the railroad for the best possible short-cut to Fantasyland or Discoveryland. However, it is usually quicker to walk if you need the fastest way back to Main Street USA.

the back which adds to the effect. Steaks are their stock-in-trade, but they also do excellent salmon, chicken and farfalle pasta. A set, 3-course meal is €25 for adults and €10 for kids, although some of the à la carte items go up to €23.50. Superb desserts add to the high quality on offer here.

Character-seekers will want to make a beeline for the **Lucky Nugget Saloon**, which offers a fabulous Tex-Mex buffet lunch from 12–3pm, plus 6.30–10pm for dinner in high season. The restaurant is wonderfully styled like a genuine, two-storey Western saloon, with a stage and a long bar, and the food is a serve-yourself buffet (€30 for adults, €15 for 3–11s) featuring assorted crudités, chicken wings, nachos, salsa, fajitas, spare ribs, chilli con carne, pasta, pizza and a large choice of desserts.

The character interaction here includes the seemingly omnipresent Chip 'n' Dale (or Tic and Tac as they are known in France), Pluto, Gideon (from Pinocchio) and Daisy Duck. If €90 for a family of four seems a touch expensive (as it does to me), check out the character tea opportunity either here or at the Plaza Gardens Restaurant.

Otherwise, your dining choices include the magnificently evocative **Cowboy Cookout Barbecue**, a counter-service barn of a place featuring spare ribs, burgers, smoked chicken and chicken nuggets. The lovely smoky barbecue smell, the cowboy ambience and the Country & Western twang (with live music periodically) add up to a memorable dining experience, even if the food is only fairly average. **Fuente del Oro Restaurante** goes down Mexico way for more counter-service, cantina style, with tacos, chilli con carne and other Mexican specialities such as fajitas and quesadillas. Finally, the **Last Chance Café** offers more cowboy fare with typical Western decor, serving turkey legs, chips and sandwiches.

Shopping is suitably cowboy orientated too, with **Tobias Norton & Sons – Frontier Traders**, a leather emporium featuring hats, boots, wallets and belts, **Bonanza Outfitters**, offering the full range of Western apparel, and the **Eureka Mining Supplies** with typical cowboy-style foods and toys, including the inevitable hats and guns.

Halloweenland

If you are here between 1 October and 2 November, remember that Frontierland becomes **Halloweenland** for the duration, with a dazzling array of spooky special effects, creepy scenery and haunted shows. A giant spider's web covers Fort Comstock, the Thunder Mesa Riverboat gets a ghoulish Mummy-style makeover, pumpkins and scarecrows abound, various Disney characters turn up throughout Halloweenland's pathways and the daily Princess Parade is taken over by Disney Villains like Cruella and Jafar. Children can get into the 'spirit' with a monstrous makeover at the **Sorcerer's Apprentice** (face painting) or the **Halloween Tiff** hair salon for a 'hair-raising' style, while a mysterious **Fortune Teller** offers to tell your creepy fortune!

> BRIT TIP: The Halloween Parties are not usually widely publicised in the UK, so they are worth making a note of and seeking out if you are visiting at the right time (or call 08705 03 03 03).

Two extra-spooky **Disney's Halloween Parties** are put on (usually the Saturday before Halloween and the evening of Halloween itself) and the Theme Park is open from 9pm–2am with unlimited access to the main attractions (in Halloweenland, Main Street USA, the Indiana Jones ride in Adventureland and Space Mountain in Discoveryland), with the addition of live music on a special stage in front of the castle and a 'haunted' disco for a separate ticket price of €26 for adults and €15 for children. My researcher Robert Rees is a confirmed Halloween fan and says there is a great evening atmosphere for the Halloween Parties, made even more memorable by the amazing costumes many guests wear.

The transformation of the whole 'land' – unlike anything attempted at the American parks – is hugely

> BRIT TIP: For that Kodak moment, try to gain a view of the castle from one of the small side paths between Frontierland and Adventureland, as there is a number of unusual perspectives offering good photo opportunities.

ambitious, but the Imagineers have pulled off quite a triumph here, making October a real must-visit month if you can.

Another unique feature of this section of the Theme Park is the latticework of paths which interconnect between Frontierland and Adventureland. This surprisingly small-scale landscaping is a notable element of the European influence behind the design of the Theme Park, and the paths are almost interwoven to provide an alternative way of getting around as well as plenty of looks at different aspects (but keep your map handy in case you get lost!).

> BRIT TIP: Adventureland is the hardest 'land' to navigate, so hang on to your map to find your way from place to place.

Adventureland

Africa, the Caribbean and the jungles of Asia combine to provide Adventureland with a host of contrasting – and thrilling – experiences, all with the great benefit of some of the most lush landscaping and use of plants and trees. In all honesty, there are the least amount of attractions here, but the whole area has such a wealth of detail and fine architecture (take a close look at Skull Rock and the castle façade of the Pirates ride), it is easy to spend a good deal of time just wandering and admiring. Even if you don't eat at most of the counter-service diners, it is worth looking into places like Colonel Hathi's Pizza Outpost and Restaurant Hakuna Matata to appreciate the interior design that gives them a real storybook feel.

Indiana Jones™ and the Temple of Peril: Backwards!: If you are coming from Frontierland, turn left by Colonel Hathi's for this 5-star thrill ride. Not content with creating a ducking and diving coaster that seems to zip along faster than it is, the designers gave it a brain-scrambling 360-degree loop and have re-configured it twice to run both backwards and forwards (for now, it has extra thrills going backwards!). The theming alone is wonderful, with the queuing area leading you through an archaeological dig in best Indiana Jones fashion, before you reach the temple and your rickety mine wagon car.

Before you know it, you are being thrown around a tight, twisting track with its sudden loop and dramatic swoops, only to come to the end of the track all too soon once your body has got the hang of it! This is definitely not the ride for you if you suffer from neck or back problems as there is quite a bit of head-jarring vibration along the way but it is also quite exhilarating and much more

6

BRIT TIP: The scary aspect of the Indiana Jones ride and its position at the innermost end of Adventureland means it is often overlooked by many park visitors, hence it is a good ride to do during the busiest parts of the day.

fun than it looks (terrifying!). Indiana Jones is a FastPass ride, which is handy for coaster-lovers as it rarely draws a big queue and means you can usually ride with only a 10–15-minute wait and then bag a FP for later on. Restrictions: 1.40m (4ft 6in). TTTT½.

Retracing your steps slightly and turning left brings you into the central portion of Adventureland, known as **Adventure Isle**. The Imagineers have worked overtime here to create something radically different from a number of existing themes in other parks, and they opted for an overgrown adventure playground of the most elaborate kind. This is a delightful pot-pourri of attractions, mainly aimed at children but which are also eye-catching and detailed enough to appeal to adults as well.

BRIT TIP: Adventure Isle is just about the only area of either park that is NOT accessible for guests with disabilities. It is simply not designed for the use of wheelchairs.

La Cabane des Robinsons: The Swiss Family Treehouse is the first you come to. The re-creation of the tree 'house' of the castaway Robinson family from the 1960 Disney film is a gentle walk-through attraction, showcasing all the clever ways in which a giant (man-made in this case) banyan tree was adapted to provide shelter, food and running water. Queues are rarely a problem here and there are some great views from the top. AAA.

Spinning off the treehouse is a high-level rope suspension bridge which takes you on to the five other sections of the Isle, **Skull Rock** (a labyrinthine stone edifice which towers over one end of the lagoon), **L'île au Tresor** (a series of lookout towers and spooky secret caves), **Le Ventre de la Terre** (a series of galleries under the tree), **Captain Hook's Galley** (a rather tame pirate ship which actually has little to explore) and **La Plage des Pirates** (or **Pirates Beach**, a clever play area of slides and climbs expressly for the little shipmates). Kids will surely want to dash off and explore Ben Gunn's Cave, Ambush Alley and Dead Man's Bridge, and it is a good area in which to let them loose for a while. TTT.

Pirates of the Caribbean: Coming off at the top end of Adventure Isle brings you to one of Disney's trademark and truly unmissable rides. The original version of this attraction was installed in *Disneyland California* in 1967 and remains an Imagineering gem to this day, highlighted by the use of their pioneering work with audio-animatronics. These are a series of life-like (or robot-like, in some cases) figures which move, talk, gesticulate and, in this instance, lay siege to a Caribbean island! Your journey starts as you wind down inside the Pirate Castle, through secret streets and sudden dungeons, until you reach your boat for a plunge into the unexpected darkness of the pirate realm.

There are two minor plunges (and slight splashes – front seat passengers may get a little wet), the first of which drops you into the middle of the island siege, with the clever – and distinctly amusing – action going on all around you, and a second which drops into the pirate treasure caverns. Skeletons and dungeons abound, and it may be a little too intense and realistic for under 5s, but there is little that is genuinely scary and the whole effect is so amazing you will probably want to have several goes to appreciate all the detail involved. While it is a popular ride, queues rarely top half an hour here and move steadily, and it is a welcome place to cool down during the hotter months. AAAAA (TTTT for under 8s). NB: See if you can spot some of the elements 'borrowed' when this ride was used as the inspiration for Disney's hit film *Pirates of the Caribbean* in 2003.

If you enter Adventureland via the main entrance off the Central Plaza, you will come into the **Agrabah Bazaar**, a magnificent outdoor/indoor shopping scenario straight out of *1,001 Nights*, and with some more suitably exotic scenery and architecture. The clever nature of the 'outdoor' street that is actually completely under cover and the wonderfully detailed decor add up to one of the real triumphs of the Imagineers' art hereabouts and mark it out as almost an attraction in its own right. Here you will also find **Le Passage Enchanté d'Aladdin**, a walk-through exhibit of the Aladdin story with some amusing tableaux and clever lighting tricks. AA.

Adventureland is also home to one of my all-time favourite restaurants of all the Disney parks, the **Blue Lagoon**, which is actually set inside the Pirates ride (so there are usually a few shouts of 'Bon Appetit!' from people setting off on the ride as you dine). You enter just below and to the left of the ride entrance, and the setting alone is worthy of perusal. You eat on a mock 'outdoor' terrace under dim lights, authentically furnished, listening to sounds that

BRIT TIP: Plan a special meal, even with the kids, in the Blue Lagoon and you won't be disappointed. Book at City Hall or with your hotel concierge. Perfect in winter when it is heated to tropical temperatures!

evoke the feeling of an evening on some distant Caribbean island. The seafood-orientated menu is also a delight, with the likes of fricassee of tuna and swordfish, steamed emperor fish and mahi-mahi, Jamaican pepper fillet of beef and chicken curry. The set menu is €25.15 (€9.90 for children), while starters range from €7 to €11 and main courses from €15 to €25, topped by the Captain's Platter, a dish of crab claws, scampi, shrimps, whelks, scallops, winkles and oysters for a princely €27. The kids' menu includes scallop of chicken, ham ravioli and pan-fried vegetables, and even the burger is proper, ground beef that actually tastes like meat (although that may not go down well with those with a penchant for fast-food burgers!).

Your counter-service options here include **Colonel Hathi's Pizza Outpost** (pizzas, salads, lasagne and spaghetti – set pizza menu at €10 – all in best *Jungle Book* style), **Restaurant Hakuna Matata** (an African safari adventure, with spiced chicken, fish nuggets, lamb kebab and a shrimp and tuna salad) and **Restaurant Agrabah Café** (a Mediterranean-African medley of dishes, including meze, couscous, tajines and fabulous pastries, all in an oriental souk setting). **Café de la Brousse** and **Captain Hook's Galley** offer various sandwiches, hot dogs, ice creams and drinks.

Shopping brings an additional

6

array of possibilities here, with **Indiana Jones™ Adventure Outpost** (safari accessories and Indy souvenirs) and **Le Coffre du Capitaine** (as you exit the Pirates ride, and with a suitable range of sea-themed treasures and toys) the pick of the bunch. The remarkable Agrabah Bazaar includes **Les Tresors de Scheherazade, La Reine des Serpents, L'Echoppe d'Aladdin**, as well as a fine Arabian-style sweetshop.

Fantasyland

Having arrived in the Theme Park's largest 'land' via Adventureland, here you will find the biggest selection of rides and the most concentrated fun for under 8s. This is the stuff of pure fantasy and the whimsical creativity on show is first class, from the huge castle down to the tiny detail of the clock façade on 'it's a small world'. Unfortunately, it is usually the most crowded section of the Theme Park, with the queues building up quickly from mid-morning and rarely abating until early evening (when it is open until 11pm). Parts of Fantasyland at the back also close from 9pm to prepare for the evening fireworks, so don't think you have the place to yourself all of a sudden!

If you have young children, this should really be your first port of call as it is likely to offer the most candidates for 'favourite ride' and it is not unknown for families to spend virtually all day here.

If you are here for 'rope drop' (highly recommended), you should head straight through the castle and try to do the Carousel, Dumbo and Peter Pan in quick succession, as these three are all terribly slow-loading rides where the queues build up almost immediately and remain painfully slow throughout the day. Excluding Peter Pan but including the Mad Hatter's Tea Cups (another

BRIT TIP: A 'secret' route goes from the main entrance all the way to the heart of Fantasyland, mainly under cover in case of rain. Take the Liberty Arcade up Main Street USA, turn sharp left into Frontierland, walk straight through Fort Comstock and follow the covered walkway into Adventureland, skirt round the side of the Restaurant Agrabah and Les Tresors de Scheherazade (briefly in the open), then pick up the walkway alongside the restaurant Au Chalet de la Marionnette and you end up at the Peter Pan ride. It is also a quick way OUT of Fantasyland when the Theme Park is busy.

slow-loader), you might also be inclined to say 'We waited all that time for THAT?' at the end of the ride. That is to say, they are not terribly exciting for grown-ups, being basically just re-themed versions of standard fairground rides. However, children will almost certainly demand to ride Dumbo at least once and, if you have managed to get it under your belt without waiting half an hour or more (and the line usually peaks at a mind-numbing hour), you will have done pretty well!

Taking Fantasyland in a clockwise direction starting at the castle, you have no less than 14 main attractions from which to choose, plus seven restaurants and seven shops that include some of the most original gift items in the Theme Park.

Le Château de la Belle au Bois Dormant (Sleeping Beauty Castle):

This is a draw in its own right having two highly contrasting things to see. **La Galerie de la Belle au Bois Dormant** is easy to miss as you scamper through, but is actually upstairs in the castle and tells the story in pictureboards and words (in French) of Sleeping Beauty. Check out the beautiful Renaissance-style tapestries which line the walls and the stunning stained-glass windows. You can also walk along an external balcony which provides a great view from both sides of the castle. AA. Underneath *le château* and accessible via three different portals (including a back door of Merlin's shop, down a winding stone staircase), is the magnificent **La Tanière du Dragon**, or dragon's lair. Here, the creature who turned many a would-be saviour of Sleeping Beauty to toast lurks in steamy, underground splendour, wrapped in reptilian fashion around the stalactites and stalagmites, occasionally rearing his audio-animatronic head to threaten fire and brimstone on all those who dare to disturb his slumbers. In the semi-darkness, it really is a convincing beast (look at the steady 'breathing' movement of its chest!) and is usually far too menacing for under-5s. TTT (for under 8s).

Stepping through the castle's rear gateway brings you to a courtyard and a great kids' photo opportunity

with the **Sword in the Stone**. Immediately in front of you then is **Le Carrousel de Lancelot**, a fairly standard horsey roundabout which youngsters still seem to love even if queuing can take an age and Mum and Dad would really rather be doing something (anything!) else. AA (TTTT for under 5s).

Blanche-Neige et les Sept Nains (The Adventures of Snow White): Right next door, this is a typically Disney kiddie ride which is a fairly dark journey into the cartoon world of the classic animated film. The soundtrack is purely in French, which detracts a little if you are unfamiliar with the story (but then, how many people is that likely to be?), and all kids can relate to this mildly scary trip into the realm of the Wicked Witch, her evil plans and the suitably happy ending. Under 5s may find parts of it distinctly menacing, but my 4-year-old was okay once he had got over the initial worries of being in the dark and was happy to ride it again several times (shouting 'Boo!' at the witch on the way round!). AAA (or TTT for under 8s).

Pinocchio's Fantastic Journey: Following on is another dark ride, this time in the company of Jiminy Cricket showing his attempts to keep the wooden puppet-boy on the straight and narrow. Again, it is a touch intense for the real young 'uns (especially with the surprise menace of the whale), but most kids find it fun rather than frightening. The special effect at the end with the Blue Fairy is well worth seeing. AAA (TTT for under 8s).

Dumbo the Flying Elephant: Needing little explanation, this is a standard fairground whirligig with elephants as your flying 'vehicle' (albeit without the requisite flapping ears, which is my main reservation about the ride). The front-seat passengers get to make the elephant go up and down while spinning

6

round and that's about it. There is little to look at while you are queuing (and the lines move painfully slowly) and the music is horribly repetitive after a while but kids all seem to get a buzz out of piloting their elephant and it is a highly visible ride, hence hard for parents to ignore! Head here first thing in the morning or expect to queue for an hour or so (the crowds do ease off a little during the parades, but there is no substitute for doing this ride early on). TT (TTTT for under 8s).

Peter Pan's Flight: Next door to Dumbo, this is Fantasyland's other serious queue-builder. It has the saving grace of being a FastPass ride, so, provided you arrive before mid-afternoon, you can benefit from the ability to return with only a minimal wait at the appointed time. Once you do, you board your pirate ship for a ride up, up and away over the streets of London, turn right at the first star and straight on to morning, all the way to Neverland and a close encounter with Captain Hook and his bunch of inept pirates.

It is another indoor dark ride (very dark as you go through the star-lit portion), but the overhead mechanism of your 'ship' and the elaborate scenery combine to create the right illusion of visiting this cartoon world. Usually a big hit with all the family and a must-do ride as far as the kids are concerned, so try to take advantage of the FP opportunity. Be aware that the waiting time can often top an hour here and much of the queuing area is out in the open, so your best bet, if the FPs have all gone (as often happens in high season by 2pm), is to leave it as late as possible or wait until a parade has just started. AAAA (TTTTT for under 8s).

Step out of Peter Pan, turn left and you come to the **Fantasy Festival Stage**, a showcase for various visiting school bands, singers and dance acts (billed under the heading of Magic Music Days) a number of times every month, as well as the venue for some of the Christmas festivities.

> BRIT TIP: When not in use, the Fantasy Festival Stage actually makes a handy place to sit in peace and quiet and sip a drink or munch a snack.

To the right of the Festival Stage is the entrance to the **Fantasyland Railroad Station** and this will usually get you back to Main Street USA much quicker than walking if there is no serious queue.

Now, all these attractions so far are relatively faithful copies of existing Disney rides, but the next three are all *Disneyland Resort Paris* originals.

Alice's Curious Labyrinth: An interactive maze leading up to the Queen of Hearts' castle, this seems to have almost universal appeal for children up to about 12, with a whole range of *Alice in Wonderland* tricks and motifs along the way, including amusing signage, squirting fountains (kids *really* gravitate towards these, trying to catch the water as it 'jumps' from fountain to fountain), an encounter with the hookah-smoking Caterpillar and several scrapes with the Queen of Hearts and her guards (in various audio-animatronic guises). It is fairly gentle stuff but keeps youngsters (and their parents) amused for a good 15–20 minutes and is another ideal place to visit when waits at Peter Pan and Dumbo are hitting an hour. AAA.

Passing further along and under the railway bridge brings you to the little area right at the back of Fantasyland which gets overlooked by some. But, if you have young children, this is somewhere you won't want to miss, both for the instant kiddie appeal and the relatively short queues here.

Le Pays des Contes de Fées: This is a gentle boat ride into a fairytale world of miniature depictions of stories like *Snow White*, *Peter and the Wolf*, *The Wizard of Oz*, *Beauty and the Beast* and *The Little Mermaid*. For the *Aladdin* section, your boat is 'swallowed up' by the giant lion's mouth cave from the story, which can be a little daunting for the youngest passengers, but the whole thing proceeds at barely walking pace, so you have plenty of time to ease any apprehensions. AAA.

> **BRIT TIP:** If you are at Le Pays des Contes de Fées at any other time than peak periods, the boat ride is usually a walk-on attraction and has the great benefit for youngsters of being able to take them straight back on for another go if they enjoy it.

Casey Jr – le Petit Train du Cirque: Another guaranteed hit for the under 8 brigade. In reality, it is a fairly tame, junior-sized coaster, themed in eye-catching style after the circus train in Dumbo. Some of the cars are designed like animal cages, others are open and, of course, two can sit up front in the 'engine'. It glides smoothly along for some 5 minutes, encountering a couple of mild dips and gentle bends, but it gives just the right illusion of excitement to those of the requisite age (and any nervous parents!). Indeed, my youngest – then aged 4 – must have set some sort of record for riding this five times in a row with great glee, delighting in trying to sit in every

different seat, front and back, along the way! AAA (TTTT for under 5s).

As you exit this two-ride miniland, you pass the disused Le Pirouette Du Vie Moulin, a bigwheel type ride which proved unworkable with even moderate queues and which has quietly been abandoned. It still looks good in non-working mode but sadly that is all you get from it.

Mad Hatter's Tea Cups: Another standard fairground ride which has been given a bit of *Alice in Wonderland* top spin to make it seem a bit more than it actually is. Kids all seem to love the chance to ride in these manically whirling cups, which have a wheel to make them spin counter to the main rotation (Uuurgghhh! says I). I must admit, going round in never-decreasing circles (or so it seems) was never my cup of tea at all, but it remains a seriously popular ride, hence it is best to do this one early in the day or later in the evening. TTT.

Continuing our clockwise tour of Fantasyland brings you next to one of Disney's signature rides.

'it's a small world': Designed under the direction of Walt himself for the New York World Fair in 1964, this ride has stood the test of time amazingly well for children under 8 and remains a big hit to this day. The exterior façade is one of the most eye-catching in the Theme Park, with all manner of moving and static elements that add up to a

> **BRIT TIP:** Hang around outside 'it's a small world' at the quarter hour and watch the wonderful clock (you can hear it ticking from quite a distance) come to life with a display of moving figures in best toytown tradition.

6

wonderfully artistic collage. Inside, all it really consists of is a slow-moving boat ride through a series of highly colourful scenes featuring audio-animatronic dolls singing and dancing in various national-themed displays, from Britain to Brazil and Africa to the Arctic. It features an insidiously catchy theme tune (I challenge you NOT to be humming it by the time you exit!) and a fabulously imaginative winter-wonderland final scene, but otherwise it just highlights the clever way in which Disney's Imagineers can take a routine kind of ride and give it a whole new style and appeal.

Once again, it proves if you give it the right scale and a proportionate amount of detail (with a little sprinkle of Disney 'pixie dust'), the ordinary can become quite extraordinary. Even many adults are captivated by the spirit and vivacity of this attraction, and it is one that bears multiple rides during the day. Queues here rarely top 20 minutes and move quite steadily, so this is a good one to do at most times, but especially in the afternoon (and when it might be hot). AAAA.

Returning to the front right of the castle brings you to **Le Théâtre du Château**, which is home to **Winnie the Pooh and Friends**, a 25-minute show in the company of Christopher Robin and his bear of very little brain, plus Piglet, Rabbit, Eeyore and Tigger. It is simple, easy on the eye (and ear) material and it is usually perfect for giving under 8s a half-hour break from the non-stop ride scenario. However, beware the hard stone benches (extremely uncomfortable by the end of the show!) and the lack of any shade at all in summer (remember those hats and sunscreen). AAA.

When it comes to eating opportunities, Fantasyland has another gourmet offering in **Auberge de Cendrillon**, with an elegant ballroom-type setting and an excellent French menu. Open

11.30am–4pm, it features ravioli, risotto, roast salmon, entrecote steak and duck pâté as well as the regular burger fare, and there is also a pleasant outdoor courtyard (with Cinderella's carriage as decoration). The set meal for adults is €28 and €10 for children. The other outlets are all counter-service types and fill up quickly for lunch at even mildly busy times: **Au Chalet de la Marionnette**, which has a rear entrance opening in Adventureland, features roast chicken, burgers, salads and chips, plus a range of German desserts; **Toad Hall Restaurant**, modelled in mock English country house style, á la Wind in the Willows, and serving fish and chips, pies, sandwiches and cakes; and **Pizzeria Bella Notta**, an Italian diner, modelled after Lady and the Tramp, with a decent range of pizzas and pasta.

> BRIT TIP: Of all the counter-service restaurants in busy Fantasyland, the Pizzeria Bella Notta is likely to have the shortest queues, as it is slightly off the beaten track.

Additionally, you can grab a snack, ice cream or drink at **March Hare Refreshments, The Old Mill** and **Fantasia Gelati**. For shopping, the interlinked group in and around the castle offers some worthwhile retail therapy, with **Merlin l'Enchanteur** (a clever little 'rock-carved' boutique featuring fine crystal, glassware – hand-made while you watch – and porcelain statuettes), **La Boutique du Château** (a Christmas-orientated offering), **La Confiserie des Trois Fées** (a great sweet shop in the company of the good fairies Flora, Daisy and Burnet from *Sleeping Beauty*), and the epic **Sir Mickey's**

featuring two distinct halves –
cuddly toys, jewellery, glass and
ceramics, and children's clothes, toys,
games and souvenirs.

Discoveryland

When the Imagineers set about
designing the fifth and final 'land' of
the Theme Park, their challenge was
to come up with a new variant on a
fairly well-worn theme. In both
Anaheim and Orlando, this area had
been developed as Tomorrowland,
an unabashed attempt to predict and
present the future in a fun and
amusing way. There is a mock retro
styling about the previous examples
but that was felt to be an over-used
idea when it came to *Disneyland
Resort Paris* and the call went out for
something new.

So, the Imagineers studied their
European history and literature and
came up with a new motif, that of a
future world inspired by technology
derived from such historical
luminaries as Leonardo da Vinci and
Jules Verne. That helped to
determine the overall look and feel
of Discoveryland (a new title too, as
Tomorrowland was felt to be too
narrow a definition), hence the
styling is a kind of 'antique' future,
with much of the architecture
bowing heavily to Verne's 19th-
century images of the future.

The two principal icons – Space
Mountain and the Café Hypérion –
are magnificent re-creations of
Vernian visions and help to create a
visual stimulus that is both bold and
exciting (can you tell I quite like this
area!). The totally fanciful exterior
of Space Mountain is one of the
greatest examples of the ride
designer's art because so much of it
is totally unnecessary to the ride
itself; it is purely and simply a
statement of style that epitomises
the creativity inherent in a Disney
Theme Park, and the rides here are
pretty good, too.

Space Mountain: This is a
breathtaking blast of a ride 'From
the Earth to the Moon'. For those
unfamiliar with the Verne novel, the
setting is the Baltimore Gun Club
and the giant cannon Columbiad,
which is designed to fire a capsule as
far as the moon. You queue up
through the heart of the ride itself,
so you get a tantalising glimpse of
what's in store before you reach your
vehicle, which is 'loaded' into the
barrel of Columbiad. The dry ice
flows, the music rolls, the lights
pulsate and then … pow! You are off
at breakneck speed into 'space',
dodging close encounters with
meteorites and other cosmic
phenomena, looping the loop and
corkscrewing twice in a scintillating
coruscation of lights and barely
glimpsed obstacles. The light show
alone throughout the high-speed,
3-minute whizz is worth seeing and,
if the description sounds disturbing,
don't let it put you off. This is one
of the smoothest coasters you will
ride and it is a big-time thrill. It is
also a FastPass ride, which is vital for
peak periods as the crowds do flock
here from mid-morning onwards.
Souvenir photos of your ride are
available at the end for €12.
Restrictions: 1.32m (4ft 3in)
TTTTT.

BRIT TIP: If you don't
visit Space Mountain early
in the day and you can't get
a FastPass, return in early
evening to beat the worst of
the queues.

Les Mystères du Nautilus: As
you exit Space Mountain, you
encounter another *Disneyland Resort
Paris* original, a clever walk-through
version of Captain Nemo's famous
submarine. The realism as you go
down 'underground' on a circular
steel staircase is all encompassing,

6

bringing you into the Nautilus itself and a self-guided tour of this amazing Verne creation. Take your time to peer into all the little nooks and crannies and admire the intricate detail, and sit for a moment at one of the big, circular portholes. Is that a giant squid moving in, too close…? You'll have to check it out for yourself! Children under 7 must be accompanied by an adult here. AAA.

Orbitron – Machines Volantes: Next door is this similarly eye-catching ride, which is really only a jazzed-up version of the Dumbo ride, spinning and climbing in regulation fashion as the front-seat 'pilot' takes the controls. The clever circulation of the accompanying 'planets' really makes this ride, however, giving it the appearance of something far more intricate, and it is another one which is fun just to watch. TTT (TTTTT under 8s).

Star Tours: Behind Space Mountain is the impressive futuristic façade of Disney's wonderful collaboration with *Star Wars*™ director George Lucas. The queuing area of this alone is something of a masterpiece, as you are drawn into the make-believe world of squabbling 'droids C-3PO and R-2D2 as they prepare your Star Speeder for the light-speed trip to Endor. This is a faithful transplant of the ride in *Disneyland California* and *Disney-MGM Studios* in Orlando, with the one exception that the commentary provided by your robot pilot is all in French.

The ride itself, though, is a 24-carat thrill, as the hugely realistic Star Speeders load and lift off for outer space, where all manner of mishaps lead you into a series of adventures. This was the bee's knees when it made its debut in Anaheim in 1987 and it is still a magical experience for Disney newcomers (although those familiar with the ride from elsewhere may feel it is a little ho-hum by now). Star Tours is also another FastPass ride, which is handy because you could spend a good 45 minutes waiting in line at peak periods. There is no height restriction, but those with bad backs or necks might want to give it a miss, and it is probably too intense for under 4s. TTTT.

> BRIT TIP: Head for Discoveryland first and you can ride either Space Mountain or Star Tours without much of a queue and then pick up a FP for the other. Of the two, Star Tours draws the heaviest and most consistent crowds throughout the main part of the day.

The exit to the ride brings you into an amusing area of interactive games, **L'Astroport Services Interstellaires**, where the main attraction is the Star Course, a kind of human pinball, from which kids all get a blast (minimum height requirement 1.02m/3ft 3in).

Behind Star Tours is the **Discoveryland Railroad Station**, but this is a good one to miss at busy times as it is second only to the Main Street station for drawing long, slow-moving queues.

Honey, I Shrunk the Audience: Right next door to Star Tours, this 3-D film show is also a major Disney trademark attraction. Pioneered in all their American parks, it provides yet another variation on Theme Park thrills. Here, continuing where the two hit films left off, you enter a wacky science world of the Imagination Institute (run by the highly amusing Eric Idle), where they are about to honour the inventions of a certain professor Wayne Szalinski.

An entertaining 8-minute pre-show sets the scene for the main part of your adventure in the awards 'theatre' and then the real fun begins once you don your 3-D glasses. The inevitable on-stage mishaps are accompanied by a sequence of special effects throughout the theatre that often have the audience in hysterics (although under-5s may find it plain scary) and which it would be a shame to spoil by revealing, so just sit back and get ready to be surprised... very surprised (and beware the sneezing dog!). This is also a show that requires a full English dialogue to follow the story, hence headphones are provided for non-French speakers. AAAAA (plus TTT).

Autopia: Another attraction which you need to visit early in the day unless you want a long wait. Rather old-fashioned, this mock Grand Prix track – a 'futuristic Formula 1 circuit' – is purely for kids and sits a little awkwardly among the other more sci-fi laden offerings. It is often closed for maintenance and it is a notoriously slow-loading ride, hence the queues can touch an hour or more and move very slowly. And, unless you are under 8, you are not likely to get much of a thrill from these tame cars that run on well-defined tracks, even if they provide the basic illusion of driving. Younger children will need to be accompanied by a parent but you are not really missing much if you bypass this one. TT (TTT for under 8s).

Le Visionarium: Returning to the more inventive, this is an attraction that worked so well on its debut here it was swiftly exported to Orlando's *Magic Kingdom Park*. It offers a truly eye-catching, not to mention amusing, 20-minute film and audio-animatronic presentation in the company of the robot, Timekeeper. A 5-minute pre-show prepares you for what's in store and then you

enter the circle-vision, 360-degree auditorium, where Timekeeper proceeds to dazzle you with his time machine, which sends robotic assistant Nine Eye both backwards and forwards in time, with some comical results. The effect of the specially shot film, which completely encircles the auditorium, is quite breathtaking, but the only drawback here is the headphones you need for the English translation, which are just not good enough to keep out the rather loud French soundtrack. AAAA.

> **BRIT TIP:** Le Visionarium rarely draws serious queues, hence it is a good show to take in during the main part of the day, or when it is wet or too hot (it is air-conditioned).

6

Videopolis: Youngsters will certainly want to make a beeline for the big theatre/restaurant inside the wonderfully elaborate Café Hypérion (a homage to Jules Verne's famous airship), where another of the main shows takes place up to six times a day. Until the beginning of April 2004 it is **Mickey's Show Time** (a 25-minute song-and-dance pastiche of various well-known Disney films such as *Aladdin* and

> **BRIT TIP:** Between shows, the Videopolis stage screens classic Disney cartoons, so, if you need a rest in air-conditioned comfort or shelter from the rain, or if your kids just can't face another queue, come into the Café Hypérion, grab a drink or a snack and kick back for a while.

Jungle Book), then from June it will change to an all-new **Lion King Show**. Geared as a classic, fun, family show, expect a true Hakuna Matata experience as Timon, Pumba and Rafiki introduce a selection of musical highlights from the classic animated film.

People start queuing for the theatre seating part of Videopolis a good 30 minutes before the show, and this is certainly the best place from which to watch. However, you can find a table up at the back (in the restaurant seating part of the cafe) and see perfectly well without having to join another queue. You can even make it a mealtime by grabbing some food from the burger-orientated cafe. The first show of the day is usually not over-subscribed either, so it is a good one to programme into your plan of campaign if you can. AAA (AAAA for under 8s). NB: Mickey's Show Time, which made its debut in March 2003, was the third show here in three years, hence it is likely to change again soon.

As a final word on the attractions, the inevitable video games make an appearance in the shape of **Arcade Alpha** and **Beta** on either side of the lower entrance to Videopolis, while a third and larger option is **Arcade Omega** just to the left of the main entrance to Discoveryland. Older children and young teens who need a break from the family shackles for a while can head to any of these and shoot up a T-Rex or similar, or play football, air hockey or otherwise indulge in video fun. TTT.

When it comes to eating, the aforementioned **Café Hypérion** is worth investigating even if you don't visit the counter-service diner, which serves cheeseburgers, chicken burgers and chicken nuggets. **Pizza Planet** (easy to miss, but it's just to the right of Honey, I Shrunk the Audience) is a rather disappointing offering if you expect something out of the *Toy Story* film.

BRIT TIP: Pizza Planet can be a bit of a godsend if you have under 5s in need of a Theme Park break. It has a soft-play climb and slide area which allows them to run around and let off some steam, while you sit and watch with a drink!

The **Rocket Café** at the back of Space Mountain offers an additional few snacks and drinks which you can consume in relative peace and quiet at the tables outside Pizza Planet.

There are also two main gift stores, the elaborate **Constellations** (the usual range of souvenirs but a ceiling twinkling with a 'universe' of stars) and **Star Traders** (for all your *Star Wars*™ related merchandise, other space toys and sports gear).

Parades and tours

If that is the full detail on each of the five 'lands', you have several other sources of great entertainment along the way. Chief among these is the daily parade (or parades if you are here in high season or a special event like Halloween or Christmas). The new (in May 2003) **Princess Parade** is the main event here, except for the

BRIT TIP: Be aware people start staking out some of the best spots to view the various parades – along Main Street USA and around the Central Plaza – a good 30 minutes in advance. At peak periods, they will start gathering an HOUR beforehand.

festive period from mid-November to early January when it is replaced by the Christmas Parade (described in Chapter 2). If you have never seen a Disney parade, this is a genuine must-see experience. Yes, the queues at many attractions do tend to shorten a little during the daily parade, but it is a shame to miss something as creative and dynamic as this just to take in another ride.

> **BRIT TIP:** For the main daily parades, the section of the route in Fantasyland is less crowded than elsewhere, while the corner of the Town Square by the Discovery Arcade is also a good place to wait as it is often overlooked and offers some shade when it's hot.

Children are truly captivated by the scale and elaboration of the huge floats, as well as the chance to see a multitude of their favourite characters at fairly close quarters. The music is memorable, the dancing amazingly energetic (especially given the heat in summer) and the splendour of floats such as Steamboat Willie featuring Mickey and Minnie, Snow White (with her Prince and the Seven Dwarfs), Beauty and the Beast, and the famous Pumpkin Coach of Cinderella and Prince Charming is totally enchanting. Sleeping Beauty and Prince Phillip brave Maleficent's transformation into the fire-breathing dragon, while Aladdin and Jasmine drift by on their Magic Carpet. Between the floats, a cortege of elegant footmen and dancers move effortlessly along to the main theme tune, stopping at strategic moments to begin the elaborately choreographed Royal Ball. The whole spectacle takes a good 25–30 minutes to pass by, and you will use up a LOT of film in the process – if you don't end up being totally side-tracked by watching children's faces around you. AAAAA.

The new **Disney's Fantillusion** parade, which has replaced the Main Street Electrical Parade, adds to the picture for the high summer and winter season evenings (usually around 10.30pm), and is equally stunning. It features an eye-popping cavalcade of Disney favourites in a high-tech setting of glittering lights and dazzling floats. This completely captivating parade comes in three parts and unfolds with an almost balletic grace, first as Mickey himself brings the Gift of Light, then a darker section as the Disney villains threaten to take over (with some spectacular special effects as Jafar transforms into a serpent, Maleficent becomes the wicked dragon and the winged Chernabog commands fire), and finally a joyful conclusion as the heroes and heroines, princes and princesses get together with Minnie to save the day.

> **BRIT TIP:** You can watch the Fantillusion Parade from the steps of the Railroad Station on Town Square, then, once it has passed by, take one of the arcades up to the Central Plaza to be ready for the fireworks while people are still watching the parade along Main Street USA!

It features a fabulous soundtrack by Bruce Healy and a seemingly endless fairytale pageant of shimmering, twinkling lights, and the overall effect is so utterly thrilling, even by Disney standards, it is worth keeping the kids up to see it, even if it is usually past their bedtime. The whole parade stops at various points for a few well-rehearsed routines from the magnificently costumed dancers, and it can take a good 30 minutes to pass by. But, whatever you do, don't miss this one! AAAAA+.

The **Halloween Parade** adds to the daily fun throughout October (check your park map for timings) and is another visual riot of creepy-costumed capers, song and dance, with various characters joining the extravaganza. Here, the Disney Villains have usurped the stage occupied by the Princes and Princesses for a darker (but still fun) cavalcade of ghosts, goblins and witches, with some wonderfully inventive, skeleton-inspired touches. AAAA.

It is worth taking a mental step back from all the clever artistry of the floats to appreciate the non-stop energy and quality of the many dancers throughout every parade, who keep up their efforts for every second of every performance, day in and day out. From talking to various Cast Members, I am aware of the immense dedication it takes, but they also have a lot of fun along the way and get a real kick out of seeing the reaction they get from their audience – especially the kids. So don't hesitate to smile and wave back as they certainly deserve all the encouragement and appreciation you can muster.

BRIT TIP: The best place from which to watch the nightly fireworks is in front of the castle or at the end of Main Street USA. The show is choreographed with, and symmetrically around, the great *château* and the visual effect is stunning.

In high season (summer and Christmas), there is also the nightly finale of **Tinker Bell's Fantasy in the Sky fireworks** and the **Sparkling Christmas fireworks** extravaganza which bring down the curtain on proceedings at 11pm each evening. This magnificently choreographed and music-coordinated event is the perfect way to conclude any Disney visit, as the company's expertise with pyrotechnic shows is legendary and well merited. Few people have the vision and capability to present fireworks in such a thrilling and well-balanced way, and the effect of

BRIT TIP: For some genuine Disney shopping bargains, check out the Plaza West Boutique, just to the right of the *Disneyland Hotel* as you exit the Theme Park. They stock a range of previous season's merchandise at greatly reduced prices, which can be well worth checking out if you have kids.

seeing the many extravagant starbursts over the Sleeping Beauty Castle is breathtaking. Be warned, however, the fireworks ARE pretty loud, and small children are often scared by the sound and scale of the shows.

Want to learn more about the *Disneyland Park*? Well, sign up for a **Guided Tour** at City Hall early in the day (subject to availability; maximum of 25 people) and you can take a full walking tour in the company of a highly knowledgeable Cast Member to point out the interesting bits. At €15 for adults (free for children 3–11), the tours last almost 2 hours and will definitely give you a novel insight

The Disneyland Park with children

Here is a rough guide to the rides that appeal to different age groups. Obviously, children vary enormously in their likes and dislikes but, as a general rule, you can be fairly sure the following will have most appeal to the ages concerned (also taking into account the height restrictions):

Under 5s
Disneyland Railroad, Main Street Vehicles, Thunder Mesa Riverboats, Pocahontas Indian Village, Critter Corral, La Plage au Pirates (Pirates Beach) play area, La Cabane des Robinsons, The Tarzan™ Encounter (although check the volume isn't too loud for young ears), Winnie the Pooh and Friends, Blanche-Neige et les Sept Nains (Snow White), Pinocchio's Fantastic Journey, Le Carrousel de Lancelot, Peter Pan's Flight, Dumbo, 'it's a small world', Le Pays des Contes de Fées, Casey Jr, Alice's Curious Labyrinth, Le Visionarium, Orbitron (not recommended for babies), Autopia, Les Mystères du Nautilus, Mickey's Show Time/Lion King Show, Princess Parade.

6–8s
All the above, plus Phantom Manor (with parental discretion), Fort Comstock, Rustler Roundup Shootin' Gallery, Big Thunder Mountain, Adventure Isle, Pirates of the Caribbean, Le Passage Enchanté d'Aladdin, La Tanière du Dragon, Mad Hatter's Tea Cups, Star Tours, Honey, I Shrunk the Audience.

9–12s
Phantom Manor, Fort Comstock, Rustler Roundup Shootin' Gallery, Big Thunder Mountain, The Tarzan™ Encounter, Pirates of the Caribbean, Adventure Isle, Indiana Jones™ and the Temple of Peril: Backwards!, La Cabane des Robinsons, Peter Pan's Flight, Mad Hatter's Tea Cups, Alice's Curious Labyrinth, Arcade Alpha, Beta and Omega, Le Visionarium, Orbitron, Space Mountain, Les Mystères du Nautilus, Honey, I Shrunk the Audience, Star Tours.

Over 12s
Phantom Manor, Big Thunder Mountain, Rustler Roundup Shootin' Gallery, The Tarzan™ Encounter, Pirates of the Caribbean, Adventure Isle, Indiana Jones™ and the Temple of Peril: Backwards!, Mad Hatter's Tea Cups, Arcade Alpha, Beta and Omega, Le Visionarium, Orbitron, Space Mountain, Honey, I Shrunk the Audience, Star Tours.

6

into the creation of this truly magnificent entertainment venue.

And that, folks, is *Disneyland Park* in all its detailed splendour. Hopefully, after a day here (even when the crowds are at their heaviest), you will agree with me in judging this to be a work of art in the business of having fun. Take the time to acquaint yourself with all that's here in advance, and you should be well prepared to get the most out of this immensely diverse range of attractions. As I advise for visiting any Disney park anywhere in the world, try to take some time along the way to slow down and appreciate all the fine, intricate detail that's involved in the park.

There is just so much packed into this Theme Park in particular, it would be a shame if you went home without seeing the history of Dapper Dan's barber shop, the nostalgia of the two arcades and the whimsy of restaurants like Pizzeria Bella Notte and the Blue Lagoon. It is a wonderfully complete and immersive environment that really does transport you a million miles away from everyday life, so make sure you get the most out of it.

A new development to look out for is the introduction of **Pal Mickey**, an electronic toy-cum-tour guide which has been pioneered at *Walt Disney World Resort Florida*. This clever little gimmick takes the form of a 30-cm (1-ft)-high cuddly Mickey with a computer-chip heart, making him a genuine Theme Park companion. Providing Disney can crack the multi-lingual barrier, your plush Pal will act as a cute guide around the Theme Parks (offering suggestions for things to do at given times or making interesting observations) and a handy source of amusement for children while waiting in queues (with three different games to play). The American version offers Mickey for hire (at around $10) or to buy (for $50), and I would expect a similar arrangement and pricing if or when he is introduced to *Disneyland Resort Paris*.

But we can't stop here. There is a whole new park to explore yet. It's on to *Walt Disney Studios Park…*!

> BRIT TIP: Unless you are particularly speedy in leaving the Theme Park at closing time, you might be better off taking the 15–20-minute walk back to the big hotels such as *Disney's Hotel Santa Fe*, *Disney's Cheyenne Hotel* and *Disney's Newport Bay Club*, as the crowds at the shuttle bus stop can mean another lengthy wait.

Walt Disney Studios Park

(or, Lights, Cameras, Action!)

If the *Disneyland Park* represents the very essence of Disney magic and imagination, where does that leave the new *Walt Disney Studios Park?* That's a good question if you expect more of the same after visiting the original park and it is a moot point as to which you should visit first as a newcomer to the resort.

Perhaps the best answer is to treat this new, smaller development as a completely different entity to its bigger brother, something that complements the first park but doesn't attempt to copy its formula of non-stop rides and fun. There are far fewer attractions packed in, but what there are tend to be much bigger in scope and offer a vastly different experience. Put simply, if the *Disneyland Park* is the Theme Park of rides, then the *Walt Disney Studios Park* is the Theme Park of shows.

There is also a major difference in the geography and topography, in addition to the newer park being just half the size of its older sibling (although with scope for expansion in years to come). It consists of just four main areas and there are no great distinguishing features of the interior three once you have passed through the entrance complex known as the Front Lot. It is also an easy park to negotiate, and getting from one area to another for the various shows is a lot less

problematical than it can be at the older park. You can also walk from one end to the other in little more than 5 minutes and it positively invites you to step outside for lunch in *Disney Village* as the simplicity and convenience are paramount.

Another notable difference is in the *sound* of the two parks. In the *Disneyland Park*, the accompanying music is really there only as a background to all the fun and rides. In the *Walt Disney Studios Park*, the music is right up front, setting the scene and providing a soundtrack almost everywhere you go, most notably in the Backlot area. This dramatic musical accompaniment underscores the film-orientated nature of the Theme Park and adds an extra layer to the overall theming.

Get with the theme

Although there are rumours of new rides being added in the next couple of years (the Tower of Terror™ in *Walt Disney World's Disney-MGM Studios* is the one most Disney fans would like to see here and is a favourite with the rumour-mongers!), at the time of writing there are just nine out-and-out main attractions, plus a daily parade, on which to concentrate. Of course, this being a Disney park, there are always some delightful extras along the way and, in the *Walt Disney Studios Park*, they go in for something they call

Streetmosphere, a series of mini street theatres, musical acts and comedians who add a lot to the atmosphere and fun.

The depth and elaboration of the theming, both architecturally and in the landscaping, is not on the same scale as the *Disneyland Park* either, although there is also an argument that the Studios environment is actually too realistic for its own good. As one Cast Member told me, 'Well, our theme is a movie studio. What do you expect a movie studio to look like, apart from a collection of big, fairly bland buildings?' Of course, there is a fair bit more to it than that, but it is a pertinent point.

The whole idea is to surround you with the magic of the movies and, to that end, the collection of large studio soundstages which house most of the attractions can look a touch functional by comparison with the neighbouring park. However, Disney's Imagineers are adding extra touches of embellishment externally all the time, and the internal effects are rarely short of spectacular (just wait until you walk into the Rock 'n' Roller Coaster for the first time!).

The one possible concern for parents with younger children is there isn't as much for them to do here as next door. There is only one main kiddie ride and one show that's purposefully for them, while several attractions are definitely not for young eyes and ears (too loud or too scary). The daily parade, however, is a genuine source of family fun, and the Streetmosphere acts add to it all. I found that my children were well entertained for most of the day (see What We Did Last Summer, opposite).

Staying dry

The other clever element of the *Walt Disney Studios Park* is the fact nearly all of the attractions are either inside or under cover, which is vital in winter and quite welcome in the hotter months, too. With the exception of the Flying Carpets Over Agrabah, they are also a much longer and more involving experience. Several of the shows last half an hour or more and that means the time passes in bigger 'chunks' than it does in the *Disneyland Park*, hence you can spend longer doing fewer things here. It is unlikely you will find yourself galloping from ride to ride as you tend to do next door, but there should still be enough to keep you occupied for a full day (with the option to move between parks with the multi-day Passport tickets – see page 85).

Another difference between the Theme Parks is the eating opportunities. While the *Disneyland Park* has a comprehensive mix of restaurants, cafes and snack bars, the *Walt Disney Studios Park* is limited to just four counter-service options, plus a series of snack wagons. With *Disney Village* just 5 minutes' walk from the front gates, it is easy to argue you have all the choice you need there (plus a chance to escape the crowds), but I would still like to see at least one full-service restaurant in the Theme Park to provide a bit of breadth and add to the studio style (anyone who has eaten in the Sci Fi Dine-In Theater or the 50s Prime Time Diner at *Disney-MGM Studios* in Orlando will know what I mean!). However, quite interestingly, there are also fewer merchandise opportunities throughout this park and you don't feel quite so much a target for the big sell.

Right on queue

What about the queues? This was a prime concern of mine when I attended the big preview event in March 2002 as, while the attractions themselves were all unfailingly enjoyable, I could foresee some fairly long waits in places. Summer

2002 was certainly busy enough and seemed to provide a good test of all aspects of the Theme Park's crowd management. With very few exceptions, the attractions coped well with everything that was thrown at them, with only the Studio Tram Tour collecting some formidably long queues. Queuing for the big Stunt Show Spectacular could also be an ordeal unless you were there half an hour early, as the line was snaking out into the main concourse of the Backlot area from midday to mid-afternoon, but it is a huge arena and most people usually get in.

The final big bonus with this park is that, even in high season, the crowds tail off considerably after the 3.30pm Disney Cinema Parade. That means, if you want to do some of the rides with virtually no queues, or take in the final show of something like Cinémagique, either hang on right to the end or come back into the Theme Park at about 5pm and you should enjoy things like Rock 'n' Roller Coaster and the Flying Carpets almost unhindered (my record is five goes on Rock 'n' Roller in the final hour of the day!).

Okay, without any further preamble, let me introduce you to – the *Walt Disney Studios Park*.

Just walking up to the gates of the new park should provide quite a thrill, as the epic icon in front of you makes it clear what's in store – film adventure and lots of fun in the inimitable Mickey style. The 33m (108ft) high water tower edifice (based on the same structure at Disney's home studios in Burbank, California), topped by a large pair of mouse ears (I kid you not), is called… wait for it… the Earful Tower (!), and sets out the visual style

---

What we did last summer

Until I took the whole family along – with my boys then aged 6 and 4 – I was of the opinion there was a lot less to do here for young children than the older park, where kids will usually keep going for as long as you let them! Our experience was extremely informative, as we had nearly a full day at *Walt Disney Studios Park*, and both boys were keen to go back the next day to see the amazing Stunt Show again. Admittedly, we didn't arrive until almost 11am, but it was then a fairly non-stop experience until the 6pm closing, at which time we called a halt for dinner back in the *Disneyland Park*. There was only a minimal wait between attractions, too, and the judicious use of the FastPass system allows you to bypass several long queues at various points.

The regular availability of the characters in the Animation Courtyard area was another plus, as the opportunity to grab autographs and pose for photos with their Disney favourites actually proved a stronger lure than some of the rides. In addition, the Streetmosphere acts are well suited to holding children's attention for a while and my eldest boy was often first to form a crowd when any of the street performers appeared!

The visual fun and imagination of the Disney Studio 1 area in the Front Lot was also a big hit with all of us, although it was a shame we weren't allowed inside the Rock 'n' Roller Coaster building just for a look, as both boys were well under the height restriction yet would have enjoyed seeing the clever film pre-show and a view of the ride itself. We have since put the repeat factor to the test and found it remains an all-day experience, with the Stunt Show providing almost never-ending fascination, along with the Studio Tram Tour, Animagique and Cinémagique.

The Walt Disney Studios Park at a glance

See full-colour map opposite page 128.

Location	Off Exit 14 of the A4 autoroute, proceed to the clearly signed car park; or turn right out of the Marne-la-Vallée RER and TGV station; or through the *Disney Village* if staying at a resort hotel
Size	25 hectares (62 acres) in four areas
Hours	10am–6pm winter and spring off-peak weekdays, 9am–6pm weekends; 9am–6pm all summer
Admission	**Under 3,** free; **3–11s** €25 (1-Day Passport, low season), €29 (1-Day Passport, high season), €69 (3-Day Passport, low season), €80 (3-Day Passport, high season), €129 (Classic Annual Passport) and €199 (Fantasia Annual Passport); **adults** (12+) €29 (1-Day Passport, low season), €39 (1-Day Passport, high season), €79 (3-Day Passport, low season), €107 (3-Day Passport, high season), €149 (Classic Annual Passport) and €229 (Fantasia Annual Passport)
Parking	€7.50
Pushchairs	€6.50 (Pushchair shop to left of Studio Photo, on right hand side of entrance courtyard)
Wheelchairs	€6.50 (Pushchair shop)
Top Attractions	Rock 'n' Roller Coaster starring Aerosmith, Moteurs…Action! Stunt Show Spectacular, Studio Tram Tour, Cinémagique
Don't Miss	Disney Cinema Parade, Rhythmo Technico, Streetmosphere performers
Hidden Costs	**Meals** Burger, chips and coke €5.95 3-course meal €20 (Rendez-Vous des Stars) **Kids' meal** €5 (at all cafes and snack bars; €10.90 at Rendez-Vous des Stars) **T-shirts** €10.50–26 **Souvenirs** €1–182 **Sundries** Face painting €8–12

in no uncertain terms, as well as providing a handy marker for much of the way around the park.

If you approach from the main car park, the Studios will be straight ahead of you as you come through the moving walkways. From *Disney Village* just bear left past the Gaumont Cinemas and, from the bus or train station, continue straight on, passing *Disney Village* on your left. The park is subdivided into four main areas, although there is no great visual distinction between them, and your adventure starts as soon as you walk through the imposing gates.

Talking tactics

Unlike the *Disneyland Park*, this is not somewhere you need to be right on opening time (although you will be able to get most of the rides done in the first hour if you do). With so much of the Theme Park's entertainment geared around the big show times such as the Stunt Show and Cinémagique, you can arrive in more leisurely style and head first for the attraction which most appeals to you, fairly safe in the knowledge you can usually get into most of them with only minimal queuing (although you will find the crowds at their heaviest from midday to 4pm in high season).

BRIT TIP: Having said the shows all have good capacities, it is still advisable to arrive 15–20 minutes early if possible so you will benefit from being among the first to be seated.

Probably your best plan is to grab a FastPass (FP) for one of the two attractions with the queue-busting system (see page 87) before going to one of the shows. The Studio Tram

Tour builds up the longest wait times (up to 90 minutes at peak periods), so it is highly advisable to come here first. Alternatively, if you have younger children, they will certainly want to ride the Flying Carpets Over Agrabah and this is one where you can use the FP system. So make this your first port of call before heading for something like Animagique or the Art of Animation.

Coaster fans will want to make a beeline for the fabulous Rock 'n' Roller Coaster starring Aerosmith and you can grab a FP for this one and then take in, say, the Stunt Show or Armageddon: Special Effects. Surprisingly, Rock 'n' Roller doesn't draw huge crowds (apart from just after the Stunt Show), and you can usually get a FP at any time (the others do tend to run out later in the day). It also has the benefit of being almost a walk-on ride early in the day and in late afternoon. Additionally, each of the main show attractions is quite capacious and it is rare for everyone waiting not to get in.

Front Lot

Once through the turnstiles, you come into a lovely Spanish-style courtyard that marks the entrance to the first main area, the Front Lot. This is the 'office' part of the Theme Park and houses the more functional elements such as pushchair and wheelchair hire, lost property, lost children centre, baby care centre, first aid station, cash dispenser and currency exchange. You will also find the **Studio Services** here, for any queries you may have about the park (like when and where to find the characters and which Streetmosphere acts will be performing). Visitors with disabilities can also pick up a *Guide for Guests with Special Needs* if they haven't done so already and the Blue Card which allows access to all attractions (see pages 25–6).

This area is an extremely elegant piece of design, with the central Sorcerer Mickey fountain, flanked by palm trees, providing a great photo opportunity. The left-hand side of the courtyard is taken up by the **Walt Disney Studios Store**, the Theme Park's biggest shop, while on the right is **Studio Photo**, for all your photographic requirements (although again, it is better to bring your own).

In the early morning, you can meet several **Disney characters** here, and it is worth pausing to enjoy the classic 1930s-style architecture as the Theme Park transports you into the world of the movies, Hollywood style.

You really get the full effect, though, as you walk through the doors of **Disney Studio 1** (remember to pick up a Park Map as you enter), which is almost an attraction in its own right, even if it is in many ways just a covered version of Main Street USA in the *Disneyland Park*. It is 70m (230ft) long, 35m (115ft) wide and 20m (66ft) high, making it the second-largest 'soundstage' in Europe (okay, it isn't actually a working facility, but the impression is pretty good). The overall effect is as if you have walked into the middle of a Hollywood film shoot, with all the paraphernalia of movie-making everywhere you look.

BRIT TIP: Need to get your photos developed in a hurry? Visit the Legends of Hollywood store in Disney Studio 1 and you can get your films processed in 2 hours. While it's not cheap, it is a great way to ensure those happy snaps do actually come out (or if they need to be re-taken!).

The film 'sets' are all unfinished and provide almost a kaleidoscopic montage of scenery in each direction, with a series of facades and hoardings, which change the perspective in a multitude of ways with the aid of some brilliant lighting effects. Down the left side is the **Legends of Hollywood** store, while the right flank is given over entirely to the **Restaurant en Coulisse**.

BRIT TIP: Restaurant en Coulisse gets pretty busy from midday to 2pm but is ideal to visit between 3 and 4pm for a late lunch or early tea.

The shop is cleverly disguised behind no less than six different facades, giving the impression of a whole movie 'street' modelled on various Hollywood stores – both real and imagined – from the 1920s to 1960s. Designs that stand out include Last Chance Gas (a mock Route 66 petrol station), The Alexandria Theater (a classic Los Angeles 'movie palace') and The Gossip Column (a news and magazine stand) and, of course, you can buy a whole range of film-related souvenirs as well as the usual Disney souvenir merchandise inside.

On the other side, the restaurant is the combination of another six imaginary 'sets', with the counter-service diner concealed behind such legendary establishments as Schwab's Pharmacy (a classic 1940s' American drugstore), The Brown Derby (the famous Hollywood restaurant in the shape of a bowler hat), Club Swankadero (an imaginary nightclub), The Gunga Den (a well-known bar) and the Liki Tiki (a wonderful South Seas tropical-themed bar, complete with thatched roof).

Here, the fare is French continental style for breakfast and standard burger style the rest of the day, with pizza, lasagne and salads as your alternatives. The Menu Mickey (a double bacon burger with chips, either a chocolate snack bar or doughnut and a soft drink) is €9, while a Maxi Menu (double chicken-grill burger) is €11.

There are actually no less than 670 seats for dining here, so it absorbs a lot of people, and the upstairs terracing – 'Carmen's Veranda' (ouch!) – also provides a great look at the whole of Studio 1.

> BRIT TIP: The Studio 1 area has a handy Restaurant Reservations kiosk, where you can book meals for later in the day at the full-service restaurants in *Disney Village* and the *Disneyland Park*.

Linger in Disney Studio 1 for a while and you are likely to meet **CinéFollies**, a group of improvisational artists who are 'filming' various comedy movie shoots that inevitably involve much chaos, a lot of fun – and members of their audience. Studio 1 is also home to three excellent musical groups, who provide various live entertainments almost throughout the day. The **Fabulous Dandies** perform classic American musical standards, the **Keystone Cops** add a slapstick touch to their renditions of classic black-and-white era film themes, and the **Studio 1 Orchestra** provides some big-band style for more well-known movie scores.

Animation Courtyard

Turn right as you exit the doors of Disney Studio 1 and you are immediately in the area of the

Waiting for opening

If you arrive half an hour before the official opening time, you will still be admitted through the main turnstiles of the *Walt Disney Studios Park*. This brings you into the Courtyard, where you are likely to meet Goofy or Pluto as they welcome you to the Theme Park. Children can stop for a photo and an autograph, and you can then pass into Disney Studio 1 and either have a bite to eat or browse the shops. Finally, at the appointed opening hour (either 9 or 10am), the crowd starts to gather at one end in front of the doors through to the rest of the Theme Park and, with a final countdown, the Cast Members open all the doors simultaneously and allow the eager throng through.

If you are looking for the thrills first, turn left and head straight for the Backlot area and Rock 'n' Roller Coaster, or go straight ahead and pick up the Tram Tour (with its visit to Catastrophe Canyon!). Alternatively, if you have young children, you will probably want to turn right and go into Animation Courtyard for the Flying Carpets Over Agrabah and the Art of Disney Animation. The Television Production Tour (in Production Central) often does not open until an hour after the rest of the Theme Park.

Theme Park which caters most for the younger visitors, Animation Courtyard. As well as more chances to meet, photograph and get autographs from the Disney characters, you have the one genuine kiddie ride here and the most enchanting of the shows.

The Art of Disney Animation: The first big set-piece attraction,

BRIT TIP: Check the Information Board as you come into Animation Courtyard to find out the wait times at each of the attractions – and the longest queues to avoid.

located under the giant Sorcerer's Apprentice hat, this is a four-part adventure into the history, creation and magic of animated film. The first section concentrates on the history and will be the area that least keeps the attention of younger children. It is basically a pre-show area, with a series of exhibits around the room, showing how animation developed from the most basic forms into the art form which Walt Disney helped to pioneer. The highlight, amid several hands-on opportunities (like a Zoetrope and a Magic Lantern), is one of only two surviving multi-plane cameras, a tool developed by Walt himself in the 1930s.

As the doors close behind you, a large video screen comes to life and Walt pays tribute to the European pioneers of animation, along with Walt Disney Company chairman Roy Disney (Walt's nephew). Annoyingly for us, it is all dubbed in French (you would have thought one of the showings would be kept in English) with English subtitles, but it sets up the next stage in the 225-seat *Disney Classics Theater*. The doors underneath the screen then open and you pass into the mini-cinema for an 8-minute highlight film of Disney classics that is sure to keep everyone happy.

Stage three is another theatre-like auditorium, set up like an animator's office, where a part live show and part film brings Mushu from *Mulan* to life and explains how this dragon-character came into being (with a highly amusing voice-over from

Eddie Murphy). The interaction between the live 'artist' and Mushu is wonderfully scripted and highly amusing and, although the on-stage presentation is in French, there are headphones to provide a full translation (watch out for the finale as the Murphy-dragon imagines himself as The Mushu of Notre Dame!).

You exit the theatre into a final room of six 'animation stations', which give you the chance to try your hand at drawing, colouring or providing a voice or sound effects for various characters. It is great fun for children of, say, 6 upwards, and the Animation Academy with a real artist is presented in both French and English. In all, it is a fascinating and thoroughly enjoyable look at the artistry of feature animation and the queues move steadily here, so you are rarely waiting for long. AAAA.

Animagique: Opposite the animation attraction, this is a unique live show featuring the innovative Czech art of 'Black Light' stagecraft and Japanese 'Bunraku' puppet manipulation. If that sounds a bit dry, prepare yourself for 25 minutes of pure Disney fun in the company of Mickey, Donald Duck and the cast of *Dumbo*, *Pinocchio*, *Jungle Book* and *The Lion King*.

The story (partly in French and Donald Duck-ese!) sees Donald stuck for inspiration at the drawing board. Ignoring Mickey's warnings, he opens the Disney vault and

BRIT TIP: Try to arrive a few minutes early for the Animagique show as the 1,100-seat theatre comes to life with a series of clever sound effects that ring and echo in delightful style around the auditorium before it begins.

unwittingly lets loose a host of animated characters who run riot on stage, with a big song-and-dance finale that will have you humming the catchy theme tune as you leave. Some excellent effects surprise you along the way which I won't spoil by revealing but be prepared for some extra fun, especially if you are in the first dozen or so rows. The startlingly high-tech show (involving digitally synchronised lighting, audio and machinery effects, in addition to all the puppeteering) is presented up to seven times a day and show times are posted both outside and on the Theme Park maps. AAAA.

BRIT TIP: If you have children, try to sit in the central section of the theatre, no more than 10–12 rows back and you will enjoy one of the neatest special effects of the Animagique show.

As you exit Animagique, children will probably want to head straight for the **Mickey encounter** on the other side of the concourse. This you will probably have to queue for, and the 'star' does need to take a break from time to time, so it can be a while, but it is a well-organised line (unlike a few of the scrimmages that can develop around the characters in some places) and children are usually quite well-behaved when they can see the famous Mouse at the end!

Flying Carpets Over Agrabah: At the innermost end of Animation Courtyard is the main children's ride, which is another variation on the Dumbo/Orbitron attraction of the *Disneyland Park*. This has been transported with a slightly different theme from the ride in Orlando's *Magic Kingdom*.

BRIT TIP: Don't head for the Flying Carpets ride just after the daily Disney Cinema Parade, as the parade finishes in Animation Courtyard and a lot of the crowd follow it and end up in the Carpets queue.

Here you line up (in a loosely themed area like a film 'green room' where actors prepare for their next scene) to take part in 'casting' for a part in a movie, with the Genie (from the 1992 Disney film *Aladdin*) as the director (in French and English). Once aboard your four-person 'flying carpet' there are controls in the front seats to make it go up and down and in the rear seats to add a bit of tilt 'n' turn. In all honesty it is a fairly tame ride, but children under 10 always seem to get quite a thrill from it. However, the queues do build up substantially, so it is advisable to grab a FP early on or wait until early evening. Be aware though, that you miss most of the film-set queuing area if you do decide to go for a FP. TT (TTTT for under 10s).

If you need a snack, the **Studio Catering Co** has two outlets here themed like truck trailers and offering hot dogs, burgers, fish and chips, club sandwiches, popcorn, ice cream, doughnuts, muffins and cookies, as well as drinks. There is only one shopping opportunity, but it is an excellent one, **The Disney Animation Gallery** at the exit of the Art of Disney Animation (inside the giant Sorcerer's Apprentice hat). This offers a rather upmarket range of souvenirs and some serious collectibles – figurines, statues, books and genuine Disney film cels – for those who enjoy the true art of Disney.

7

Production Courtyard

Retracing your steps past Studio 1 (or turning left out of the doors) brings you into Production Courtyard. This is the middle section of the Theme Park and offers three contrasting main attractions.

Cinémagique: One of the Theme Park's undoubted highlights and a real tour de force of imagination, this half-hour film show, exclusive to *Disneyland Resort Paris*, starts out superficially as a tribute to the history of both European and American cinema, but soon takes a dramatic turn for the unexpected. It ends up as a hilarious series of scenes featuring comedian Martin Short as a hapless 'time traveller' through a whole range of cinematic genres that are linked together by a wonderful love-interest storyline.

The show includes numerous funny scene shifts (the 'cowboy shoot-out' scenario is truly inspired) and a couple of eye-popping special effects that I won't reveal but which add hugely to the fun (hint: an umbrella might be a good idea!). French actress Julie Delpy is the co-star of the show and the whole thing takes place inside a beautiful 1,100-seat theatre with an art deco theme that harks back to the classic movie palaces of the 1930s' era in Hollywood.

It probably won't hold the attention of younger children (say, under 4s) for the full 30 minutes, but there is enough amusing on-screen action to keep most entertained and adults will enjoy the clever interweaving of scenes, with Short popping up in all manner of unlikely well-known film scenarios. AAAAA.

Just outside the Cinémagique theatre, the circular podium is home to **Rythmo Technico**, a wonderfully inventive four-piece 'film technician' group, who create some amazing percussion effects à la

BRIT TIP: Waiting in the holding pens for Cinémagique is fairly dull, but the large capacity of the theatre ensures everyone usually gets in, while you can often wait until the last minute and still find a seat. There are up to 10 shows a day in high season, starting at 9.30am, and it is perfectly possible (if not advisable) to visit here a couple of times in one day.

Stomp, and also have a visual comedy thread running through all they do. Starting off like clumsy props men, they quickly evolve into an energetic rhythm section, using anything that comes to hand, including film cases, tools, brooms and boxes. You name it and they can drum up a beat on it, providing some engaging live entertainment for all ages for 20 minutes at a time, four times a day. Don't miss them! AAAA.

Studio Tram Tour: The biggest attraction of the area (and arguably of the whole park), this large-scale, 15-minute ride experience has been adapted from the *Disney-MGM Studios* park in Orlando and enhanced with several brand new elements. Cleverly arranged by language into three sections, this is a tram tour of mind-boggling proportions.

The tram takes you on a behind-the-scenes movie studio tour, learning some more tricks of the film world trade, such as location sets, props, costumes and special effects. Each tram has a video screen with a full commentary (the English version supplied by a wonderfully laconic Jeremy Irons) that points out

7

BRIT TIP: At the entrance to the Studio Tram Tour, look for the British/French flag to ensure you end up in the right part of the tram. Otherwise, you will be listening to the tour narration in Spanish/Italian or German/Dutch!

the key areas along the way. You pass a whole array of film props and scenery (notably the imposing Waterfall City facade from the Dinotopia mini-series) before entering the tour highlight, **Catastrophe Canyon**.

Here, you are supposed to get a dry-run version of a hugely elaborate special effects situation but the 'director' mistakes the tram for his film 'extras' and starts the action sequence with you in the middle! Before you know it, the tram has been subjected to earthquake, fire and flood, and the culmination, when 265,000 litres (58,300 gallons) of water are dumped on the flaming set, is quite breathtaking.

Having 'survived' the canyon, you continue on past some more film props (look out for some planes from *Pearl Harbor*) and the costume studio, before passing the **Star Cars** garage exhibit of well-known movie

BRIT TIP: Young children can be scared by all the dramatic special effects. Try to explain to them what's going to happen and reassure them that it is all quite safe and just another film trick. The left-hand side of the tram may get a little wet.

vehicles (like Cruella de Vil's car from *101 Dalmatians*, the Humvee from *The Rock* and the sports car from *Runaway Bride*).

Finally, you enter the smoking ruins of London, circa 2022 (or at least a remarkable film set facsimile). Here, for anyone familiar with the summer 2002 blockbuster film *Reign of Fire*, you get a close encounter with one of its 'stars'. Well, not actually one of the dragons, but a fairly 'hot' close-up of their fiery breath, which blasts out twice on the right side of the tram. The shock effect, the noise of the fire and the feel of the heat will definitely scare young children (and some adults!), so you do need to think carefully before taking your youngster on this tour. However, the encounter is over pretty quickly and the rest of the set is really something to marvel at. Avoid this just after a Stunt Show has finished in the Backlot area, as many of that 3,000-strong crowd head straight here, and during the main part of the day as queues often top an hour (and there's not much to see while waiting). AAA/TTTT.

Television Production Tour: The final attraction in Production Courtyard is this rather tame walk-through of the actual Walt Disney Television Studios here. The French version of the Disney Channel is all filmed here, and you do get a good look inside the studios, but that is as exciting as it gets and will not hold the attention of young children for long (it has already been given two revamps to make it more interesting).

There is a multi-lingual welcome presentation and then you enter the Transmission Control Room, where a human presenter interacts with various Disney characters to explain how the TV studios work (children may find the English sub-titles hard to follow). You then move into a viewing room that affords a grandstand look into the real working part of the studio but, unless there is a programme being filmed, it is not the most enthralling of scenes.

The tour is rescued at the end however, by a completely new final section (added in August 2002), which provides a whole array of interactive Disney games, puzzles – and the brilliant CyberSpace Mountain. Taken from the now-defunct Chicago DisneyQuest, this is a coaster simulator in a massive box, with all the twisting, turning fun of the real thing. You choose and design your track first and then head up to the 'pods' to check out how it works. Huge fun for kids (especially the grown-up ones!). AA (plus TTTT).

When it comes to grabbing a bite to eat, the Production Courtyard has the best of the Theme Park's dining in the shape of the **Rendez-Vous des Stars Restaurant**, a cafeteria-type diner in full art deco style. The speciality is a meat carvery but the range of food is extremely broad, from grilled salmon Louisiana style to pasta Bolognese, roast chicken, vegetable lasagne and a variety of salads. It is worth taking a look inside to appreciate the decor, which includes a fine array of authentic Hollywood photographs and film

> BRIT TIP: For that extra special occasion, you can order a birthday cake at the Rendez-Vous des Stars at the beginning of your meal. It costs €22 and serves 4–8. But this is also the restaurant to avoid when the Stunt Show has just finished and 3,000 people are in the vicinity!

memorabilia, including one of the 26 Oscars won by Walt during his long movie career.

Alternatively, **La Terrasse** is a covered area in the middle of the Production Courtyard, with a 264-seating capacity for the six **Studio Catering Co** outlets sprinkled around here. Nearby, look for the **Bug's Life photo spot** with a giant Flick the ant!

The Backlot

The Backlot area is past the Rendez-Vous des Stars and features the most action-packed offerings in the park, with three highly contrasting top-drawer thrill elements.

Key to Walt Disney Studios Park Map

Front Lot
1 Walt Disney Studios Store
2 Studio Photo
3 Disney Studio 1
4 Legends of Hollywood
5 Restaurant en Coulisse

Animation Courtyard
6 Art of Disney Animation
7 Animagique
8 The Mickey encounter
9 Flying Carpets Over Agrabah
10 The Disney Animation Gallery

Production Courtyard
11 Cinémagique
12 The Studio Tram Tour
13 Catastrophe Canyon
14 Television Production Tour
15 Rendez-Vous des Stars Restaurant
16 La Terrasse
17 Rythmo Technico

The Backlot
18 Armageddon: Special Effects
19 Rock 'n' Roller Coaster starring Aerosmith
20 Moteurs ... Action! Stunt Show Spectacular
21 Le Café des Cascadeurs
22 Backlot Express Restaurant
23 Rock Around The Shop

WALT DISNEY STUDIOS

DISNEY VILLAGE

Top and above left: Buffalo Bill's Wi
  West Show
Above: Planet Hollywood
Below: Café Mickey
Left: Disney Village entrance

©DISNEY

BEYOND THE PARKS

Left: Val d'Europe
Top left and above: Sea Life Centre
Below: Manchester United
      Soccer School
Below left: Disney Golf

VAL D'EUROPE

DISNEY

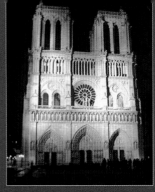

PARIS*attractions*

Left: Lido de Paris
Above clockwise from top right:
Eiffel Tower,
Sacré Coeur,
Moulin Rouge
Arc de Triomp
River Seine,
Rose Window
Nôtre Dame
Nôtre Dame

BRIT TIP: The props on display in the pre-show area of Armageddon: Special Effects include the spacesuit worn by actor Ben Affleck in the film.

Armageddon: Special Effects:
This unique, wonderfully elaborate show that puts YOU at the heart of the action (although it's not one for young children) is the first of the thrills. You enter into a pre-show area, full of models, exhibits and diagrams from the blockbuster film, starring Bruce Willis (there are two studios for this purpose, 7A and 7B, and the array of models, etc, does vary), where a Cast Member greets you and acts as the show's 'director'.

With the help of your director and a video that explains the eye-popping scenario of the film, your role as 'extras' in a special effects scene is explained in amusing detail (in English and French). The screen is then turned over to a tribute to Frenchman Georges Méliès, who is credited with inventing film special effects. It shows how the movie world has taken his ideas and developed them with astonishing creativity in the last 100 years.

The video continues with the explosive arrival of Michael Clarke Duncan, another of the *Armageddon* stars, who explains how the film's technical wizardry was carried out. You are then invited to come and see

BRIT TIP: It is a good idea for an adult to experience an attraction first to check on its suitability, if you are worried that something might be too scary for your children.

for real how it is done and walk through, under 'directorial' guidance, into an amazing mock-up of the movie's Russian space station – just as it comes under threat from a meteor shower! The ensuing chaos, as the station almost literally blows up all around you, is brilliantly scripted and the array of effects incredibly realistic, with smoke, sparks, bursting pipes, buckling doors and a huge central fireball that adds some very real heat to the proceedings.

In my opinion, the sights and sounds (and it is pretty loud, too) are really much too intense for young children (anyone under 7, I would say), but there are no real warnings of this outside. However, the space station itself is a work of art and the hectic action is suitably breathtaking. They could do with adding a bit of interest to the extremely plain waiting area outside though. TTTT.

Rock 'n' Roller Coaster starring Aerosmith: This next attraction is a real blast of a ride that rockets you from 0–100kph (62mph) in just 2.8 seconds! It is a slightly revised version of the ride of the same name at Orlando's *Disney-MGM Studios*, making it a different experience.

7

BRIT TIP: Listen out for Aerosmith lead singer, Steve Tyler, completing a clever 'sound-check' as you board the Rock 'n' Roller Coaster – it all adds considerably to the fun.

Here, you enter the rock 'n' roll world of the American supergroup Aerosmith, as they discuss the creation of this unique rockin' ride, a 'revolutionary musical experience' produced by Tour De Force Records.

As the record company's VIP guests, Aerosmith invite you to enter

BRIT TIP: The queue for the Rock 'n' Roller Coaster drops off during a performance of the Stunt Show next door but it should be avoided just after it finishes as many people make a beeline for the nearest ride.

the 'research and development' area to try it out at first hand and you pass into the launch area, complete with 'sound engineers' and computer models of the ride systems, which feature 'Soundtracker' cars. These are fitted with five state-of-the-art speakers per seat so you literally 'ride the music'.

Once you are firmly harnessed into your seat, the countdown begins and you blast off into a topsy-turvy 'rock video' that features two loops and a corkscrew as well as some eye-popping lighting effects on the way round. There are five different music tracks that accompany the ride, hence there are five variations on the ride experience. Aerosmith have even re-recorded a couple of their tracks, so see if you can notice the new lyrics (hint: the 'adapted' songs are *Love In An Elevator* and *What Kind of Love Are You On?*). A FastPass attraction, it is advisable to grab one at peak periods as the normal waiting time can top half an hour. However, there is rarely much of a queue for the first couple of hours and from late afternoon. It is not recommended for anyone with back or neck problems or for pregnant women. Restriction: 1.2m (3ft 9in). TTTTT.

Moteurs…Action! Stunt Show Spectacular: Next door to the Rock 'n' Roller Coaster, this is one of the most remarkable shows ever. Full of genuine high-risk stunts

and hugely skilful car and motorbike action, it will have you shaking your head in amazement for quite a while afterwards.

BRIT TIP: People start queuing for the Stunt Show a good half an hour before a performance at peak times and the middle shows of the day are always absolutely full. It is better to head for the first one, or stay until the last to minimise your wait.

Seating starts a good 15–20 minutes before one of the three or four shows every day, and there is some amusing pre-show chat (in English and French) and freestyle show-boating by one of the bike riders to keep people amused before the serious stuff starts. Various audience members are recruited to help in one of the scenes and a roving cameraman picks out people from the crowd to highlight on the big video screen in the centre of the 'square'. The huge set is based on a typical Mediterranean village and is magnificently crafted to have an 'aged' appearance.

Once the preliminaries are completed, you are treated to a 45-minute extravaganza of daredevil stunts, with a Car Ballet sequence, a Motorbike Chase and a Grand Finale that features some surprise pyrotechnics to complete a truly awesome presentation (keep your eyes on the windows below the video screen at the end!). Each scene – featuring a secret agent 'goody' and various black-car baddies – is set up and fully explained by a movie 'director' (and the need for bilingual commentary is handled skillfully). The results of each 'shoot' are then played back on the video screen to

BRIT TIP: If you have young children, be aware there is some (loud) mock gunfire during the show, which can upset sensitive ears, while the motorbike scene includes a rider catching fire, which can be quite frightening for them.

show how each effect was created and how it is all spliced together to create the desired end product.

All the cars were specially created for the show by Vauxhall and there are some extra tricks (including an amusing appearance by Herbie from *The Love Bug* film) in between the main scenes. The whole thing was designed by Frenchman Rémy Julienne, the doyen of cinematic car stunt sequences, who has worked on James Bond films *Goldeneye* and *Licence to Kill* and other epics like *The Rock, Ronin, Gone in 60 Seconds* and *Enemy of the State.*

It all adds up to a breathtaking show however, and kids are sure to want to come back to this (mine certainly did), which is another good reason to see it early in the day. There is nothing like it in any other theme park in the world (until they open a similar version in *Disney-MGM Studios* in Orlando in 2005), and the fact so much of it involves genuine, live co-ordination makes it a truly thrilling experience.

However, the exit is quite a scrum as 3,000 people have to leave through two fairly narrow thoroughfares and it can take 10–15 minutes to get clear of the auditorium, so if you can sit towards the front either on the right or left of the grandstand, you will be out quicker. TTTTT.

When you need to stop for something to eat in the Backlot, **Le Café des Cascadeurs** is an imaginative little diner (themed like

an art deco studio cafe for the stuntmen and women) around the corner from Armageddon, serving a fairly simple selection of salads, sandwiches, hot dogs and crisps, but the train carriage setting is good fun. The **Backlot Express Restaurant** is a counter-service café with another highly themed interior – like a studio's art department, full of props, tools, light fittings, furniture and other film accoutrements – that makes dining fun. The food is fairly ordinary – toasted sandwiches, pizza, baguettes, bagels and salads – with the standard Menu Mickey at €10 and the kids' menu at €5, but it holds up to 500 inside, plus there is some outdoor seating in the summer. Look out for the big model suspended from the ceiling – the motor speeder from *Star Wars VI: Return of the Jedi.*

BRIT TIP: In Le Café des Cascadeurs, help yourself to a selection or two on the classic 1950s-style jukebox.

There is only one shopping opportunity here, **Rock Around The Shop**, at the exit to the Rock 'n' Roller Coaster, for a range of Aerosmith and rock-related merchandise, plus the chance to buy your photo from the ride itself (€12 and €19).

Here comes the parade

In best Disney park fashion, no visit is complete without the daily procession and here it is, the **Disney Cinema Parade**, at either 1.45pm or 3.30pm according to the season. Starting between the Backlot Express Restaurant and the Rock 'n' Roller Coaster and winding down into Animation Courtyard, it is a positive extravaganza of kids' favourites, from *Mary Poppins* to *Toy*

The Walt Disney Studios Park with children

Our guide to the attractions which are most like to appeal to the different age groups in this park (taking into account any height restrictions):

Under 5s
The Art of Disney Animation, Animagique, Flying Carpets Over Agrabah, Meet Mickey, Studio Tram Tour (with parental discretion), Moteurs … Action! Stunt Show Spectacular (also with parental discretion), Disney Cinema Parade, Rythmo Technico

6–8s
All the above, plus Disney Studio 1, Cinémagique, Armageddon (with parental discretion), Streetmosphere

9–12s
All the above, plus Rock 'n' Roller Coaster starring Aerosmith

Over 12s
Disney Studio 1, Art of Disney Animation, Animagique, Studio Tram Tour, Cinémagique, Armageddon, Rock 'n' Roller Coaster starring Aerosmith, Moteurs…Action!, Streetmosphere, Rythmo Technico

Story and *Monsters Inc.* The series of elaborate floats – starting with Minnie and ending with Mickey Mouse – also include *The Lion King*, *Pinocchio* and *101 Dalmatians* and a host of characters on foot, while a handful of guests are also chosen to ride aboard with Mickey. The whole thing takes about 25 minutes to pass as it stops at regular intervals for the cast to interact with onlookers (especially children) along the route, backed by another wonderfully infectious theme song. It is also an easy parade to catch and watch in relative comfort as it doesn't usually draw the huge crowds of the *Disneyland Park*. Wait in front of the Rendez-Vous des Stars restaurant and you should get a great view. AAAA.

The park's additional fun is provided by the **Streetmosphere** performers, various alternating acts who patrol the Theme Park and turn up unexpectedly for impromptu shows that have a central theme but with some improvisation, too.

There are special acts for seasons like Halloween (12 different acts) and Christmas (including an *a capella* carol group), which vary from day to day, so you never know who's going to turn up. However, keep a special eye out for the following three.

The **Sound System** is a wacky duo (a 'mad scientist' and his hapless assistant) who push a strange musical contraption and inveigle guests to get involved in helping to produce various sound effects which they then work into a plot.

The **Italian Cine Band** brings a touch of Italian tragicomedy to proceedings, a group who start off in fairly cacophonic style but quickly work into a repertoire of music made famous in Italian films such as *La Strada* and *La Dolce Vita*.

The **Knights** are another crazy group, with an Italian director trying to film a medieval spectacular. Trouble is, he has only two actors for his epic, so he has to recruit – guess who? – yes, you the guests, into his increasingly manic production.

For those keen to learn more about the Theme Park, there is a 2-hour **guided tour** (€10 for adults, children 3–11 free), which gives an in-depth view of the history and architecture. Book at Studio Services when you first arrive (subject to availability).

As with the *Disneyland Park*, the *Walt Disney Studios Park* looks even better in early evening, when all the clever (and hidden) lighting effects come into play. There is definitely some room for improvement and enhancement in time along with some more attractions (and the 'rumour mill' was in full turn at the time of writing, see below).

The high quality however, of virtually everything here still provides a rich and rewarding experience. You will also come out with an improved knowledge of the movie business and a heightened respect for all those who work in it.

The essence of a theme park is that it envelops you with its sense of design and purpose and this, I believe, the *Walt Disney Studios Park* does, ensuring you believe you have truly had a movie-world adventure.

Right, that should be your fill of the Theme Parks for now. But the fun doesn't stop here. Oh no! There is still plenty to do and see when we visit the *Disney Village*, Val d'Europe and more. It's time to go beyond the Theme Parks...

7

The rumour mill

Hints and stories of supposed new construction at the *Walt Disney Studios* have been pretty constant right from the park's opening. The announcement in October 2003 of increased losses by Euro Disney SCA seemed to sound serious alarm bells for any immediate future development. However, the park management is aware of the need to keep enhancing its offering, so it will not be surprising to see some new elements added in the next year or so.

Top of the agenda would appear to be a children's playground (*Disney's California Adventure* in Anaheim recently added Flick's A Bug's Land, which may be hint of things to come) to give some much-needed extra fun for the youngest age group and it would be logical to extend that into a fully fledged 'land', with an accompanying children's-style ride to go with it (something like the highly kid-popular Buzz Lightyear's Space Ranger Spin from Orlando's *Magic Kingdom Park* would make sense). There is certainly room to add a 5-star thrill ride like Orlando's Tower of Terror (which has already been 'exported' to *Disney's California Adventure*), and that is a fairly persistent rumour, but it is hard to imagine such a major project being completed before 2006, even if the funding were in place. Once again, the News & Rumours pages of www.dlp-guidebook.de provides an excellent source of up-to-date reference.

Beyond the Theme Parks

(or, Let's Shop 'Til We Drop and Other Fun Pursuits)

Having led you, quite literally, up the theme park path, it is now time that I took you beyond those confines and explored some more of what makes this resort – and this whole area of the Ile de France region – such an enticing one.

To backtrack slightly and put things in context, the Ile de France is the central region of France, the 'island' around which lie the other great regions of Normandy, Picardie, Champagne-Ardennes and Burgundy. The Ile itself is made up of eight *'départements'*, namely **Yvelines, Essonne, Seine-et-Marne** and **Val d'Oise** (which form a large outer ring) and then **Hauts-de-Seine** (immediately to the west of the city), **Seine-St-Denis** (to the northeast), **Val-de-Marne** (to the southeast) and **Paris** itself. The *département* of Val-de-Marne should not be confused with Marne-la-Vallée, where *Disneyland Resort Paris* is located, in the *département* of Seine-et-Marne.

Prior to 1989, when construction began, there was little here apart from sugar beet fields, but the development since has been swift and dramatic. There is, in fact, no real town or village of Marne-la-Vallée, it is a made-up name given to the RER/TGV station here, which acts as the terminus for the RER's Line A. The nearest sizeable village is Chessy, hence the RER station is properly known as Marne-la-Vallée Chessy. However, to all intents and purposes, Marne-la-Vallée IS the site of *Disneyland Resort Paris*, hence this is how the majority refer to it.

Marne-la-Vallée is also (highly confusingly) a sub-district of the Seine-et-Marne *département* closer to Paris (between the towns of Noisy-le-Grand and Lognes). When driving, therefore, you should always aim for 'Les Parcs Disneyland'.

More to see and do

When it comes to the associated attractions 'beyond the Theme Parks', there are six distinct topics to cover. First and most obvious is all the fun, fine shopping and dining of **Disney Village**. Second, Disney has also developed its own sporting connections – at **Disneyland Golf**. Third is another sporting venue but this time for children – the **Manchester United Soccer School** (for ages 7–14) from spring 2004. Next, the neighbouring development of **Val d'Europe** offers another scintillating array of great shops and restaurants, including the Auchan supermarket and the additional outlet shopping of **La Vallée**. Finally, the highly family-friendly **Sea Life** aquarium centre is situated inside the Val d'Europe shopping centre and is another excellent reason to go beyond the Theme Parks.

Disney Village

1 Planet Hollywood
2 Annette's Diner
3 King Ludwig's Castle
4 Sports Bar
5 New York Style Sandwiches
6 Billy Bob's Country Western Saloon
7 The Steakhouse
8 Rainforest Café
9 Café Mickey
10 McDonald's
11 The Disney Store
12 Buffalo Trading Co
13 The Disney Gallery
14 Team Mickey
15 Hollywood Pictures
16 World of Toys
17 Gaumont Cinema
18 Buffalo Bill's Wild West Show
19 Hurricanes
20 Central Stage
21 Lake Disney Marina
22 IMAX Cinema (summer 2004)

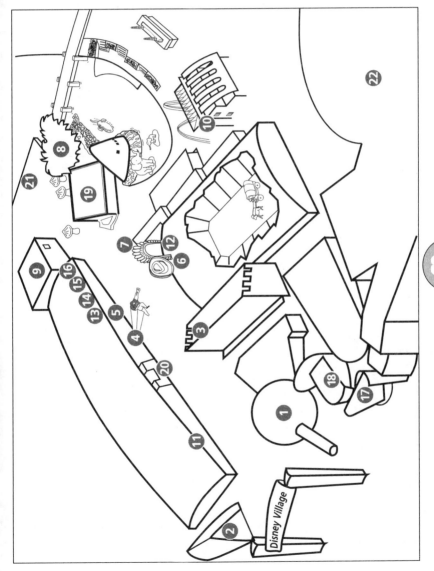

The golfing opportunity is obviously primarily for devotees of the sport but the other four should all be on your must-see list if you are here for 4 days or more (or if you are on a repeat visit). As this is primarily a new-town area (the great Disney trail-blazing has given rise to a flurry of modern suburban development all around), there are not many other out-and-out tourist attractions here, but it does make a great base from which to explore Paris and some of the more genuinely historic points of interest in the region (notably the towns of Provins and Meaux), as will be made clear in Chapter 9.

Disney Village

Starting at the top, it is almost impossible to miss this hugely colourful and imaginative entertainment centre situated between Disney's hotels and the Theme Parks. This impressive complex was designed by American architect Frank Gehry, who was also responsible for the Guggenheim museum in Bilbao, Spain, and it features a host of complex, almost abstract ideas designed to link the village to the railway station.

If you come straight in by car or train, you just *might* not notice *Disney Village* on your left as you scamper headlong for the *Disneyland Park*, but otherwise it is fairly obvious. From one end (nearest the Theme Parks), it is dominated by a massive gateway topped by a huge red banner with *Disney Village* emblazoned across it. From the hotels end, you enter via the Lake Disney entrance, with a spread of restaurants – Café Mickey, Rainforest Café and McDonald's – before you.

In one way, it is easy to see the Village as just one big merchandising opportunity. There are a dozen different ways to spend money here – from the shops to video games –

and even some of the restaurants have their own gift store. But, ultimately, this has the hallmark of the Imagineers once again (even if the Rainforest Café, Planet Hollywood and McDonald's all have their own internationally recognisable style). It has a wonderful outdoor cafe style, especially in the evening and the brilliant way the overhead lights are arranged to form a 'ceiling' at night is well worth stopping to see. Famously, Cast Members tell of the family who were into their second day in the resort when they stopped a shop manager to ask where all the rides were – they hadn't yet made it out of *Disney Village!*

The main Central Stage provides live entertainment most evenings (weather permitting), and there are other stalls, vendors and street performers from time to time, which all help to build up the carnival atmosphere (as well as set-piece seasonal events, such as St Patrick's Day, the Festival Latina in June and the Christmas festivities). When you add in the entertainment possibilities of Buffalo Bill's dinner show, the cinema complex, the live music of Billy Bob's and the late-night disco, Hurricanes, you have a serious array of choice. The one thing, perhaps surprisingly, they don't have here is a good coffee bar.

The Village is an on-going development programme, continually updating, refurbishing and changing the variety on offer and no one else does it with such thoroughness and creativity as Disney.

What's there

Roughly speaking, you can divide the offerings of *Disney Village* into the **Restaurants and bars**, the **Shops** and the **Entertainment**. But, to get maximum enjoyment, you need to be aware of a couple of things. Firstly, the restaurants normally start to fill up from around 7pm. In high summer, when the Theme Parks are open until late, the peak period for the restaurants and shops is more likely to be 9pm. Unless you have made a booking (and only four of the restaurants actually accept bookings), you are likely to find queues of up to half an hour to get into places like The Steakhouse, Planet Hollywood and even Annette's Diner.

The other factor is the weather. On a fine evening, you will usually find it easier to get a table while, if it is wet, everywhere fills up extremely quickly, so you need to try to anticipate the rain to avoid being left out in it!

> BRIT TIP: The restaurants at the Theme Parks end of *Disney Village* fill up quickest, with Planet Hollywood the most popular venue of them all.

It is also worth pointing out the village is relatively quiet during the day, hence it is the ideal spot for a more relaxed lunch away from the Theme Parks, and some leisurely afternoon shopping. You have free pick of all the restaurants (apart from Billy Bob's, where the buffet is evenings only) and it is particularly convenient if you are in the *Walt Disney Studios Park*, where there is no table-service dining choice.

The restaurants and bars

Planet Hollywood: Taking *Disney Village* from the Theme Parks end, as soon as you come through the gateway you face the immediately recognisable 2-storey edifice of this popular international chain. Planet Hollywood is a hugely popular draw from early evening until late

(reservations can be made in the early evening only, which takes care of most of the queues but, if there is a line, there is a great bar area and some snazzy bar staff to make the wait more fun). An unhurried lunch is also available from 11.30am during the day. If the queue can be seen outside, you are looking at a good 30-minute wait for a table.

> BRIT TIP: When the *Disneyland Park* is open until 11pm, head out to Planet Hollywood for dinner at about 6pm and you will have your pick of the best tables.

The huge variety of movie models, costumes, portraits and other memorabilia in this 500-seat restaurant is subdivided into differently themed areas, each with its own video screen that shows well-known film clips, music videos and (well worth looking out for) special trailers for forthcoming movies. The memorabilia, which will certainly get film buffs wandering around to study it, varies from James Cagney to Wesley Snipes, Arnold Schwarzenegger and Sylvester Stallone, and the upstairs section includes a sci-fi dining area and an adventure area, as well as the lively bar, while downstairs there is a *Raiders of the Lost Ark* type section and the Zebra Room (for obvious, stripy reasons). The inevitable gift store is also downstairs and you will probably find the Planet Hollywood merchandise a bit cheaper here than in their London store.

Curiously, different nationalities seem to eat at different times of the day. The Brits tend to eat earlier, hence there will be a predominance of British people in the restaurant from 5–7pm, while the Spanish are

8

BRIT TIP: Need to check your email? Planet Hollywood has two internet terminals for you to use for a small charge while you are waiting for a table.

almost invariably the last ones out! Usefully, they offer a Cinema Special meal, a set, 2-course dinner, which they can usually turn around quickly if you are in a hurry. The menu has also been slightly tailored and adapted for the more European mix of customer here, hence several dishes have been tweaked (Spinach Dip replaces the more usual nachos, and their lasagne is a house speciality) and several regional specialities have been added (like the typically French Croque Monsieur, a glorified ham and cheese toastie).

The full range is salads (€10.50–13), sandwiches and burgers (€12.50–13.50), steak, chicken, ribs, salmon, grilled lamb and fajitas (€17.50–22), pasta dishes (€13.50–15), while desserts include chocolate cake, cheesecake, ice cream and an excellent white chocolate bread pudding. I must say, of all the Planet Hollywood restaurants I have visited around the world, the food here is consistently the best, which I ascribe to that extra bit of French flair. They also freshen the menu from time to time and in 2003 added draught beer along with a Happy Hour offering a 'pint for the price of a half pint'. TVs in the bar show all the major sports events and the latest football results are usually available.

If you haven't been to a Planet Hollywood before, you will probably be wowed by their lively entertainment mix (even their soundtrack is carefully balanced so you can talk at the table without having to shout), and you should make a beeline for this one. If you

are already familiar with their style, head here anyway and try their LA Lasagne (a layered pasta that is rolled, cut in half, deep fried and then smothered in their tomato sauce), which will make your taste buds quiver with delight and your waistline shudder!

I'll admit to being slightly biased in my liking for the brash cinema-style motif that is Planet Hollywood but I also reckon it is one of the best dining experiences in the whole resort and it stays open until the last person goes.

Annette's Diner: Opposite PH stands this classic 1950s' rock 'n' roll style restaurant. Straight out of *Grease* and *Happy Days*, the bright, vivid decor provides a suitably fun, family atmosphere, with waiters and waitresses who dance on the bar top at various moments.

The large icons are all typical Americana from this period, and the menu is equally in keeping with the theme, with the usual line-up of burgers, hot dogs, salads and sandwiches. On two levels, the mezzanine floor offers the best views of the restaurant, which also features a classic Cadillac and Corvette photo opportunity at the entrance.

The kids meal (for under 11s) is €8.40, while the burgers range from €7.20–11.20. The desserts are possibly their best feature, with a range of ice creams, sundaes and shakes to appeal strongly to those with a sweet tooth. When the queues get long (as they do regularly), there is a handy takeaway window to the side, while Annette's is open from 11.30am–11pm Sunday

BRIT TIP: To book any of the restaurants in *Disney Village* you can call 01 60 45 71 14 or make a reservation through the concierge at your hotel.

to Thursday, and 11.30am–midnight (Friday and Saturday).

King Ludwig's Castle: Continuing along the main *Disney Village* thoroughfare brings you next to this hugely elaborate new establishment, which opened in a blaze of publicity in June 2003. Inspired by Neuschwanstein Castle in Bavaria (built by 'mad' King Ludwig II), King Ludwig's has been designed primarily for German visitors but will, I think, appeal widely to anyone who enjoys good beer, Bavarian food and castles in general. With 297 seats (a substantial increase on the Rock 'n' Roll America bar/diner which it replaced) on two floors, the interior of the restaurant is redolent with castle theming, including wooden panelling, flags and ornate carvings.

The menu is designed to appeal to international tastes, with starters such as Vienna Sausage with Sauerkraut and Mustard, Pickled Herring Roll Mops with Potato Salad and Onions and Goulash Soup, and main courses like Wiener Schnitzel, Braised Pork Shank with Sauerkraut and Bread Dumplings, Sauerbraten (marinated German-style pot roast) with Roasted Potatoes and Goulash, while desserts include King Ludwig's famous strudels and Black Forest Gateau. There are also more straightforward salads and pastas, plus a simple kids' menu, but the feature dishes are all quite delicious.

This can all be washed down with a good choice of beer and schnapps and there is even their own version of the Oktoberfest beer festival on Friday and Saturday evenings and Sunday lunchtimes (mid-September to 5 October), with a set menu at €20 per person (including a 1-litre beer) and Bavarian bands. A quite magnificent design, both inside and out, the Castle has a more fantasy-orientated and whimsical touch rather than the usual more formal, stern approach. The menu is around

€17 for lunch and €20 for dinner, and a gift shop at the entrance sells branded merchandise – glass, porcelain and the inevitable swords – under the mark of Prince Luipold of Bavaria (a direct descendant of King Ludwig II and the owner of the famous Kaltenberg brewery).

Sports Bar: A regular haunt for many Brits, this is the nearest the village gets to a proper pub and stands diagonally opposite the Castle. With an outdoor terrace, indoor seating and a cinema-style video screen at one end (plus a dozen TV screens sprinkled through the bar), this is the place to come for a British-style beer, a quick snack and, more importantly, the footy on telly at weekends and midweek! They show a great variety of European action and keep all the latest scores and tables on big blackboards behind the bar.

Popular with Disney Cast Members, the Sports Bar can be a lively place most evenings, but especially at weekends when the locals come out to play. The draught beers are Kronenbourg 1664, Budweiser, Beamish and Carlsberg, while there is a good choice of bottled beers, including Foster's, Heineken, Corona, Guinness, Beck's, Stella Artois, Kriska and Hoegaarden.

Open from midday to 1am (until 2am on Friday and Saturday), hot dogs, chips and crisps are also available. It is usually packed for the big European football games and does get very smoky, so it is not ideal for children, although they are welcome.

8

BRIT TIP: For smokers, the Sports Bar has a tobacco kiosk at the front which is open from 10.45am–midnight daily.

New York Style Sandwiches: Immediately next door to the Sports Bar (and sharing the same outdoor terrace), this deli-style, rather nondescript diner/takeaway offers baguettes, sandwiches, salads, ice cream, fish and chips, hot dogs, crisps and drinks. The set children's menu (choice of ham sandwich, fish and chips or chicken nuggets and chips, plus a yoghurt and a drink) costs €6.50, while main menu items run from €3–9. The deli is open from 9am–midnight every day (9am–1am Saturdays).

Billy Bob's Country Western Saloon: Just down from King Ludwig's Castle, you come to this wonderful mock cowboy saloon, with a large bar and a stage for live music every evening (with occasional guest bands in addition to the excellent house band, the Moody Brothers). The 3-storey Grand Opry-style building (copied from an original in Austin, Texas) is superbly designed inside (anyone who has been in the old Cheyenne Saloon in Orlando will know the idea), with tiered balconies all providing a good view of the stage. You can learn to line dance here or just sit back with a drink and enjoy the Moodys, who are genuine American exponents of the Country & Western genre (even if it's not your usual musical cup of tea, their live style is worth checking out).

Bar snacks include chicken wings, spare ribs and nachos, or try out the excellent **Billy Bob's Buffet**, which is at the top of the bar at the back (go up the stairs to your left and keep going!). The buffet is available from 6–10.30pm, Sunday to Thursday and 6–11pm on Friday and Saturday, and it offers a great value meal (€25 for adults and €10 for kids) featuring salads, roast pork and beef, fajitas, chilli con carne, fresh salmon and vegetables, chicken wings, spare ribs, cheese tray and a huge choice of desserts. Billy Bob's can be booked in advance through your hotel concierge.

Billy Bob's is open from 4pm–1am Sunday toThursday and 4pm–2am Friday and Saturday and midday–1am on Sunday, with snacks served from 6–10.30pm. Early evening usually sees a kids' dance session when the saloon is given over to a more youthful, energetic vibe ideal for the 8–14 brigade. To book, call 00 33 1 60 45 70 79 from the UK.

The Steakhouse: Right next door, this offers the real fine-dining opportunity in *Disney Village*, in fact, only the California Grill in the *Disneyland Hotel* and Hunter's Grill in *Disney's Sequoia Lodge* can rival this for quality. It is a spectacular venue, with a Chicago-style warehouse interior in three sections, the main warehouse, the smart bar and the conservatory-like annexe. It is all decorated in 1930s' Americana, with lots of dark woods, rich upholstery, wood panelling and elaborate candelabra lighting effects. The bar area is straight out of the TV programme *Cheers*, but it is also extremely elegant for such a large restaurant and provides a great backdrop for a special occasion meal (although it is also popular with families early in the evening and you will find a lot of children here).

The mouth-watering menu is pretty broad-based, too, although the obvious speciality is steak (filet, entrecote, rump steak, sirloin and steak tartare) along with a couple of excellent fish dishes (try the roast cod with pecans, endive and apples),

> BRIT TIP: If the other restaurants are heaving, try Billy Bob's Buffet for a more out-of-the-way meal. Not many people actually notice it and it is usually possible to get a table without much of a wait.

chicken, wild boar, veal, pork and a lamb curry, as well as a vegetarian main course and another house speciality – an escalope of duck foie gras with lentils. The à la carte prices are not too outrageous (the steaks run from €21–27, while the starters vary from €6–17), and there is a set menu for €34 which offers a choice of four starters, main courses and desserts.

For children, the Mickey's Menu (€14) is also a cut above the usual kiddie fare (although they can still get the ubiquitous chicken nuggets). Reservations are highly recommended at most times and the restaurant is open daily from midday to midnight. This is also the place to come for their superb Sunday Brunch with Disney characters, from midday to 3pm. It's a tad pricey at €32/adult and €16/child (that's almost €100 for a family of four), but it does make for a memorable meal and it is rarely crowded, which means the kids get plenty of time with the characters. To book from the UK, call 00 33 1 60 45 70 45.

Rainforest Café: This unmistakable, international chain restaurant, providing a larger-than-life jungle adventure and whose decor owes a lot to the artistry of the Imagineers, is next up on the grand village restaurant tour. Here you will find tropical aquaria, waterfalls, streams and a host of (animatronic) animals to accompany your meal, all in a realistic rainforest setting punctuated by thunderstorms and rainfall. You don't just go to eat here you go 'on expedition' and it is as much the decor as the food that creates the experience.

In truth, the food is fairly regular diner fare just given a bit of a twist and a few fancy names (Rasta Pasta is penne pasta with chicken, broccoli, peppers and spinach tossed in a cream sauce, while Mojo Bones is BBQ ribs with coleslaw and chips), but the portions are huge and usually work out good value for money. Salads, pasta, burgers and grills (try the Jungle Salmon – steamed salmon steak in a mild paprika butter – or Siva's Curry – chicken and shrimp with pineapple in a mild, creamy curry sauce) range from €12–25, while the starters vary from €6–12. Cocktails and desserts are both specialities, and the Chocolate Diablo Cake is worth coming in for on its own (along with the Key Lime Pie and Carpaccio d'Ananas).

Children in particular love the rainforest style and pick up on the many environmental messages, while the kids' menu (€12.50) is one of the best. The Café doesn't accept reservations, so you just have to turn up and wait your turn, but there is a huge gift shop to inspect before you eat and plenty of audio-animatronics to keep the kids happy (the big 'alligator' outside seems to provide an almost endless source of amusement).

The Rainforest Café is open from 11.30am–midnight every day, with the gift shop open from 9.30am.

Café Mickey: New in spring 2002 (replacing the Los Angeles Bar & Grill), Café Mickey is another really fun and lively venue which has the great benefit of staging character meals throughout the day. Once again, the decor is both bright without being garish and amusing without being obvious. TV screens showing classic Disney cartoons help to keep children happy if the food doesn't (and the food is way above average), but it is more likely to be the excellent character interaction that makes their day.

A big breakfast buffet runs from 7.30–10.30am (with two separate seatings at 7.30 and 9.30), while lunch and dinner are available from noon–11pm (Sunday to Thursday) or noon–midnight (Friday and Saturday), and the dinner menu is basically an

8

extended version of the lunch one.

Perhaps here you can see the most European influence at work, providing a wide-ranging choice and a highly thoughtful and appetising selection (from pizza and pasta standards to seafood, vegetarian dishes and even a curry), way above usual diner fare. Try the Beef Carpaccio starter or the Compôte of Vegetables, then progress to Captain Hook's Fresh Salmon (with mashed potatoes and lemon butter sauce) or Aladdin's Curried Chicken Tanjine, followed by a wonderfully tempting dessert buffet. The 3-course set meal is €30 for adults. The upstairs dining area also boasts a magnificent view over Lake Disney from the terrace.

Children (under 12) get their own menu (€14) and a special Mickey surprise at the end. The characters circulate fairly constantly to keep everyone happy and the smart decor ensures adult sensibilities are not forgotten either. Booking is highly advisable, though (with the possible exception of lunchtime). In France, you can call 01 60 45 71 14.

> BRIT TIP: Tigger, Pluto and Co appear outside Café Mickey (weather permitting) in early evening to strut their funky cartoon stuff and amuse the younger crowd.

McDonald's: Completing the impressive spread of restaurants throughout the Village is the inevitable McDonald's, albeit quite a smart, almost high-tech version of the ubiquitous American burger chain. Open from 8am–midnight (8am–1am on Saturday), it is a major draw in the evenings as it is obviously one of the cheaper options, but it also has a high capacity with an outdoor terrace,

providing a pleasant place to sit given the right weather. The original architecture is based on Italian theatre and the split-level arrangement also offers a games area for the kids.

Finally, if you're after a late-night snack, there are various **hand-carts** throughout the village where you can grab a hot dog, popcorn, crêpes, ice cream or toffee apples, to send you on your way.

> BRIT TIP: If *Disney Village* is too crowded for your tastes or you can't get a table for dinner, try going to *Disney's Hotel New York* (see page 62) for their Parkside Diner, where you can usually get a table at any time, or even the upmarket Hunter's Grill at *Disney's Sequoia Lodge* (see pages 64–65). Both have wonderful bars, too.

Shopping

Okay, if that sums up your eating opportunities in the village, your retail therapy opportunities aren't quite so wide-ranging, as you will find some of the merchandise recurring in different shops. However, there is still a wonderfully imaginative array of gift stores and it is worth wandering through the likes of The Disney Store and the Rainforest Café shop just to check out the decor.

Entering the Village from the Theme Parks end, first on your left is **The Disney Store**, the biggest in the resort, selling the full selection of character and souvenir wares, from books and cuddly toys, to videos, watches and jewellery plus an extensive clothing selection and, nearer the festive season, an array of Christmas decorations, too. Kids will love browsing in here (if they can be prevented from trying to buy everything in sight) and above their heads are a load of fun things to watch, a whole series of large-scale moving models and mobiles – including Mickey Mouse flying a spaceship. Almost opposite is the **Planet Hollywood gift store**, for restaurant souvenirs and movie memorabilia, and next door the new **King Ludwig's Castle** restaurant also has a specialist shop.

Continuing down the right hand side of the main thoroughfare brings you to the **Buffalo Trading Co**, which offers a wide variety of Disney-branded merchandise, all with a Wild West theme (plus some smart Western gear, like overcoats, leather jackets and waistcoats). You may be hard pressed to extricate your offspring without buying them some kind of cowboy paraphernalia. This also becomes the Halloween store for September and October, with some suitably spooky special effects and lighting.

Opposite is the **Disney Gallery**, which offers a more upmarket selection of gift items for cinema and art fans. Disney collectors will want to make a beeline for here to check out the range of limited series of lithographs and original animated film cels. There are some great books (here's where you can get a copy of Didier Ghez's superb book *Disneyland – From Sketch to Reality*) and photographs, and it also has the latest collections of china figurines and snow globes, plus novelties like a Mickey telephone (every home should have one!).

Immediately next door, you enter one of three shops that are actually interconnected (handy in the rain) and, while you will probably already have seen some of the merchandise on offer, there is more novel stuff, too. **Team Mickey** is a sports-

themed emporium, **Hollywood Pictures** offers an array of film-themed clothing, photo albums and gifts (and the inevitable cuddly toys) and **World of Toys** is almost a reprise of The Disney Store, with yet more kids' play things (beware the pirate paraphernalia and swords!), Disney costumes and a big sweet counter.

Finally, inside the main entrance to the **Rainforest Café** lurks an animal-themed gift shop just waiting to ensnare the unwary with another line-up of soft toys, games, clothing and environmentally aware souvenirs. Their audio-animatronics make it fun for children too, and should keep youngsters amused while the grown-ups browse.

Essential services are provided by a **bureau de change** next to The Disney Store, while there is also a big **tourist information office** just outside the *Disney Village* gates in front of the train station. There used to be a **post office** located inside the village but that is now just inside the station, facing the tourist office.

A **first aid station** can be found behind the video arcade in the middle of the Village, through the (unmarked) doors in the back left corner.

Village entertainment

If all that isn't enough to keep you occupied, then Disney has a third array of opportunities to entertain and amuse. Foremost of these is Buffalo Bill's show, plus Hurricanes nightclub, but there is also live music and other street performer-type entertainment throughout the Village (weather permitting, once again). When you consider the big seasonal events, like Christmas, Chinese New Year, St Patrick's Day and the Festival Latina, which are all either based or have a significant presence here, this can be an exceptionally lively scene at different times of the year.

8

One of the most eye-catching features of the Theme Parks end of the Village, however, is the fully modern 15-screen **Gaumont Cinema** complex, which is largely a French-language operation and the soon-to-open (scheduled for June 2004) **IMAX Cinema**. However, Monday night is Original Language night (usually at 7.45 and 10.30pm) and there is always one major current-release film shown in English without the drawback of French sub-titles or dubbing. The IMAX will be able to offer both the signature giant-screen films and 3-D movies, as well as DMR productions – digitally re-mastered versions of normal-screen films (like the *Matrix* series) which can be shown in clear, sharp pictures on the IMAX screen. Expect a predominance of French language presentations, as at the Gaumont, with the occasional English film.

Buffalo Bill's Wild West Show

Next door to the Gaumont – and arguably the most prominent feature of the village – is **Buffalo Bill's Wild West Show**, a near 2-hour sit-down dinner spectacular that relives the myths and legends (and realities) of America's cowboy country. The huge indoor arena, some eye-catching stunts and the full Western style ensure this is a hit with all the family (but especially children in the 4–12 age range).

BRIT TIP: Buffalo Bill's is not advisable for anyone who suffers from asthma or other respiratory complaints as the animals kick up a fair bit of dust in the indoor arena.

The food is unremarkable, but there is always plenty of it – chilli con carne, chicken, ribs, sausage, corn on the cob and potatoes, plus apple cobbler, ice cream and either tea or coffee – and there is a separate children's platter (roast leg of chicken, sausage, corn on the cob, potatoes and chocolate mousse, plus a soft drink or mineral water), which always seems to go down well (I thought my eldest son – then 5 – was going to eat his own weight in food as he was so taken with the whole environment!). There is also a constant supply of either beer or Coca-Cola (with the meal only – you pay for your drinks in the pre-show 'saloon' area) as part of the entrance price. Everyone gets a straw cowboy hat to wear, and you sit in one of four colour-coded sections corresponding to the different cowboys in the show, who go through a series of games and competitions to decide the 'numero uno' for the evening.

BRIT TIP: In summer, watch out for Wild Bill's cavalcade in the *Disney Village* at 6pm as a prelude to the first show of the day.

You need to be in best audience participation and hat-waving mood as you cheer and clap for your cowboy and hiss and boo the others, and it all adds up to good, fun, raucous stuff. Annie Oakley, the 'Queen of the Winchester', puts in an appearance and literally shoots the lights out (there are some magnificent horse-riding tricks and skills on show, too), and much of the narration is carried out in English as the 60 performers are nearly all American. A Native American element also features and, at one point, the curtain at one end of the auditorium rises to reveal a majestic rocky outcrop, which complements the superb lighting and sound effects. There are wagon trains and cattle drives, cavalry charges and rodeo games, along with a big finale with the inevitable stagecoach – and it is all performed with great gusto and zest by the large cast.

The degree of authenticity is also remarkable, with the Native Americans from a variety of tribes (including Blackfeet, Sioux and Cherokees), the buffalo from Canada, longhorn cattle from Texas and the horses all original Pintos and Appaloosas (for the Native Americans) or quarterhorses (for the cowboys). It is staged twice a night – at 6.30 and 9.30pm. Guests can arrive up to 45 minutes early and enjoy the saloon bar atmosphere and live music, and, while it is on the expensive side at €52 for adults and €32 for children (3–11), it provides an excellent mix of entertainment, spectacle and fun. You can book in advance by calling (from the UK) 00 33 1 60 45 71 00.

Hurricanes

If the Wild West is not your scene, then the dance club **Hurricanes** may be (especially if you can arrange child-minding or baby-sitting for the evening through your hotel concierge). Here, upstairs and to one side of the Rainforest Café, the late-night crowd can really expend some energy as Hurricanes only gets going at 11pm and keeps bopping until 4am every morning. The weekdays are usually quieter (especially out of season), but

Fridays and Saturdays can be extremely lively as it is a big draw for the locals, and the place will be buzzing for the duration. The dance floor is pretty big, the sound system excellent and, if the bar service is a little slow when it's busy, that is only a minor quibble.

Hurricanes offers free entry for all Disney hotel guests (with hotel ID) and Annual Passport holders, otherwise it costs €10/person. The usual evening line-up is Sunday, Singles Night; Monday, International Night; Tuesday, Ladies Night (free for ladies); Wednesday, 1980s' Night; Thursday, Tropical Heat Wave; Friday, Revival Night; and Saturday, Night Fever Party.

Of course, you can also check out the live music (and dance) at **Billy Bob's Country Western Saloon** (see page 140) with two or three sessions a night (highly recommended if the Moody Brothers are playing), plus a Trapeze act twice every Saturday night (7.30 and 9pm) or the soccer on the big TV screens in the **Sports Bar** (see page 139). The 1970s makes a return in the Sports Bar every Thursday at 8pm with the Folie Disco, so dig out those flares and kipper ties!

Central Stage

In the heart of *Disney Village*, the **Central Stage** is another outlet for live entertainment of various kinds, from music to circus acts, hula-hoop contests to quizzes. When the stage is not in use, a live DJ keeps the music going in this area, creating a party atmosphere through much of the early evening. The majority of the big set-piece events take place here (notably at Christmas and during the Festival Latina), while the big video screen adds another fun element. Regular free concerts from up and coming bands (usually around 8.30pm) are also staged here.

8

Older children will certainly gravitate towards the **video arcade** (immediately behind the Central Stage), where they can indulge their passion for the latest games and shoot-'em-ups, with air hockey, football, basketball, skittles, skating, surf-boarding and motor-racing all on offer, among many others.

Fun and games

The Village is also sprinkled with various types of **fun games** (all of which require an extra few euros), such as mechanical bull riding and Ring the Bell (the typical fairground attraction). Strictly for kids, there are three variations on the remote-control driving games, with boats and trucks.

Then, from the **Marina** on Lake Disney, you can hire pedaloes, pontoons and canoes from 1.30pm every day until early evening (again, weather permitting – and it is not a great attraction even in the dryer moments in winter!). They cost from €5–12 for 20 minutes and you need to wear a life jacket at all times.

Finally, at peak times and for seasonal events, the Village comes alive with a series of **street performers** such as jugglers, stilt-walkers and diabolo throwers, which all helps to enhance the carnival nature and intent of this long entertainment thoroughfare. It is definitely a lively, and occasionally even raucous, affair (not a big hit with seniors usually), although the atmosphere is decidedly different in the cold and/or wet.

If you are staying at a Disney hotel or even if you are at a hotel nearby, you are very conveniently placed for *Disney Village*, and there is a big car park which brings you up close to McDonald's. Once on site, everything is within a short walking distance and it is so easy to just wander around, sample a variety of different establishments, and then

wend your way 'home' again in this safe, well-organised and thoroughly entertaining environment.

Of course, for those without a car or a Disney hotel booking, the usefulness of the RER station is paramount. Here, you can enjoy the convenience of a public transport system that runs on schedule 99 times out of 100 and keeps working until a little after midnight each day, ensuring you can get back to the great number of hotels linked to the Line A (and within walking distance of the stations along the way). It may not be America (for those who think in such terms), but it is still efficient, user-friendly and good value. Miss out on a night in *Disney Village* at your peril!

Disneyland Golf

Golf aficionados will certainly be keen to indulge in their favourite sport at the **Disneyland Golf Course** in the neighbouring village of Magny-le-Hongre, which is barely 10 minutes' drive from the resort itself. Although quite a modern set-up, it has all the characteristics of something a lot more mature and its three nine-hole courses should provide a good test for all standards of golfer, as well as providing what amounts to three different 18-hole rounds. All three start and finish in front of the clubhouse and so can easily be combined.

Open year-round, 7 days a week, the facilities are second to none in the Paris area (there is another good course at nearby Bussy-St-Georges, but the variety and challenge at *Disneyland Golf* are far superior). A driving range and practice green (complete with a certain well-known Mouse head profile!) are situated to either side of the clubhouse, which has an extremely pleasant bar and restaurant, and an outdoor terrace to enjoy the best of that summer weather (which somehow seems to be that bit more, well, summery in Paris).

From the striking circular restaurant building, the view out over the green of what is, effectively, the 18th hole, the driving range and the practice green is quite superb and highly conducive to a satisfying lunch. There is also a well-equipped pro shop which can hire out both electric and manual carts, full sets of clubs and golf shoes, as well as offering the usual range of equipment and clothing to buy. A TV lounge, changing rooms and showers complete the clubhouse set-up, and there is plenty of car parking space right outside.

Green fees start at €26 for a winter weekday 18-hole round and go up to €52 for a summer round on a weekend or bank holiday. For a nine-hole round, prices range from €22–37, with reduced rates for under 18s. Club hire is €6 per club or €25 for a full tailor-made set, while hand-carts are €5 and electric ones €25 for an 18-hole round. A bucket of 30 balls for the driving range costs €3, five buckets is €12 and 11 buckets €24. Tuition is available from one of the two fully-qualified instructors at the course, from €23 for a half-hour lesson to €70 for an accompanied round. For more details, visit www.disneylandparis.com and click on the Golf section.

Manchester United Soccer School

Want to learn to bend it like Beckham? Well now you can at this special venture (new in spring 2004) between Disney and the famous Manchester United soccer club. Aimed at youngsters aged 7–14, it is designed to offer 2½ hours of specialised technical training under the supervision of professional coaches from the Old Trafford proving ground (but no, Ryan

Giggs and Paul Scholes are not likely to appear!).

A whole new soccer facility is opening next to *Disney's Sequoia Lodge* hotel, including a full-size pitch, changing rooms and training equipment. Each coach will hold three sessions per day, during which they oversee various skills training like passing, dribbling and, of course, free kicks. All children taking part will collect an official Manchester United training diploma and a Nike souvenir (United's commercial partners).

The 2½-hour lessons will cost €25 per child and you are likely to need to book at least a week in advance on 0870 5030303, although all the main tour operators should also be able to book this for you in their *Disneyland Resort Paris* packages.

Val d'Europe

Right, it is finally time to leave the immediate environs of *Disneyland Resort Paris* behind and venture a little further afield (although not very far, in this instance!). If you are staying at *Disney's Newport Bay Club* (or you peer over the back walls of the *Walt Disney Studios Park*), you will be able to see, across the fields

8

BRIT TIP: Need petrol? The Shell service station in the Val d'Europe car park is rated the cheapest in the Ile de France, so it is the ideal place to fill up for the journey home. However, you CANNOT use the ground-level petrol pumps (they accept only French credit cards), so you must use the services below in the underground car park.

BRIT TIP: If you are finding it too expensive to feed your brood at *Disney Village*, head for Val d'Europe where prices are much lower and you can stock up on snacks, etc, at the Auchan hypermarket.

in front of the hotel, the huge, sprawling structure (still surrounded by cranes and other building construction) that is the **Val d'Europe** shopping and leisure complex. Barely 3 years old (it opened on 25 October 2000), it has its own stop on the RER line and has given rise to a mini-city development all around it. Covering some 24.5 hectares (60 acres), it is basically a glorified (but highly attractive) mall, with two additional elements in the central part (the Sea Life Centre and a big health and fitness centre called Moving) plus the associated development of La Vallée outlet shopping village (in an outdoor 'street' at one end).

For anyone who enjoys retail therapy, this should definitely be high on their list of priorities. The 2-level mall itself has a huge number of high-quality shops (some 130), many of which are internationally recognisable brand names (like Gap, Zara, Benetton and H&M) or uniquely French and wonderfully chic. Choose from the likes of Occitane en Provence (candles, perfumes and cosmetics, made with plants and flowers from southern France), Yves Rocher (make-up and beauty products with the accent on health), Carnet de Vol (men's fashion and sportswear), Carré Blanc (household items like towels and carpets, all with that essential French style), Paraffinesse (artisanal home-made candles and perfumes), Artès (an antiquities and art store), Petit

Bateau (the must-have women's T-shirts), Armand Thierry (men's and women's fashions), Le Tanneur (leather handbags, luggage and wallets), Arthur (pyjamas, slippers and dressing gowns) and – women take note – Orcanta lingerie. There are seven shoe shops (check out Taneo and San Marina for the latest fashions), nine jewellery outlets (including a Swatch Store and Swarovski), five children's clothing shops (with Sergeant Major offering a whole range from 1 month to 14 years) and two sports stores.

There is even a high-quality Paris souvenir shop, Articles de Paris, where you can get that essential mini Eiffel Tower!

BRIT TIP: If you regularly take the car to Calais to stock up at the many hypermarkets there, Val d'Europe offers a much more civilised and user-friendly way to do that much-needed shopping.

Services

The clean, airy, uncluttered confines of the mall, some wonderful architecture (inspired by the great Parisian styles of the late 19th century) and the user-friendly way of doing things all add up to a true 21st-century shopping experience, enhanced by an array of tempting cafes and rest areas (around 250 armchairs are dotted throughout the mall). If you avoid the weekend, you will also find it free of crowds and easy to negotiate – no queues here! There are five 'welcome points' (including two in the huge car park) to assist with finding what you need, along with baby-care centres for nursing mothers where hostesses can even provide jars of baby food. In addition, four free play areas are available for children, with a variety of slides and climbs (excellent for the 3–8 age group). Other services include valet parking, shoe repairs, photo printing, hairdressers (two) and opticians (three).

Hypermarket

Also here, and on both levels, is the **Auchan hypermarket**. If you have brought the car, this is where you can fill up with all those essentials such as wine, beer, spirits and a host of other items. The lower level features all the food (a huge choice, and in serious quantities!) while the upper (ground floor) level stocks a massive range of domestic goods, clothes, books, CDs, toys and even furniture. The two levels are linked by a sloping moving walkway, which means you can take your trolley around the whole store with ease.

The Auchan chain is well known all over France and offers considerable savings on comparable goods in the UK, so it is worth having a good look round. The whole store covers some 21,000sq metres (more than 5 acres!) and is open from 8.30am–10pm, independent of the rest of the mall.

Les Terrasses

The Val d'Europe RER station is only 5 minutes from Marne-la-Vallée, and the mall is only a couple of minutes' walk from the station (turn right as you exit and it is straight in front of you). Walk right through the mall and you come to the main cafe area, **Les Terrasses**, a monumental conservatory-style annexe, with luxurious vegetation filling this iron-and-glass construction. Here, your choice of dining options is both wide and mouth-watering, from a fine teahouse and crêperie (just called Paul) to a proper Italian pizzeria, a fine

seafood restaurant (the boat-themed La Criée), an elegant Chinese (Le Dragon d'Europe, with set menus at €8.50, €12, €13.50 and €19.50, plus a kids' menu at €7.50), a wonderfully fresh and inviting cafeteria, the eclectic Hippopotamus (beef, lamb – and ostrich!), and the inevitable McDonald's (although even that has a much smarter appearance than usual). You will also find live entertainment, with shows for the children and music in the evenings for an older audience.

The shopping part of the mall is open from 10am–9pm from Monday to Saturday (closed Sunday) but Les Terrasses is open 9am–10pm every day. For more details on this retail wonderland, look up www.valdeurope.fr (then click on English version and 'Vos magasins').

> BRIT TIP: For a really excellent cup of tea and the chance to sample some exquisite crêpes, give yourself a break at Paul and just sit and admire the architecture of Les Terrasses.

8

Sea Life Centre

On the lower level of Les Terrasses (down the escalators) is the Moving health and leisure centre and the excellent **Sea Life Centre**. If you have children aged between 2 and 12, this interactive aquarium (part of the UK-based Merlin Entertainments Group, which has six similar Sea Life Centres in Britain and another eight in Europe) will keep them amused for a good couple of hours, and provides a welcome diversion from all the hectic theme-parking.

Many hotels offer a free daily shuttle to La Vallée, hence you can usually come straight here, or you can just get a bus to the Marne-la-Vallée RER station and take the 5-minute train ride. Seasonal special offers for Sea Life – such as 'free child entry with every full-paying adult' – are worth looking out for. Opened in April 2001, this 'aquatic park' offers a marine journey through 30 contrasting displays, exhibits and shows that trace an underwater journey from the source of the Seine river out into the Atlantic and on to the Caribbean. From tiny shrimps to menacing sharks and moray eels, from small tanks to the gigantic main aquarium holding 700,000 litres (154,000 gallons) of water, there is plenty to amuse, entertain and even educate young minds.

BRIT TIP: The Sea Life Centre is a good alternative when the weather turns cold and wet. It is also worthwhile when the temperatures go sky high, as it is fully air-conditioned and is therefore blissfully cool on hot days.

The journey starts with a theatre experience (in French but with English sub-titles), which offers a strong environmental message about sea life conservation. The 5-minute film introduces you to the aquarium and all it portrays, including the hands-on stuff for the kids. Children can also pick up a scratch card at the entrance, which invites them to visit the 10 question panels throughout the centre and choose the right answer on their card. Get more than eight correct and they win a prize! All the explanations are fully bi-lingual and staff can also give talks and answer questions in English.

Each fish tank and aquarium is

presented in a different way, and the highlights are the walkthrough underwater tunnel (a 360-degree experience, with sharks, rays and other fish swimming all around you), the Lost City of Atlantis exhibit, the Stingray Pool (where children can actually touch one of these fascinating creatures if they are patient and gentle), a film presentation on the Atlantic Ocean (and how deep-sea exploration developed), and the Coral Reef tank.

The whole interactive theming, with different walkways, passageways and alcoves, invites you to explore every nook and cranny – and learn quite a bit along the way. Talks and demonstrations with the sharks, stingrays and touch-pool are given at regular intervals, while various feeding times add still further to the experience. At the end, a great little cafe invites parents to sit for a while and unleash their offspring on the two children's play areas, with a ball pool, slides and various things to climb in, on and around.

BRIT TIP: You can come and go as you please once you have purchased your Sea Life admission. That means you can go shopping and come back later in the day if there is a particular show or demonstration you want to see. The Sea Life Centre is also fully accessible for the disabled.

Their newest feature in 2003 was Sharks – the True Story, a fascinating look at this often misunderstood creature, with the largest collection of sharks (more than 20 species) in France.

Sea Life is open from 10am–8pm every day and costs €11 for adults,

€9.50 for senior citizens and €8 for children 3–11 (under 3s free, and children under 14 must be accompanied by an adult). For more details, call 00 33 1 60 42 33 66 (from the UK) or visit their excellent website, www.sealife.fr.

La Vallée

Now, step through the doors of Les Terrasses and you enter **La Vallée**, right outside the Val d'Europe complex, and one which will appeal most to dedicated shoppers, for this is an outlet shopping village – meaning major bargains on big-name brands. All prices are guaranteed to be reduced by at least 33% on high street retail stores and you can save considerably more in many instances.

The 60-plus shops (with more opening in 2004) vary from homeware, luggage, shoes and accessories to high fashion, but most are clothing stores, with the accent on designer names and famous labels. The village design, with its winding streets, encourages you to stroll the length of the complex, and all the shops are unfailingly inviting, with courteous staff who seem light years away from the usual high street surliness and disdain. There is a useful Welcome Centre to get you started, a well-designed children's play area and clean, well-maintained toilets.

For homeware you have the choice of Bodum, Haviland (a famous china store), Anne de Solène (household linens), Sia and Guy Degrenne (one of the leading French brands), while the Samsonite store, the French Lancel and Lamarthe, and the Italian Furla and Mandarina Duck offer luggage, handbags and accessories. For outlet children's wear, you have Donaldson, Tartine et Chocolat and Miniman (both famous French brands) and Bebebo (the Italian version). Teenagers can choose from well-known names such as Miss Sixty, Energie, Murphy NYE and Cerruti Jeans. If you are hunting for designer shoes, check out Charles Jourdan, Robert Clergerie, Maud Frizon (all French) or Camper (Spanish).

Women's high fashion is represented by Anne Fontaine, Arayal, Batiste, Kenzo, Mariella Burani, MaxMara, Nitya and Ventilo, plus Chantelle for lingerie, while the men can choose from Café Coton, Charles Tyrwhitt, Gianfranco Ferre and Kenzo. International brands abound such as Diesel, Nina Ricci, Polo, Christian Lacroix, Salvatore Ferragamo, Ralph Lauren, River Woods and Tommy Hilfiger, plus other well-known names such as Reebok, Timberland, Dunhill and Burberry. For serious shoppers, it is a veritable Aladdin's cave of desirable items, and all with some major mark-downs which make you wonder why we ever bother paying the usual high street rip-off prices (you can tell I enjoy shopping here!).

La Vallée is open 10am–8pm Monday to Saturday (7pm, from 1 October to 30 April) and 11am–7pm on Sunday. A daily shuttle bus service operates from the Disney hotels, which is well worth taking. Check with your hotel concierge for details. Bert's is a good place for a meal and you can look up more details on www.lavalleevillage.com.

And that sums up all the various alternative fun and entertainment on offer away from the Theme Parks. A meal in Les Terrasses is highly recommended at any time, while the general opportunity to travel easily thanks to the great convenience of the RER line (and the good road system) comes as a major bonus for those who like to explore a little.

But let's not stop here. There is still more great sight-seeing to be had in the city itself, so let's conclude by having a brief look at the main attractions of Paris itself…

8

9 The Attractions of Paris

(or, Getting an Eiffel of the City)

Okay, I will admit to a certain bias here but Paris is a wonderful city and I reckon you'd be crazy to spend several days just 32km (20 miles) away and not consider paying a visit. Even with children to keep amused, there is a huge amount of family-friendly fare on offer, while the Eiffel Tower itself remains one of the greatest sources of child fascination and wonderment in the world.

Given that it is so easy to get into the city centre from Marne-la-Vallée on the RER (and even easier from some of the off-site hotels in the vicinity of Line A), visiting some of the great monuments, parks and museums of Paris is a natural adjunct to all the Theme Park frolics. Public transport around the city is both plentiful and reliable, and is far and away the best, cheapest and most

---

BRIT TIP: Arguably the best ticket in town is the *Paris Visite*, a travel card enabling you to use all the public transport services. The all-day, go-anywhere pass covers the RER, Métro and bus systems, and a 1-day pass costs around £12 (see pages 153–4).

---

hassle-free way to see the sights (driving – and the seemingly eternal bugbear of parking – is not recommended, even if you are comfortable with using your own car in France).

It takes just 35–40 minutes to go all the way from Marne-la-Vallée into the city centre, which means there is nothing to stop you having almost a full day in one of the Disney parks and then heading off for an evening in Montmartre, the Latin Quarter or just a stroll along the Champs Elysées. Paris is absolutely chock-full of evening entertainments of all kinds, from humble bars to fabulous restaurants and full-blown dinner cabarets like the Moulin Rouge and (a much better prospect, to my mind) the **Lido de Paris**. For couples, it is hard to imagine a better city and a more tempting array of possibilities, especially for a meal out.

Now, it is not my intention here to go off on a detailed description of all Paris has to offer. Our principal topic is *Disneyland Resort Paris* after all and there are plenty of other guidebooks to provide an in-depth examination of the city itself. I can't however, let the opportunity pass without providing a brief look at what makes Paris so special, highlighting the real must-see and must-do opportunities of this fabulous metropolis – and also point out the most relevant of them, those that the whole family will enjoy.

The city is fairly easy to get to grips with and should be able to provide you with a decent perspective in just a day or two (and the organised bus tours are a great way to start here – see page 154), even if the heavy traffic sometimes makes it seem like one of the most chaotic places on earth.

Introducing the city

Paris is laid out like an architect's dream in 20 districts or *arrondissements* all running out in a spiral from the first at the very centre (and all locations in the city are referenced according to their *arrondissement*, hence the Louvre is in the first, the Arc de Triomphe in the eighth, and so on).

The core of the city dates back to Baron Haussman in the 19th century, whose urban development programme from 1852–70 essentially created the outline plan we see today, with its grand boulevards, wide streets and geometrically elegant squares. It is city design on an epic scale (although constrained within relatively modest confines – the whole of Paris covers just 106sq km/41sq miles – less than *Walt Disney World Resort Florida*, which is 122/47!), punctuated at key points by great monuments such as the Arc de Triomphe (Napoleon's 'Arch of Triumph' commissioned in 1806 and finally finished long after his death in 1836), the Place de la Concorde (dating back to 1755), the monumental Ecole Militaire (the army school and museum of the 18th century) and the Louvre (arguably the greatest art gallery in the world and home to the *Venus de Milo* and the *Mona Lisa*), the oldest part of which dates back to 12th century.

Paris is also effectively split in two by the River Seine, the **Left Bank**, or southern half and the **Right Bank** or northern sector of the city. The most famous landmark though, is 'only' 115 years old and the brainchild of Gustave Eiffel. Built for the International Exposition of 1889, La Tour Eiffel is instantly recognisable the world over and offers three stages up its 324m (1,063ft) height, with a view from the topmost of up to 80km (50 miles). More modern developments have seen the construction of the city-encircling Périphérique highway (1973), the modernist Pompidou Centre (1977) and the Louvre Pyramid (1989).

Getting around

Thanks to the comprehensive public transport, a truly integrated system involving the trains (RER, or Réseau Express Régional), underground (the Métro) and buses, getting around to all the sights is a doddle. Signposting is usually clear (especially on the modern fleet of buses, which have a map of the route and a board indicating each stop) and reliability is outstanding.

The Métro system will get you to every major (and not-so-major) tourist site in the city with only the minimum of walking and it runs until around 12.30am every day, while the last RER service back from central Paris to Marne-la-Vallée is around midnight (check www.ratp.fr for all the public transport details – the site is in English as well as French).

The **Paris Visite** card is almost an essential adjunct to sight-seeing, and can be purchased at any Métro, RER and SNCF train station, bus terminal counters, both main airports and all Paris tourist offices.

The card provides unlimited travel on the whole Paris public transport system, including the SNCF (suburban) trains and the Montmartre funicular. The system is divided into eight regional zones,

9

BRIT TIP: You can pick
up a *Paris Visite* card at the
Eurostar ticket offices in
Waterloo and Ashford.

and *Disneyland Resort Paris* is situated
in zone 5. An adult 1-day *Paris
Visite* card is €16.75 for zones 1-5,
a 2-day card would be €26.65 and a
3-day card €37.35 (€8.35, €12.95 and
€18.25 for children 4–11; under 4s
ride free on all public transport).

The card also comes with an array
of discount deals and special offers
with a host of tourism partners in
the city, including 50% off a second
ticket on the Bateaux Parisiens boat
tours, €2 off entry at the Cité des
Sciences (the excellent Museum of
Science), €4 off L'Open Tour (open-
top bus ride of the city) and a 10%
discount card for the Galeries
Lafayette department store.

BRIT TIP: The *Paris Visite*
card offers 10% off a set
menu at one of the four à la
carte restaurants in the
Disneyland Park, so, if
you're definitely heading
out to the city for some
sight-seeing, it pays to buy
the card before you go to
the Theme Park.

Do it all with Disney

With all these possibilities virtually
on the doorstep, it stands to reason
Disney would be quick to see a way
to give their guests even more value
and purpose to staying on-site. So
they have teamed up with the
Cityrama bus tours, offering a daily
sight-seeing excursion into and
around the city on one of their big,
modern double-decker coaches.

They run daily at 10am from
Disney's Hotel New York and have
quickly proved immensely popular,
so it is advisable to book early – with
your tour operator in advance or at
the hotel concierge desk when you
check in. The tour returns about
6pm, so you still have some park
time left at the end of the day, and
the buses Cityrama uses are all
extremely comfortable and well
equipped, with air-conditioning,
toilets, drinks service and a full audio
commentary on multi-lingual
headphones.

The basic route takes you into the
heart of the city to start with, and
provides a well-narrated overview of
the geography, architecture, art,
history and culture. The history is
graphically illustrated with sites like
La Bastille (one of the city's oldest
districts, now transformed into a
more upmarket and happening area,
with nightclubs, restaurants, piano
bars and cafes) and **Le Marais**
district, a mini city in its own right,
full of original little streets, markets
and several substantial mansions,
now occupied by some chic art
galleries, cafes, health food shops
and piano bars.

BRIT TIP: Going
shopping in Paris? The key
word to look for in any
window display is 'Soldes'.
This means 'Sales' for all
keen bargain hunters!

At the heart of Paris is the **Ile de
la Cité**, the original settlement site,
which dates back to the third
century BC. The tour continues
through the **Quartier Latin** (Latin
Quarter), the famous Left Bank
district that has been the centre of
the city's university life for more
than 700 years, and offers a cheaper
selection of cafes and shops for more
student-like budgets. You then pass

the magnificent **Palais du Luxembourg**, with its 20-hectare (50-acre) gardens, and travel along **Rue Bonaparte**, Paris' version of Bond Street for some exclusive shopping.

The Louvre

Across the **Pont Neuf**, one of the 12 main bridges which link the two halves of the city, you drive past the **Louvre**, the massive repository of just about every example of artwork known to mankind. Its principal claims to fame are the exhibits of the *Venus de Milo*, *Mona Lisa* and Van Gogh's *Sunflowers*, but you can easily spend a day or more investigating the wealth of art on display. It is divided into seven departments – Oriental Antiquities (including Islamic Art); Egyptian Antiquities; Greek, Etruscan and Roman Antiquities; and, for the modern period, Paintings, Sculptures, Art items, Prints and Drawings. Open 9am–6pm daily (with late opening on Wednesdays to 9.45pm), entry is €7.50 (or €5 after 3pm and all day Sunday). More details can be found on www.louvre.fr.

BRIT TIP: Many Paris museums are free on the first Sunday of the month (although queues are longer than normal). The museums owned by the Ville de Paris (except the Catacombs) are free every Sunday from 10am–1pm.

Notre Dame

Having whetted your artistic appetite, you then stop back in the Ile de la Cité for lunch and an opportunity to visit the stunning cathedral of **Notre Dame** (open 8am–6.45pm daily). This masterpiece of Gothic architecture was built between 1163 and 1345, and is free to enter to sample the awe-inspiring serenity of its vast interior. There are some serious queues here at most times of the day (you'll be used to that at Disney!), but they move steadily. There is a small fee to visit the belfry and you may have to wait a good 30 minutes or so for your turn. The bus stops here for 90 minutes, so it is up to you to divide your time between the cathedral and lunch.

BRIT TIP: There are two handy quiet restaurants on the Quai de Montebello, on the south bank of the river flanking Notre Dame, which make an ideal lunch venue. Just stroll to the rear of the cathedral, turn right across the bridge, and the crowds quickly disappear.

Back on board the bus, you head back along the Left Bank and through the St Germain area, passing the **Musée d'Orsay**, another of the great repositories of French artwork. A conversion of the Orsay Railway Station inaugurated in 1900, it houses an art gallery of the finest order, from the period 1848 to 1914. Open from 10am–6pm Tuesday to Saturday, 9am–6pm Sunday (with late opening to 9.15pm on Thursdays), entry is €7 (€5 on Sundays; €5 for 18–25s; under-18s free). More information on www.musee-orsay.fr.

Champs Elysées

A drive around the vast octagonal expanse of the **Place de la Concorde** then reveals some more of the outstanding design of Baron Haussmann, especially as you continue along the **Champs Elysées** and into the **Place Charles de Gaulle** (aka Etoile), at the centre of which stands the magnificent **Arc de Triomphe**.

Along **Avenue Kleber** you can marvel at some more monumental architecture of the fascinating cityscape, especially as you enter **Place du Trocadéro et du 11 Novembre**, with its statue of the First World War military leader Marshall Foch and a grand vista representing three centuries of architecture. The view here across the Seine to the Eiffel Tower is simply breathtaking and on a par with the great landmarks of the world like the Sydney Opera House, the Acropolis and the Statue of Liberty.

The **Hôtel des Invalides** is another significant 17th-century landmark and its Musée de l'Armée showcases some 2,000 years of military history, from Antiquity to the end of the Second World War,

in an opulent setting. The Dôme within contains the tomb of Napoleon Bonaparte and is open from 10am–4.45pm from October to March, and 10am–5.45pm April to September, with a €6 entry fee for adults, €5 for children 12–17 (free for under-12s).

River trips

After all this coach-bound sight-seeing, it is time to step on to a different mode of transport (all part of the Cityrama tour) and view the city from the river on the **Bateaux Parisiens**.

Here, either under a glass roof or out on deck soaking up the sun, the English commentary continues to cover just about every angle of the city, ensuring you get a well-rounded experience and an in-depth view of the history and accomplishments of Paris and its people (or just a fabulous view if you choose to put your feet up and watch the vistas sail by).

Les Bateaux Mouches

Paris is famous for its river tours along the Seine, providing both a great view of many well-known monuments as well as a relaxing and highly enjoyable form of transport. The collective name for the half a dozen or so companies which run these tourist boats is Les Bateaux Mouches, and they ply their trade along the central section from the Eiffel Tower to the Ile de la Cité and back, with plenty of history during the day and a generous helping of romance in the evening, when you can choose just an alternative view of Paris by night or a more elaborate dinner-cruise.

In low season (November to Easter) they run every hour from 10am–1pm and 5–8pm, and every half-hour from 1–5pm and 8–10pm; in high season (Easter to 31 October) they are every half-hour from 10am–11pm, and cost around €9 for adults and €4.50 for children (under 12). A dinner cruise (from 8–11pm) costs from €90–125, but needs to be booked in advance. There is also a special **Children's Cruise** (in French only) for 1 hour every Saturday, Sunday and bank holidays, and during French school holidays every day at 1.45 and 3.45pm. It costs €9.50 per person, or €32 for a family package (two adults and two children). For more information, call 00 33 1 44 11 33 44 (from the UK) or visit www.bateauxparisiens.com.

Up the Eiffel Tower

After your hour's cruise, you return to the marina at the Port de la Bourdonnais in front of the **Eiffel Tower** and finish off in style with a visit to the tower itself. Your tour guide will lead you up the steps and across the Quai Branly to one of the lifts and a trip to the first floor (the second and third floors are extra). This 324m (1,063ft), 10,100-tonne steel edifice is a breathtaking sight close up, and the trip up by elevator or stairs is a rewarding one, both for the view and the way the story of the tower is told along the way.

BRIT TIP: At peak times during the summer (midday to around 5pm), the Eiffel Tower often stops selling tickets for the top deck, and the second floor becomes very crowded too.

The perspective on the city is quite startling (especially from the glass-sided lifts between the first and second floors!) and totally unequalled and there is even a high-quality restaurant on the second floor – the Jules Verne – which you can book separately. If the price tag at the Jules Verne (in excess of €100) puts you off, try the first floor Altitude 95 instead, with its decor reminiscent of a 1930s' airship (book from the UK on 00 33 1 45 55 20 04 for Altitude 95 and 00 33 1 45 55 61 44 for Jules Verne).

The Eiffel Tower has three lifts (at the north, east and west legs) and three staircases (south, east and west) and ticket office queues reach up to an hour in high summer. However, arrive early and you will enjoy this amazing attraction at its very best, while the evening sees it in truly sparkling mode, with a magical lighting presentation (new in summer 2003). From dusk until 2am (1am in winter), the Tower's 20,000 special light bulbs (requiring 40km/25 miles of electrical cord and 120kw of power) come to life in a glittering display each hour on the hour for 10 minutes. Once you have been up this modern marvel, you can then walk the gardens of Le Champ de Mars for the full ground-level perspective.

BRIT TIP: The Eiffel Tower draws some sizeable crowds during the day attracting the inevitable vendors (selling bottled water and trinkets) who are a constant nuisance. Take extra care with your belongings.

At the north leg you can check out the memorial to Gustave Eiffel, while ticket-holders have access to the clever elevator machinery which he designed under the east and west pillars. A Bureau de Change can be found in the concourse under the Tower, plus a Paris Tourist Office (not to be confused with the ticket office) and several souvenir shops (as well as those on the Tower itself), plus a cafeteria-style snack bar.

For those coming here independently, the nearest RER station is Champ de Mars/Tour Eiffel (on Line C; from Marne-la-Vallée, change at Châtelet Les Halles, go one stop south on Line B, then it's four stops west on C), while you can also use the Métro at Ecole Militaire or Trocadéro.

The Eiffel Tower is open every day, 9.30am–11pm for the lift and 9.30am–6.30pm for the stairs 1 January to 13 June and 1 September to 31 December; and 9am–midnight from 14 June to

9

31 August. To take the lift to the first floor costs €3.70 for adults and €2.30 for children (under 12; under 3s free); to the second floor is €7 and €3.90; and to the top is €10.20 and €5.50; the stairs (up to the second floor) are a single rate of €3.30. For more info, visit www.tour-eiffel.fr.

All in all, the Cityrama day tour provides a pretty comprehensive beginner's guide to the great city of Paris and the perfect way to get a thumbnail appreciation of all the main sites in the space of a few hours. For Disney resort guests, it costs €61 for adults and €31 for children 3–11 (lunch not included). Prices valid until April 1st, 2004.

Two new tours

Cityrama's **Illuminations** tour (from 1 October to 3 April), organised by Disney, is basically the city by night. Paris fully deserves its alternative title of 'The City of Light', and the tour portrays this aspect to the full. The English commentary, via individual earphones, is especially adapted to the ambiance of Paris by night, bringing its history to life with a series of amusing stories, accompanied by background music and French songs that celebrate the city. The Cityrama coach departs every Tuesday, Thursday and Saturday at 8pm in front of *Disney's Hotel New York*, and returns to each Disney Hotel around midnight (depending on traffic). It costs €42 for adults and €12 for children (the tours are not available on December 24 and 31).

A new excursion for summer 2003 (4 April to 2 November) was **Vaux-le-Vicomte**, a truly magnificent and historic château some 50km (20 miles) southeast of Paris. In the rich land of Brie, this pinnacle of 17th-century architecture – created by some of the period's greatest artists, including Le Vau, Le Brun and Le Nôtre – was the source of inspiration for the Château de

Versailles. Here you will discover the full splendour of Vaux-le-Vicomte, from the kitchens to the magnificently decorated reception rooms (which have served as a background to many films).

> BRIT TIP: After a guided visit of the Château de Vaux-le-Vicomte, you have some free time in the wonderful French gardens, designed by André le Nôtre, who was also responsible for the Jardins des Tuileries in Paris, plus a visit to the Carriage Museum.

The Cityrama coach departs every Monday, Wednesday and Friday at 2.30pm from in front of *Disney's Hotel New York*, and returns to each Disney hotel at around 6.30pm, depending on traffic. It costs €48 for adults and €24 for children.

And there's more

Of course, the bus tours are only a snapshot (albeit a fairly wide angle one) of the city and there is plenty more in store for the keen sight-seer. A great number of attractions are geared for families, which are worth highlighting here.

Montmartre: One of the must-sees of Paris, this district was a separate village up until the 19th century and became the intellectuals' and artists' quarter. Its two main focal points are the **Place du Tertre** (peaceful and serene during the day, humming with activity in the evening) and the breathtaking church of the **Sacre Coeur** (Métro Anvers), set on a hill overlooking the city with fabulous views. Entry to the church is free, but to visit the Dome and the Crypt costs €5.

You can also enjoy the highly child-friendly funicular ride up to the Sacre Coeur (included in the *Paris Visite* card).

Pompidou Centre: (Métro Hôtel de Ville) This will appeal to all lovers of modern art and is arguably the world's finest collection of modern and contemporary art, from 1905 to the present, featuring Miró, Giacometti, Dubuffet, Picasso, Matisse, Léger, Chagall, Warhol and much, much more. The wacky ultra-modern design of the building is not to everyone's taste, but it is somehow a fitting showcase for the contents within. Open every day (except Tuesday) from 11am–10pm, it costs €10 for adults and is free for under-18s (www.centrepompidou.fr).

Parc de la Villette: Perhaps right at the forefront of the great new family opportunities is the futuristic complex of this science park. Set in the 19th *arrondissement* in the northeast corner of the city (just inside the Périphérique, on the Porte de la Villette Métro stop), it consists of a comprehensive, 52-hectare (128-acre) panorama of science and technology, but in an extremely entertaining, hands-on fashion. It includes the science museum itself (**Cité des Sciences et de l'Industrie**), with a wealth of exhibitions, shows, models, lectures and interactive games, plus the Planetarium, the Mediterranean aquarium, Louis Lumière cinema (films in 3-D), and multimedia library.

In the park, there is also the *Argonaute* – a real submarine – La Géode, a giant sci-fi IMAX cinema with a 1,000sq m (10,764sq ft) hemispherical screen and Cinaxe, a large-scale simulator ride. Open from 10am–6pm Tuesday to Sunday (10am–7pm on Sunday), it costs €7.50 for a Cité Pass, €5 for the Cité des Enfants, €8.75/adult and €6.75/child for La Géode, €2.50 for the Planetarium, €3 for the

Argonaute and €5.20 for Cinaxe. The Aquarium is free (call 00 33 1 40 05 80 00 from the UK, or visit www.cite-sciences.fr).

> BRIT TIP: At the Parc de la Villette children (3–12) will enjoy a junior version of the science village at La Cité des Enfants which has an adventure playground, Electricity (5–12s) and Techno Cité (11 and up) and lots of hands-on experiments.

Bois de Boulogne: Out in west Paris (Métro Porte Maillot) this 846-hectare (2,090-acre) park is ideal family territory, providing a multitude of walks and pleasant spots. Special attractions for children include the 24-lane **Bowling de Paris** and the **Musée en Herbe** in the **Jardin d'Acclimatation**, a dedicated children's museum set in an imaginative play garden with a carousel, train ride, hall of mirrors, go-karts and mini-menagerie (€2.30 for entry to the gardens with extra tickets for rides and attractions, a book of 20 tickets costs €35. It is open from 10am–7pm daily, 10am–6pm October to May). In fine weather, people flock to the banks of

9

> BRIT TIP: In the Bois de Boulogne, bikes may be hired opposite the main entrance of the Jardin d'Acclimatation every day from mid-October to mid-April and Wednesdays, weekends and public holidays from mid-October to mid-April.

the two lakes, where you can go rowing (10am–7pm, from mid-February to end of October) or just watch the model yachts at play.

Shakespeare plays are put on at the **Théâtre de Verdure** in the Jardin Shakespeare by the Pré Catalan park in the centre of the woods and there are 35km (22 miles) of cycle routes along with 28km (17 miles) for horse riding.

Parc Zoologique de Paris: (Métro Porte Dorée) For animal lovers (and most kids!), this excellent zoo is another ideal place for children to visit, extending over 15 hectares (37 acres) in the middle of the Bois de Vincennes in the southeast corner of the city. It houses some 1,200 species – from lions, elephants and giraffes to the little microcebe from Madagascar – in a series of naturalistic settings (no tiny cages here). Open 9am–6pm in summer, 9am–5pm in winter, it costs €8 for adults and €5 for children (4–16).

Aqua Boulevard: Paris can even offer the more up-to-date children's fun of an indoor water park out on the southerly outskirts (by the Balard Métro station). The wonderful tropical theming is divided into three sections – The West Indies (especially for young 'uns), Réunion Island and Polynesia – with a whole series of seven giant slides, wave machines, water cannons and waterfalls all set around a large central lagoon.

Year-round warm weather is guaranteed and there is even an outdoor beach when the summer is in full swing. It is open from 9am–11pm (Monday to Thursday), 9am–midnight (Friday), 8am–midnight (Saturday) and 8am–11pm (Sunday), with an entry fee of €10 for adults (€11 at weekends and public holidays) and €7 for under 12s (€8 at weekends and public holidays).

Parisian gardens: When it comes to the more small-scale delights, try a stroll in the thoroughly British **Champs Elysées gardens** (Métro Champs Elysées-Clémenceau), where you might discover a puppet show (hourly on Wednesday afternoons and weekends), or the **Jardin des Tuileries**, adjacent to the Louvre (Métro Concorde), with its child-friendly pony rides, trampolines and fun fair in July and August. Both are open year-round (except for public holidays) free of charge.

Versailles: The final must-see attraction of the city is a trip to the magnificent château at Versailles (actually a 30-minute ride on the RER line C to the southwest of the city centre). Another of the world's most famous heritage monuments, it was commissioned by The Sun King, Louis XIV, in 1668.

The buildings trace the architectural styles of the 17th and 18th centuries and include the Royal Apartments, the Hall of Mirrors, the Chapel, the Royal Opera and the Museum of the History of France. The park, designed by Le Nôtre, is tastefully adorned with statues, flower beds, ponds and fountains, with several further buildings, the Grand and Petit Trianon, the Temple de l'Amour and the hamlet of Queen Marie-Antoinette.

The château is open 9am–6.30pm (May to September) and 9.30am–5.30pm (October to April). Admission is arranged into different categories: **state apartments** €7.50

BRIT TIP: The immediate environs of the Château de Versailles are also worth exploring, with a series of narrow streets and quaint shops, not to mention several mouth-watering crêperies!

(under 18s free); **audiotour** of King's Chamber €4 (under 10s free); **guided visits** with a lecturer €4 (1 hour), €6 (90 mins) and €8 (2 hours) for adults, €2.70, €4.20 and €5.50 for 10–18s; **Le Grand and Petit Trianon** €5 (under 18s free); **park and gardens** €3 (€5 with a guided tour); **coach museum** €1.90 (under 18s free). For more info on this gem, call 00 33 1 30 83 78 00 or visit www.chateauversailles.fr.

Lido de Paris

Having geared the majority of the chapter towards family activities and sight-seeing, here's one that is definitely for parents only and is highly recommended as one of the most entertaining – and surprising – shows in the city. The **Lido de Paris** is one of several internationally renowned cabarets, but is, to my mind, easily the most sophisticated and eye-catching.

It is also extremely popular, with both couples and singles right across the age spectrum (although the majority tend to be couples in the

> BRIT TIP: The Lido dinner show is totally fabulous but beware the drinks' prices – a half bottle of champagne will set you back around €40.

45–55 age group), and it even draws a family crowd with the French (children's menu, €25). It is a touch risqué, with topless dancers at various points, but it is all extremely tasteful and highly glamorous. You can opt for the dinner-dance and the full 90-minute show or just the dazzling show itself.

For dinner, there is a choice of three separate menus, all of which have been designed by top French chef Paul Bocuse and which include

a half-bottle of champagne. Within the three options (Panache, Passion and Prestige, respectively €40, €55 and €65) there is a choice of three starters, main courses and dessert, and even the Panache menu is barely less than spectacular, meaning the Prestige lives up to the very highest standards of cuisine (the starters include duck foie gras and Oriental lobster salad, while the main courses offer filet mignon, rack of lamb or a vegetarian speciality). The meal takes a leisurely 2 hours to serve and clear away, and there is dancing to a large orchestra throughout.

The large-scale show – *C'est Magique!* – then follows for the next hour-and-a-half, with a remarkable mix of spectacularly choreographed dancing, live music, ice-skating, acrobatics and magic, all cleverly interwoven into four themed sections. The staging is quite breath-taking at times, with some truly stunning special effects, and the high quality and originality of the acrobats and magician lend an air of grand pageantry to the whole

> BRIT TIP: Getting to the Lido from *Disneyland Resort Paris* couldn't be easier. You simply take the RER from Marne-la-Vallée to Charles de Gaulle-Etoile Station (about 45 minutes), then change to the Métro and go one stop to George V, and the Lido is right outside the station. If you go for the first show, you exit just after 11.30pm and there is an RER service back to Marne-la-Vallée from Charles de Gaulle-Étoile at 12.02am.

9

extravaganza (and if the acrobats don't leave you with your jaw on the floor, you need to check your pulse!). The majestic finale as the whole stage seems to unfold before your eyes provides a fitting conclusion to what can only be described as superb entertainment.

Admittedly, it is not a cheap option (the show on its own is €90, while the three dinner options total up to €130, €145 and €160) but I do feel it is terrific value for money and you will not be disappointed. There are two shows a night, the first at 9.30pm preceded by the 2-hour dinner-dance, and the second (a show only) at 11.30pm. For more information, call 00 33 1 40 76 56 10 (from the UK), or visit www.lido.fr. There is also a handful of Sunday lunch-show matinees at 1pm, plus a special children's show several times a month, with an array of aerial ballet, giant fountains, ice-skating and song and dance to positively mesmerise the younger audience.

Paris info

Of course, there is much, much more to Paris than this fairly brief overview. There are dozens more museums, churches, monuments, gardens, memorials and parks, not to mention the shops, restaurants and nightclubs and other modern city paraphernalia that make Paris such a delicious a heady brew. For all the essential information, you should contact:

Maison de la France: 178 Piccadilly, London W1J 9AL; **France Information Line:** 09068 244123 (60p per minute), e-mail: info.uk@franceguide.com or visit www.franceguide.com.

Ile de France Tourist Office: Tel 00 33 1 44 50 19 98 (from the UK), or www.paris-ile-de-france.com.

Paris Tourist Office: Tel 08 92 68 31 12 (in France), or www.parisbienvenue.com.

> BRIT TIP: The *Carte Musées-Monuments* costs just €13 and gives no queuing, no-limit access to more than 60 museums and monuments in Paris. It is on sale at Métro stations, the tourist office and FNAC shops.

Further afield

If you would prefer to escape from the hubbub for a while, the Seine-et-Marne region can offer some more down-to-earth but equally enchanting sources of fascination. With a car, there are some wonderful possibilities a little more than an hour's drive from the resort, and where you can get a feel for rural France untouched by the hectic rush and modernity of the city.

Bohemian **Barbizon** is about 70km away (44 miles) to the south (down the N104, A5B, N105 to Melun, N372 and the N37). Here, against a backdrop that an array of famous landscape painters have made utterly timeless, you can discover the Auberge Ganne, a museum-home of the 19th century and a tribute to an era of artists who influenced the world.

Take a slight detour to the southeast and you come to **Fontainebleau**, with its 16th century château, home to the kings of France from the Middle Ages. Another major architectural and artistic gem in the panoply of French monuments, its extensive gardens and the Napoleon Museum offer a fascinating glimpse into another world.

Travel still further (about another 10km/6 miles) southeast again and you come to **Moret-sur-Loing**, a medieval city curled up between the banks of the Seine and Loing rivers. Wander the town and see why it was the inspiration for some of the Impressionist painters such as Monet, Renoir and Sisley.

Closer to home

Nearer to Marne-la-Vallée (just off the A4 at Ferrières-en-Brie), you have the **Château de Ferrières**, a sumptuous pastiche of Renaissance architecture, embellished with one of the most extraordinary English parks in France. Travel east for 20km (12 miles) on the N34 to **Coulommiers**, another medieval town whose Commander's residence was built by the Knight Templars in fortress style in the 12th century. Make sure you visit the St-Anne Chapel and the round dovecote, too.

Just a short drive to the northeast is another town high on Middle Ages character, that of **Meaux**. The impressive St-Etienne Cathedral is well worth a visit, along with the Episcopal Palace (which now houses the Bossuet Museum) and the Jardin Bossuet.

> BRIT TIP: Don't leave Meaux until you have tried the local culinary speciality – Brie and mustard.

In between Meaux and Coulommiers you will also find the **Abbaye de Jouarre**, the region's most outstanding sacred site, with 12th century crypts displaying some astonishing sarcophagi which date back to the early Merovingian era. Food lovers will be interested in the Musée Briard, which traces the history of Brie country and its cheese-making traditions.

Provins

The jewel in the region's crown, to my mind, is the medieval city of **Provins**, some 60km (37 miles)

down the D231 to the southeast. Pass the 12th-century ramparts and you are truly transported back to the Middle Ages, with narrow streets, half-timbered houses, monuments (and dungeons!).

Here you can even try your hand at various medieval crafts, like calligraphy and stained glass, design coats of arms and watch the free-flying birds of prey.

Provins provides the perfect setting for various period events (visit www.provins.net for the amazing array of happenings organised every summer) and, if you happen to be in the area during the last week of August, definitely stop by to experience some of the week-long Carnival, which is one of the highlights of the Seine-et-Marne region.

Auvers-sur-Oise

Art lovers may well be lured away to the northwest of Paris to spend a half-day or so in the utterly charming village of **Auvers-sur-Oise**, the burial place of Vincent Van Gogh. Although the great artist lived here for only three months before his untimely death, the stay produced some of his most startling work, and its inspiring influence is still present today (not surprisingly, as Cezanne, Pissarro, Daubigny and others also painted here). The village also hosts a grand International Musical Festival every year (late May–June), which attracts some high-quality performers.

Start by visiting the Office de Tourisme on rue de la Sansonne to see the 15-minute audio-visual presentation on the village and Van Gogh, then wander out and drink in the wonderful scenery, the quaint farms (and the cafés!) that inspired so many great painters.

To reach Auvers-sur-Oise, take the A15 out of Paris to Exit 7 (Mery-

9

sur-Oise), then pick up the N184 alongside the River Oise into the village. For more details visit www.auvers-sur-oise.com.

Now it's up to you!

And that, my friends, is that. You now have all the essential wherewithal to not only plan and prepare for your holiday in *Disneyland Resort Paris*, but also to get the most out of it when you are there. As you can see from the last two chapters, there is a lot more to a holiday there than just theme park frolics (although, if you choose to do just that, you will still have a pretty good time!).

It is a world of almost infinite charm and substance, a combination of Imagineering pixie dust and ages-old culture and allure. The Walt Disney Company wasn't that crazy when it brought its major slice of Americana to Europe and, while it was not an instantly comfortable fit, the Franco-European influences now sit comfortably and enjoyably alongside the transatlantic ones.

Most of all however, I hope you have taken on board how much sheer artistry is involved in providing such obvious entertainment, whether it be on the rides, the shows, the restaurants or the hotels. The resort is the product of 50 years of imagination, perspiration and inspiration, with some pretty amazing architecture and engineering thrown in along the way (not to mention the vast backdrop of Paris and her environs).

After countless dozens of visits (I lost count when I got to the 50s!) to Disney theme parks, I still find them absorbing, fascinating and downright fun. There is so much involved I would hate for anyone to pay their hard-earned money and then miss out on some of the essential 'magic'.

So, I challenge you to keep this book with you at all times, read and inwardly digest the contents before you go, and then get out there and have FUN!

Bonnes vacances…

Your Holiday Planner

Here is a way to help you decide what you can do given 3 or 4 days in *Disneyland Resort Paris*. This planner is simply designed to give you an idea (from my own practical experience) of what a typical family might be able to achieve in the time allotted. Obviously, you are free to make up your own schedule (on the blank form at the end), but be aware of the different requirements of the Theme Parks and associated attractions. The two examples are designed around a visit in high season (the summer), and are for different modes of transport and different durations (reflecting two of the most popular packages being booked in 2003). Have fun with your planning!

Example 1:
2-night/3-day trip with Eurostar

DAY	SCHEDULE	NOTES
One	Dep. London Waterloo 9.39am	
	Arr. Marne-la-Vallée 1.29pm.	*Check bags in with Disney Express at station*
	Have lunch in *Disney Village*	Nice and quiet in Planet Hollywood!
	Head to Disneyland Park 2.45pm (closing time 11pm)	*Princess Parade at 3pm*
	Visit Frontierland and Fantasyland	The Tarzan™ Encounter at 5.15pm; Winnie the Pooh and Friends, Too at 7.15pm
	Stop for dinner at 7.45pm	*Great pizza in Pizzeria Bella Notte!*
	Leave park at 9pm	Walk back to *Disney's Hotel New York* – check in; bags already arrived!
Two	Head for buffet breakfast in Parkside Diner	Bit of a late start – not up until 9am! Book Billy Bob's Buffet for dinner tonight
	Off to Walt Disney Studios Park at 10am	*Get FastPass for Flying Carpets ride*

DAY	SCHEDULE	NOTES
Two	Do TV Studio Tour, then 11am Moteurs...Action! Stunt Show, 11.45am return to Flying Carpets ride with FastPass, followed by 12.15pm Cinémagique showing	
	Lunch at Backlot Express	
	Afternoon – do all the attractions of Animation Courtyard	*Did Animagique twice!*
	Catch the 3.30pm parade	
	Stop for refreshment in En Coulisse Restaurant	Watch the Keystone Cops playing – good fun
	Return at 5pm to see the Stunt Show again	*It's loud but the boys love it!*
	Have dinner at Billy Bob's at 7.15pm	*Then it's on to the Disneyland Park*
	See Winnie the Pooh show at 8.45pm, then do Star Tours and Autopia in Discoveryland	
	10.15pm – it's time to find a spot for the Fantillusion parade	*Head back to Town Square for the best view!*
	10.45pm – time to take two tired but happy boys back to the hotel	Catch the bus at the station – no crowds, as the fireworks haven't finished yet
Three	Another slow start – not up until 9.30am! Just time for breakfast	Check bags in at hotel with Disney Express system. We'll see them later! Book late lunch at Blue Lagoon
	10.30am – off back to the Disneyland Park	*Get FastPass for Peter Pan and spend morning in Fantasyland; lots of rides of Casey Jnr and 'it's a small world'.*
	2.15pm – time for lunch in our favourite restaurant	Chance for kids to play after lunch on Adventure Isle, as many people watching the 3pm parade
	Do Pirates of the Caribbean and the Haunted Mansion as our last main rides	*Stop to play in Fort Comstock on the way out*
	6.30pm – head back to the station	
	7.35pm – return on Eurostar to London	
	Arrive Waterloo at 9.30pm	Boys both asleep – tricky final journey home!

Example 2:
4-night/5-day coach trip
with Leger Holidays

DAY	SCHEDULE	NOTES
One	Pick up from home bus station at midday	
	1.30pm – arrive Dover for 2.15 P&O ferry to Calais	*Stock up with drinks and snacks on the ferry for the 4-hour coach journey to* Disneyland Resort Paris
	Arrive Calais 4.30pm; brief stop at hypermarket	Don't forget the 1-hour time change!
	Long, rather dull drive through northern France. Arrive at Disney's Hotel Santa Fe *9.30pm*	*Check in and go straight to room*
Two	Up for 8am hotel breakfast. Off to the *Disneyland Park* at 9am	Book character lunch at Lucky Nugget Saloon at hotel front desk
	Whole day in Disneyland Park	*Get FastPass for Peter Pan*
	Stop for lunch at 1pm at Pizzeria Bella Notta	Catch the 3pm parade; 5.15pm Winnie the Pooh show
	Leave park at 6.30pm – head for Disney Village	*Dinner at Planet Hollywood – only 10-minute wait for table*
	8.30pm – slow wander back to hotel via *Disney Village*	
Three	Slow start this morning – not up until 9am!	Book character breakfast for tomorrow at Walt's – An American Restaurant in the *Disneyland Park*
	10am – head for Walt Disney Studios Park	*Catch 11am Animagique show*
	Stop to watch Rhythmo Technico percussion group	Dad goes to get FastPasses for Flying Carpets!
	Do the TV Studio Tour then head next door to Cinémagique	*Just missed midday Cinémagique – go on to Art of Animation instead*
	1pm – FastPass time!	
	Stop for lunch at En Coulisse Restaurant	*Live Music from the Studio 1 Orchestra while we eat! Stop at concierge desk in Disney Studio 1 to book dinner at Silver Spur Steakhouse in* Disneyland Park

10

DAY	SCHEDULE	NOTES
	Queue for 20 minutes to get in to 2.30pm Moteurs…Action! Stunt Show	
	3.30pm – time for the Disney Cinema Parade	
	Catch the 4pm Cinémagique	Stop for a drink at Studio Catering Co outside after show
	7pm – head next door and have dinner at Silver Spur Steakhouse	
	Head back to Fantasyland for boys' favourite rides	
	10pm – bag a prime spot to watch evening Fantillusion parade on Main Street USA	*Dad goes off to get drinks! Long queues at most of the counter-service cafes still*
	Straight back to the hotel on the bus after parade	
Four	Manage to get everyone up and out to make 8am breakfast booking in *Disneyland Park*	Stop at City Hall to book evening meal at Blue Lagoon
	9am – off to Fantasyland!	*In the first hour, we do Peter Pan, Snow White, Pinocchio (twice!) and the Carousel before the crowds arrive*
	11am – leave park for RER Station	Catch train to Val d'Europe – 5-minute journey
	Visit Sea Life Centre	*Spend 2 hours looking round all the exhibits, and boys finish up in the soft-play area!*
	Have great lunch at pizza restaurant	
	On to La Vallée Outlet Shopping Village	*Boys get to play in playground while Dad enjoys a coffee!*
	Quick tour of Auchan hypermarket before catching train back to Disney	
	Catch 5pm Animagique show at Walt Disney Studios Park	*Quick refreshment stop at La Terrasse*
	One last Flying Carpets ride before 6pm closing	Time to leave for *Disneyland Park*
	8pm – dinner at Blue Lagoon	*Boys learn to shout Bon Appetit back to Pirates riders!*

DAY	SCHEDULE	NOTES
Four	Just time for another trip to Fantasyland!	
	9.30pm – back to Disney's Hotel Santa Fe *on shuttle bus*	*Pack cases for coach tomorrow*
Five	Up at 8am – straight off to breakfast	
	10am – coach departs for Calais	Non-stop to Calais hypermarket; then on to ferry at 3pm (2pm UK time)
	Arrive back at home bus station at 4.30pm. Mission accomplished!	

10

Blank form:
Your holiday; have fun now!

DAY	SCHEDULE	NOTES

DAY	SCHEDULE	NOTES

10

Further Reading

Disneyland Paris – From Sketch to Reality, by Alain Littaye and Didier Ghez (Nouveau Millenaire Editions; €45). A truly sumptuous book, only available in *Disneyland Resort Paris* (see page 143), in full colour and with a wealth of brilliant photography and illustrations, it charts the building of the *Disneyland Park*, *Disney Village* and the hotels. It also provides a magnificent insight into the creativity of the Imagineers themselves, with an in-depth look at how they arrived at the various rides and attractions, and is the perfect aid to full appreciation of all the original development.

Walt Disney Imagineering - by The Imagineers (Hyperion, £21.99). Another lavish 200-page volume providing a riveting look at how Disney's creative force thinks and works, with a fascinating series of original concept illustrations from their attractions worldwide. If you really like to know how it all works, this book is for you.

Disney - The First 100 Years (David Smith and Steven Clark; Hyperion £27.50). For true fans of all things Disney, this lovingly crafted 203-page epic charts the full story of Walt and all his creations, from his humble beginnings to the 100th year after his birth, with an annual look at each of the accomplishments and landmarks of the man and the company he created.

Acknowledgements

The author wishes to acknowledge the help of the following in the production of this book.

The Walt Disney Company, Euro Disney SCA, Maison de la France (French Government Tourist Office, London), Eurostar, Leger Holidays, Eurotunnel, P&O Ferries, Hoverspeed, Thomas Cook Signature, Port of Dover, Air France, Ségécé (Val d'Europe), Cresta Holidays, Thomson Holidays, Lido de Paris, Aéroports de Paris, Cityrama, Bridge Travel, Newmarket Group, Inter Continental Hotels, Accor Hotels, La Vallée Outlet Shopping Village, Planet Hollywood, Sea Life Paris, Seaview.

In person: Nicole Walsh, Nikki Palmas, Claire Fine (Walt Disney London), Ian Benjafield, Karine Moral, Samira Boulamlouj, Louise Crawford (Walt Disney Paris), Francois Gaspar (Euro Disney SCA), Ann Noon (Maison de la France), Ian Henry, Huw Williams (Leger Holidays), Sarah Berridge, Roger Harrison (Eurostar), Barbara Cottage (Eurotunnel), Will Waters, Jan Locke (Cresta), Rob Radmore (Thomson), Nicholas Hobbs (Thomas Cook), Phil Jenkins (Bridge Travel), Jeremy Griffin (Newmarket), Anneliese Morris, Katie Hulme (Air France), David McBeth (Planet Hollywood), Emma Doggart (InterContinental), Nick Stevens (Hoverspeed), Chris Laming, Brian Rees (P&O Ferries), Anne Monteil (Val d'Europe), Gwenaële Morel (Sea Life), Vanessa Guillemette (La Vallée), David Simpson (Seaview).

Special plaudits go to several others who have all provided help, advice and fact-checking above and beyond the call of duty: principal research assistant Robert Rees; and Annelies Trulls, Jason Bevan and Karen Marchbank.

Special thanks to Pete Werner and all the crew at the DIS (www.wdwinfo.com) and to Caroline Radula-Scott for all her input and creativity.

Readers' tips from: Jarrett Holland (Worthing, West Sussex), Stephen Gilmore, Shirley Ahmed and family, Craig Adams, Theresa Parvin, Marie from Denmark, Richard Liversidge and Mark Roberts (via e-mail).

Page references in *italics* refer to maps or
tables; those in **bold** refer to major
references. (D)= Dinner show
(R)= Restaurant (S)= Show (T)= Tour operator

11